SMALL ARMS
1945–PRESENT

**THE ESSENTIAL
WEAPONS IDENTIFICATION GUIDE**

SMALL ARMS

1945–PRESENT

MARTIN J. DOUGHERTY

amber
BOOKS

This edition published in 2012 by
Amber Books Ltd
Bradley's Close
74–77 White Lion Street
London N1 9PF
United Kingdom
www.amberbooks.co.uk

A catalogue record for this book is available from the British Library.

ISBN: 978-1-908273-17-8

Project Editor: Michael Spilling
Design: Hawes Design
Picture Research: Terry Forshaw

Printed in China

PICTURE CREDITS
Art-Tech/MARS: 11, 22, 26, 36, 43, 46, 72, 73, 104, 112, 160
Cody Images: 24, 25, 30, 50, 52, 53
Corbis: 67 (Sygma/Patrick Robert), 70 (Bettmann), 76 (Sygma/Patrick Chauvel), 158 (Reuters/Kimberly White),
    179 (Reuters/Chico Sanchez), 185 (Military Picture Librry/Eric Micheletti)
Getty Images: 102 (Gamma), 105, 107, 128 (Gamma), 130 (Time & Life Pictures), 161 (Hulton/Alex Bowie),
    162 (Hulton/Alex Bowie)
United States Department of Defense: 6, 7, 8, 10, 19, 92, 120, 122, 123, 143, 148, 170
United States Marine Corps: 145

All artworks courtesy of Art-Tech

Contents

Introduction

The invention of firearms placed long-range killing power in the hands of anyone with access to a weapon. Maximum effectiveness is difficult to achieve, however, and requires good tactics as well as marksmanship.

T HE TERM 'SMALL ARMS' was coined long ago to describe firearms that could be carried by a single person, i.e., gunpowder weapons lighter than artillery. Over the years, distinct types of small arms began to appear, each optimized to a particular role. The line between artillery and small arms was blurred when firearms heavy enough to be classed as support weapons began to appear. Light enough to move with infantry but more potent than standard personal weapons, battlefield support weapons greatly increased the firepower of an infantry force.

The invention of personal automatic weapons was another profound leap forward. Where previously, group action was necessary to provide intense firepower, now a single individual could target multiple opponents or deliver suppressing fire into an area. The increasing frequency of urban combat

during World War II was another influence on the development of small arms and infantry support weapons. Whereas previously most engagements were at relatively long ranges of several hundred metres, which required accurate aimed rifle fire, urban battles were characterised by vicious short-range firefights. German troops armed with bolt-action rifles found themselves outgunned in such engagements by Red Army soldiers armed with submachine guns. Swapping rifles for submachine guns would have been an effective counter for urban combat, but in longer-

▼ **Sniper team**

Snipers from the US 82nd Airborne Division provide security from a rooftop for Afghan forces in Dey Yak, Afghanistan, 2007. The sniper on the right is armed with a Mk.14 Mod EBR, an updated version of the M14. His companion is armed with an M40A1 fitted with an AN/PVS-10 day-and-night vision sniper scope.

range engagements the rifle was still the weapon of choice. The answer was an intermediate weapon, smaller, lighter and faster firing than the traditional battle rifle, but still retaining good accuracy out to a respectable range, and reasonable penetrating power. Thus was born the assault rifle, and with it came a change in emphasis from groups of riflemen trained to a high standard of marksmanship towards smaller units capable of delivering intense firepower within their local vicinity.

A group of militia or gunmen will normally fight as individuals with whatever weapons they can get, but formal military forces are organised in a way that optimises the effectiveness of their weapons. Various approaches have been tried in order to obtain maximum combat effectiveness, and the success of one does not necessarily mean another is wrong.

Typically, an infantry squad consists mainly of riflemen armed with a basic personal weapon; usually an assault rifle. The squad will normally contain a support weapon of some kind. This may be a general-purpose machinegun (GPMG) or a lighter squad support weapon. GPMGs tend to be chambered for battle rifle calibres; their ammunition is not compatible with the lighter cartridges used in assault weapons. However, GPMGs are powerful and offer good sustained firepower, out to ranges that lighter weapons cannot effectively reach.

Squad (or light) support weapons are sometimes little more than a variant of the standard infantry rifle, which has the advantage that magazines can be shared and any soldier can take over the support weapon. Mobility is better, too, since the weapon is lighter. However, a light support weapon does not have the hitting power or the sustained firepower of a GPMG.

Other weapons are generally used for supporting purposes. Handguns are carried as sidearms, shotguns are primarily used for security (and sometimes counter-ambush) applications, and an infantry force may be supported by grenade launchers and/or personnel armed with extremely accurate and often high-powered precision rifles.

Other approaches have been used, and successfully. For example, Chinese forces in the Korean conflict made extensive use of massed submachine guns in the assault role, while the British Army long considered marksmanship with a semi-automatic rifle more effective than automatic suppressive fire.

In the final analysis, although the capabilities of a weapon are important, what really matters is the user. Good tactics and skilled marksmanship can overcome the limitations of a mediocre weapon system, while a truly great weapon cannot make a rabble fight any better. It is when training, tactics and fighting spirit are combined with an effective weapon that great things are achieved.

▶ **Girl soldiers**

Armed with M1 carbines, female volunteers of the People's Self-Defense Force of the village of Kien Dien north of Saigon, patrol the hamlet's perimeter to discourage Viet Cong infiltration, 1967. More than 6.5 million M1 carbines of various models were manufactured, and the weapon was used widely during World War II, the Korean War, the Indochina war, Algerian War and Vietnam War.

Chapter 1

Korean War, 1950–53

At the end of World War II, Korea was
partitioned along an arbitrary line based on the positions of
Western and Soviet forces operating against the Japanese in
the region. These areas grew into very different nations and,
in 1950, Communist North Korea invaded South Korea. This
invasion drew in forces from many nations, but notably the
United States, to defend South Korea. International forces
pushed deep into North Korea before Chinese intervention
brought the conflict to a stalemate. The war was fought
for the most part with World War II-era tactics
and weapons, which were available to both
sides in huge numbers.

◀ **Taking a breather**
A soldier from the US 32nd Regimental Combat Team, 7th Infantry Division, rests following the capture of
a Chinese bunker along the slope of Hill 902 north of Ip-Tong. He is armed with an M1 carbine. Next to
him lies an abandoned Soviet-made DP light machine gun.

Introduction

After World War II ended, there was a feeling in some quarters that large conventional forces had become obsolete. Any future major conflict would surely involve a nuclear exchange, which might make war unthinkable.

HOWEVER, AT THE SAME TIME the divisions between the Communist East and the democratic West were deepening, leading to the armed standoff of the Cold War. The Korean conflict of 1950–53 was the first major armed clash of the new, post-war world. Like many later conflicts, each side was backed by East or West, turning the whole conflict into a proxy war between democracy and communism.

The war proceeded through fairly distinct phases, and was greatly influenced by external factors. Initially the North Korean forces were vastly superior to their South Korean opponents, who in particular lacked the ability to stop armoured assaults by Russian-supplied T34 tanks. These were the same excellent vehicles that defeated the Panzer divisions of the *Wehrmacht* a few years previously, and although Western tank design had advanced sufficiently that they might not be effective against European/US forces, the T34 was entirely capable of overrunning anything South Korea could put in its path.

International response

As North Korean forces advanced rapidly southwards, an international response began. Led by American forces redeployed from Japan, troops from

▲ **Machine-gun squad**
A machine-gun squad armed with a Browning M1919A6 from the US 2nd Infantry Division keeps watch north of the Chongchon River, 1952.

▲ **Firefight**
Soldiers from the 3rd Battalion, Royal Australian Regiment, armed with SMLE No. III rifles exchange fire with North Korean forces, 1951.

many nations began landing in South Korea to help defend the unoccupied portions of the country. This intervention was sanctioned by the United Nations (UN), and ultimately resulted in what amounted to a war between the UN and North Korea plus North Korea's Communist backers.

The international response was just in time to prevent the complete conquest of South Korea, but for a period the UN forces struggled to hold a relatively small perimeter around the port of Pusan in the south of the country. A counter-offensive was needed, but a conventional attack would be costly. At this point, recent US experience of amphibious warfare in the Pacific theatre came to the fore.

The deadlock was broken by an ambitious amphibious operation and simultaneous land offensive. Amphibious forces landed at Inchon, close to the South Korean capital of Seoul. Taking the capital cut the supply lines to North Korean forces

fighting in the south of the country, and greatly assisted the breakout from the Pusan perimeter.

Push north
With their supply lines cut, the North Korean forces in the south collapsed quickly, and UN troops were able to push into North Korea almost as far as the Yalu River. Chinese intervention at this point brought tens of thousands of troops into the fight on the Northern side, driving the UN back down the country. A defensive line was established at the 38th Parallel, more or less where the original demarcation line had been, and from 1951–53 the conflict took on the character of World War I static warfare.

After months of artillery bombardment and savage fighting over fortified positions, little had been achieved by either side and a ceasefire came into effect in July 1953. Tensions still run high between North and South Korea, however.

North Korean forces
1950–53

North Korea had prepared for war, and could deploy forces that were both better equipped and more experienced than their opponents.

THE FORCES OF NORTH KOREA could draw upon large numbers of personnel who had fought in World War II alongside Soviet troops. Others had participated in the recent Chinese Civil War. Although the North Korean People's Army (NKPA) was by no means composed entirely of such veterans, it was, overall, an experienced and confident force. It was also highly politicized, with Communist fervour being especially prevalent among those who had fought alongside Mao Zedong in China.

The NKPA had around 150 T34 tanks of Soviet origin. Although North Korean crews were perhaps not up to the standard of their Soviet or European counterparts, this armoured force was a formidable one in any theatre of war, and especially so against an opponent who lacked the weapons and training to counter an armoured assault. The armoured force, along with the rest of the army, had received training from Soviet advisors since the end of World War II in 1945 and had a good grasp of how to make use of its mobility and firepower.

The majority of the North Korean forces were arrayed as eight full-strength infantry divisions, each of which was supported by 122mm (4.8in) towed artillery pieces and 76mm (3in) self-propelled guns. Additional forces included two half-strength divisions and a motorcycle reconnaissance formation. Other formations were held back in reserve or deployed for rear-area security.

Invasion tactics

The withdrawal of US troops from the Korean peninsula in July 1949 created an opportunity for North Korea to invade. A period of increasing tension ensued, with raids launched across the border, before the NKPA finally launched its offensive in June 1950. The attack came as a complete surprise to the UN troops, catching many units understrength due to troops being on leave. Korea's mountainous terrain funnelled the invasion into predictable routes, but with the South Korean forces caught by surprise there was no real opportunity to exploit this advantage. The main thrust was directed down the west coast, needing to cover a fairly short distance to reach Seoul. Offensives were also launched in the central mountains and along the west coast.

The North Korean armoured brigade was used as a spearhead for assaults as resistance developed. The

◀ **Nambu Pistol Model 14**
North Korean People's Army / 109th Armoured Regiment, 1950
The Japanese Nambu pistol was a poor, unreliable weapon firing a weak cartridge. Its weaknesses were not much of a liability, however, since handguns were more status symbols and discipline tools than combat weapons.

Specifications

Country of Origin: Japan	Overall Length: 227mm (8.93in)
Date: 1906	Barrel Length: 121mm (4.76in)
Calibre: 8mm (.314in) Nambu	Muzzle Velocity: 335m/sec (1100ft/sec)
Operation: Short recoil	Feed/Magazine: 8-round detachable box
Weight: .9kg (1.98lb)	magazine
	Range: 30m (98ft)

tactics were simple but effective: a tank force would punch through the enemy position and rally at a safe distance on the far side. An unsupported attack of this sort might bring about disaster against an enemy that possessed good anti-armour weapons, but the South Koreans did not. Their positions were thrown into chaos by the armoured attack, then units were prevented from retreating by the tanks' presence in their rear.

Exploiting chaos

Meanwhile, NKPA infantry forces attacked the disorganized positions from the front and passed around the flanks, crushing resistance with an attack from all sides. The demoralized South Korean army could do little to prevent defeat in these circumstances, and it was not until international forces arrived with the training and equipment to stop the T34s that the situation was stabilized.

Chinese Infantry Section

The idea of the three-cell infantry section (i.e. a small combat unit made up of three sub-units capable of functioning semi-independently) seems to have arisen in China in the 1930s. The weapons available to the People's Volunteer Army (the name given to Chinese forces operating in Korea) were not uniform, though there was a distinct move towards entire battalions armed with versions of the Soviet PPSh-41 submachine gun. A theoretical Chinese infantry section consisted of three 'cells' or squads, each of three men, all armed with PPSh-41 or Chinese copies. The section was commanded by an NCO who was armed the same as his men. Sometimes a four-man machine-gun team was added to a section, but this depended upon the availability of support weapons.

Cell 1

Cell 2

Cell 3

▲ Type 56 (SKS) rifle

North Korean People's Army / 12th Division, 1951

The SKS was one of the first weapons chambered for the 7.62x39mm M43 round later used in the AK-47 and RPD.

Specifications

Country of Origin: China/USSR	Overall Length:1021mm (40.2in)
Date: 1945	Barrel Length: 521mm (20.5in)
Calibre: 7.62mm (.3in)	Muzzle Velocity: 735m/sec (2411ft/sec)
Operation: Gas short-stroke piston	Feed/Magazine: 10-round integral box magazine
Weight: 3.85kg (8.49lb)	Range: 400m (1312ft)

Although the North Korean armoured brigade represented the most potent force in the NKPA arsenal, the offensive's success owed much to the fighting power of its infantry forces. These were primarily equipped with weapons of Soviet origin. Mosin-Nagant bolt-action rifles and more modern SVT-40 semi-automatic rifles were common infantry weapons, along with a version of the Soviet SKS carbine, the Chinese designated Type 56. The SKS used a lighter 7.62x39mm round, rather than 7.62x54mm of the Mosin-Nagant and SVT-40 battle rifles.

North Korean troops also made good use of the Soviet PPSh-41 submachine gun, which delivered high firepower along with great reliability. Its accuracy and effective range were somewhat better than those of the typical submachine gun, so North Korean troops were not significantly disadvantaged in more open terrain.

Other equipment came from a variety of sources, including weapons left behind by the Japanese, who had occupied Korea for several decades. Most support weapons were of Russian origin, but some equipment did come from China. However, China had only recently been unified at the end of the Chinese Civil War, and its arms industry was just beginning to develop. Many Chinese weapons of the time were copies of Soviet equipment.

▲ PPSh-41

Specifications

Country of Origin: USSR

Date: 1941

Calibre: 7.62mm (.3in) Soviet

Operation: Blowback

Weight: 3.64kg (8lb)

Overall Length: 838mm (33in)

Barrel Length: 266mm (10.5in)

Muzzle Velocity: 490m/sec (1600ft/sec)

Feed/Magazine: 35-round box magazine or
   71-round drum magazine

Range: 120m (394ft)

North Korean People's Army / 7th Division, 1952

Soviet-supplied PPSh-41 submachine guns were used in Korea under their own name, and alongside license-built versions such as the Chinese Type 50 and North Korean Type 49.

▲ Tokarev SVT-40

Specifications

Country of Origin: USSR

Date: 1940

Calibre: 7.62mm (.3in)

Operation: Gas

Weight: 3.9kg (8.6lb)

Overall Length: 1226mm (48.27in)

Barrel Length: 610mm (25in)

Muzzle Velocity: 840m/sec (2755ft/sec)

Feed/Magazine: 10-round detachable box
   magazine

Range: 500m (1640ft) +

North Korean People's Army / 6th Division, 1951

The SVT-40 used the same 7.62x54mm ammunition as the proven Mosin-Nagant rifle, and its 10-round internal magazine could even be loaded using the same 10-round stripper clips. It was an effective combat weapon, though eclipsed by the new first-generation assault rifles then emerging.

Specifications

Country of Origin: USSR	Barrel Length: 719mm (28.3in)
Date: 1943	Muzzle Velocity: 850m/sec (2788ft/sec)
Calibre: 7.62mm (.3in) Soviet	Feed/Magazine: 250-round belt
Operation: Gas, air-cooled	Cyclic Rate: 650rpm
Weight: 13.6kg (29.98lb)	Range: 1000m (3280ft)
Overall Length: 1120mm (44.1in)	

▲ **Goryunov SGM**

North Korean People's Army / 4th Infantry Division

Firing the same 7.62x54mm ammunition as the SVT-40, the Goryunov machine gun served in a variety of roles on tripod or wheeled mounts. A licensed version was manufactured in China.

US forces
1950–53

The first US troops deployed to Korea from Japan, where they had been undertaking occupation duties. They were unprepared for a major war.

AT THE MOMENT OF INVASION, South Korea's military was armed mainly with obsolete US equipment. Half of its eight divisions were badly understrength, and none had adequate anti-tank weapons. Those formations that were at establishment were deployed forward near the 38th Parallel and took the brunt of the initial assault, being rapidly reduced to ineffectiveness. The remainder had to function in a chaotic situation where defensive lines were overrun faster than they could be established.

Morale plummeted and many soldiers defected to the North Korean side. As the remnant of the South Korean army was driven south, US forces began landing to give assistance. Bombing missions against North Korean targets were launched, but had no immediate effect on the conflict. Nor did the first US troops to arrive. The 24th Infantry Division, followed by two more divisions, arrived from Japan via Pusan and began moving north to confront the advancing North Koreans. However, these troops had come from 'soft' occupation duties and were not combat-ready. The US intervention force was roughly handled by the North Koreans, and forced to retire towards Pusan. Particularly demoralizing was the difficulty in stopping the Koreans' T34s. Despite a series of determined stands the US force was pushed all the way back to the Naktong River, where it managed to hang on to lines that became known as the Pusan Perimeter. Into this small area came reinforcements from the United States and the rest of the world, eventually enabling a counter-offensive to be made.

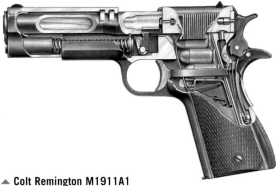

▲ **Colt Remington M1911A1**
US Army / Task Force Smith, Osan, 1950
The M1911A1 was the standard-issue sidearm for US officers and vehicle crews. Firing a hard-hitting .45 ACP round, it was an effective tool for last-ditch self-defence.

Specifications

Country of Origin: United States	Barrell Length: 127mm (5.03in)
Date: 1911	Muzzle Velocity: 255m/sec (835ft/sec)
Calibre: 11.43mm (.45in)	Feed/Magazine: 7-round detachable box
Operation: Recoil	magazine
Weight: 1.105kg (2.436lb)	Range: 100m (328ft)
Overall Length: 210mm (8.25in)	

For a time the perimeter was under severe threat, and was only narrowly saved from collapsing. However, the NKPA was operating at the end of a long supply line and UN strength around Pusan was growing. North Korean attacks became less effective as time went on and in September 1950 the NKPA failed in its last major effort to break through.

UN forces broke out of the Pusan perimeter with the assistance of an amphibious operation to retake Seoul via landings at Inchon. This was an incredibly daring operation, conducted in very difficult conditions. After the landings, Seoul was retaken in bitter street fighting, where submachine guns such as the Thompson M1A1 and fast-firing semi-automatic rifles showed their worth.

With mobility restored to the campaign, and assisted by forces of tanks and other armoured vehicles landed at Pusan, UN forces drove rapidly up the country and seemed within reach of total victory when China intervened. Lacking armoured forces, the Chinese used infantry tactics to overwhelm their UN opponents.

The 'human wave' assaults used by the Chinese People's Volunteer Army (PVA) were not suicide attacks as such, though they did result in heavy casualties. They were launched as a series of waves, with personnel expected to press forward as best they could. If an assault failed the survivors would go to ground and provide forward covering fire as the next wave advanced, then join it and begin moving forward again.

Against such attacks, firepower was the only effective defence. The primary US infantry weapon was the M1 Garand, an excellent semi-automatic rifle using an eight-round internal magazine. Some troops were armed instead with the M1 carbine, an entirely different weapon despite its similar designation. The

▶ **Smith & Wesson M1917 .45 revolver**
US Marine Corps / 1st US Marine Division, Inchon, 1950
Although semi-automatic pistols had become prevalent as military sidearms, some units were issued with revolvers firing the same round.

Specifications

Country of Origin: United States	Overall Length: 298mm (11.75in)
Date: 1917	Barrel Length: 185mm (7.3in)
Calibre: 11.4mm (.45in)	Muzzle Velocity: 198m/sec (650ft/sec)
Operation: Revolver	Feed/Magazine: 6-round cylinder
Weight: 1.08kg (2.4lb)	Range: 20m (66ft)

Specifications

Country of Origin: United States

Date: 1942

Calibre: 7.62mm (.3in) Carbine

Operation: Gas

Weight: 2.5kg (5.47lb)

Overall Length: 905mm (35.7in)

Barrel Length: 457mm (18in)

Muzzle Velocity: 595m/sec (1950ft/sec)

Feed/Magazine: 15- or 30-round detachable
  box magazine

Range: c.300m (984ft)

▲ M1A1 carbine

US Eighth Army / 2nd Infantry Division / 38th Infantry Regiment, 1951

The M1A1 carbine was a lightweight weapon intended for officers and non-combat specialists. It was prone to malfunction in very cold conditions.

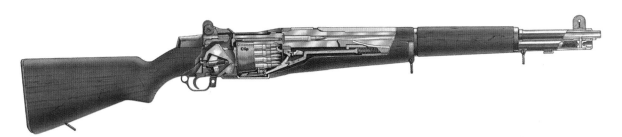

▲ M1 Garand

US Eighth Army / 24th Infantry Division, Pusan, 1950

The M1 Garand offered the US infantryman hard-hitting long-range firepower. One of the finest weapons of World War II, it remained an excellent rifle in the 1950s.

Specifications

Country of Origin: United States

Date: 1936

Calibre: 7.62mm (.3in) US .30-06

Operation: Gas

Weight: 4.37kg (9.5lb)

Overall Length: 1103mm (43.5in)

Barrel Length: 610mm (24in)

Muzzle Velocity: 853m/sec (2800ft/sec)

Feed/Magazine: 8-round internal box magazine

Range: 500m (1640ft) +

Specifications

Country of Origin: United States

Date: 1903

Calibre: 7.62mm (.3in)

Operation: Bolt action

Weight: 3.9kg (8.63lb)

Overall Length: 1115mm (43.9in)

Barrel Length: 610mm (24in)

Muzzle Velocity: 823m/sec (2700ft/sec)

Feed/Magazine: 5-round stripper clip,
  box magazine

Range: 750m (2460ft)

▲ Springfield M1903A4 sniper rifle

US Marine Corps / 1st US Marine Division, Inchon, 1950

Developed in 1943, the sniper version of the veteran Springfield bolt-action rifle saw action in every theatre during World War II and again in the Korean War, especially with US Marine units. It had an effective range of about 750m (2460ft), with the main limit on long-range accuracy coming from its very low power telescopic sight (2.5x).

M1 GARAND MANUFACTURE		
Manufacturer	Serial	Quantity
Springfield		
	4,200,001–4,399,999	1,999,998
	5,000,000–5,000,500	499
	5,278,246–5,488,246	210,000
	5,793,848–6,099,905	306,057
International Harvester		
	4,440,000–4,660,000	260,000
	5,000,501–5,278,245	277,744
Harrington & Richardson		
	4,660,001–4,800,000	139,999
	5,488,247–5,793,847	306,600

Post-World War II production totals: (approx.):
Springfield Armory: 661,747 (from 1952–56)
Harrington & Richardson Arms: 428,600 (from 1953–56)
International Harvester Corporation: 337,623 (from 1953–56)

M1 carbine fired a pistol-calibre round and was effective only at short range, though its fully-automatic M2 variant was useful at close quarters.

US forces also made use of the Thompson submachine gun, whose powerful .45 ACP round was highly lethal in close-quarters combat. The primary support weapon was the Browning M1919, which started life as a water-cooled weapon (M1917) in the trenches of World War I. By 1950 it had matured into a robust and reliable support weapon that could be deployed in the field or aboard almost any vehicle.

Close assault role

The Communist forces gradually moved more and more away from rifles and towards entire units equipped with submachine guns for the close assault role. Coupled with a willingness to accept massive casualties and a tactic of trying to break UN positions by concentrating on the poorly equipped South Korean forces wherever possible, this emphasis led to a clash of UN firepower versus dogged Communist aggression.

The Chinese intervention eventually resulted in stalemate along the 38th Parallel for many months. In this static phase of the war, snipers and skilled marksmen with accurate rifles were highly effective. There were still bitter close-quarters fights, however, as one side or the other tried to capture a strategic location and break the enemy's line.

The Korean War did not last long enough for major changes in US weaponry to take place; it was

Specifications

Country of Origin: United States
Date: 1936
Calibre: 7.62mm (.3in) Browning
Operation: Recoil, air-cooled
Weight: 15.05kg (31lb)
Overall Length: 1041mm (41in)

Barrel Length: 610mm (24in)
Muzzle Velocity: 853m/sec (2800ft/sec)
Feed/Magazine: 250-round belt
Cyclic Rate: 400–600rpm
Range: 2000m (6560ft) +

▲ **M1919A4 Browning**

US Eighth Army / 1st Cavalry Division, 1951

In addition to its infantry support role, the .30-calibre M1919, or 'thirty-cal', was used aboard a variety of armoured and soft-skinned vehicles.

fought with World War II-era equipment. Yet the character of the war changed several times, ranging from defensive positional warfare through mobile armoured operations and amphibious landings to street fighting. The flexibility of US equipment and combat doctrine was tested to its limits during the three years of involvement in the Korean conflict.

▶ **Sniper response**

US Marines move warily through an urban landscape somewhere in Korea. The Marine in the foreground is aiming an M1 carbine, while his comrades are both armed with M1 Garand rifles.

Commonwealth forces
1950–53

Although many nations assisted with the UN effort in Korea, by far the largest non-US contribution came from Britain and the Commonwealth.

DESPITE ALSO HAVING TO DEAL with insurgencies in Malaysia and Africa, Britain and the Commonwealth responded to the Korean crisis by making a major commitment of troops. Most nations that sent assistance contributed infantry formations ranging in size from a company to a brigade; few possessed the sealift capability to deploy large combined-arms forces. Britain and the Commonwealth had both the manpower and the means to transport it. The Commonwealth contribution included two British and one Canadian infantry brigades plus infantry battalions from Australia, plus an armoured brigade and artillery formations from Britain and New Zealand. The British naval contribution was also very significant.

By combining Commonwealth troops from different nations it became possible to field a complete division. Many British and Commonwealth forces fought as part of the 1st Commonwealth Division, which was formed in 1951, though some units were detached. For example, 41 Royal Marine

Commando was attached to the 1st US Marine Division at the time of the battle of Chosin Reservoir in late 1950. The Commonwealth forces had recent wartime experience in a variety of terrains and proved highly competent in both large-scale set-piece battles and the more confused fighting that resulted when Chinese forces launched a wave attack on dispersed positions.

Like the US contingent, the Commonwealth forces arrived in Korea equipped largely with the weapons they had possessed at the end of World War II. Unlike the US Army, who had gone over to semi-automatic rifles as their main infantry weapon, British and Commonwealth troops were primarily armed with bolt-action Lee-Enfield rifles. A tradition of rapid aimed fire and good marksmanship made these weapons deadly in medium- to long-range engagements but when attempting to repel a close assault they were less effective.

British and many commonwealth troops used the Sten submachine gun in Korea. Although trials were at that time underway to find a replacement for the cheap and crude Sten, its successor (the Sterling submachine gun) would not be available in time for the conflict. Stens were effective at close range but their rounds reportedly lost velocity fast over distance, adversely affecting the weapon's already fairly poor accuracy and caused stopping power to drop off sharply.

Some Commonwealth nations used their own indigenous equipment, such as the Australian Owen submachine gun, but much equipment was common across the various contingents. The standard support weapon was the Bren gun, whose accuracy allowed it to be used for sharpshooting as well as suppressive fire. The Bren used the same .303-calibre round as the infantry's rifles, simplifying ammunition supply.

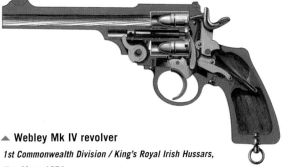

Specifications

Country of Origin: United Kingdom	Overall Length: 279mm (11in)
Date: 1899	Barrel Length: 152mm (6in)
Calibre: 11.55mm (.455in)	Muzzle Velocity: 198m/sec (650ft/sec)
Operation: Revolver	Feed/Magazine: 6-round cylinder
Weight: 1.5kg (3.3lb)	Range: 20m (66ft)

▲ **Webley Mk IV revolver**

1st Commonwealth Division / King's Royal Irish Hussars, Han River, 1951

Dating back to the beginning of the century, the Webley Mk IV fired a .455 round that made it one of the most powerful military handguns ever fielded. The Webley was not completely replaced in British Army service by the Browning Hi-Power until 1963.

▲ **Lee-Enfield Rifle No. 4 Mk I**

1st Commonwealth Division / 1st Battalion, The Gloucestershire Regiment

The Lee-Enfield rifle had proven its worth in half a century of conflict, though not long after the end of the conflict it was phased out in favour of the semi-automatic FN-FAL.

Specifications

Country of Origin: United Kingdom	Barrel Length: 640mm (25.2in)
Date: 1939	Muzzle Velocity: 751m/sec (2464ft/sec)
Calibre: 7.7mm (.303in) British Service	Feed/Magazine: 10-round detachable box
Operation: Bolt action	magazine
Weight: 4.11kg (9.06lb)	Range: 1000m (3280ft) +
Overall Length: 1128mm (44.43in)	

▲ **De Lisle silent carbine**

British/Commonwealth Special Forces

Developed to shoot a .45 ACP round almost silently, the De Lisle carbine was available in limited numbers to British special operations units.

Specifications

Country of Origin: United Kingdom	Barrel Length: 210mm (8.26in)
Date: 1943	Muzzle Velocity: 260m/sec (853ft/sec)
Calibre: 11.4mm (.45in)	Feed/Magazine: 7-round detachable box
Operation: Bolt action	magazine
Weight: 3.7kg (8.15lb)	Range: 400m (1312ft)
Overall Length: 960mm (37.79in)	

Full-bore rifles such as the Lee-Enfield are known as 'battle rifles' as opposed to the new generation of 'assault rifles' that were then emerging. Assault rifles use an intermediate round of lower power, trading hitting power and long-range accuracy for volume of fire and lightness.

The Commonwealth battle rifles were most effective in open engagements, but when facing Chinese troops armed with submachine guns at close range they were disadvantaged. A variety of weapons were nicknamed 'burp guns' by the US and Commonwealth forces in Korea. The term was applied to any fast-firing submachine gun. Most commonly this was a Soviet-made PPSh-41 or one of the Chinese or North Korean copies. These were less accurate and well-made than the Soviet originals, but retained the extremely high rate of fire. Both sides tried to play to their strengths; the Commonwealth forces trying to break up an assault by marksmanship, artillery fire and air support, and the Communists trying to get close enough to take advantage of their massive firepower.

Commonwealth Rifle Platoon

British and Commonwealth forces entered the Korean conflict with much the same organization and equipment that they had in World War II. Organization varied in practice, and few units were ever up to their 'paper' strength. A rifle platoon would consist of a HQ squad and three rifle squads, each containing a Bren LMG.

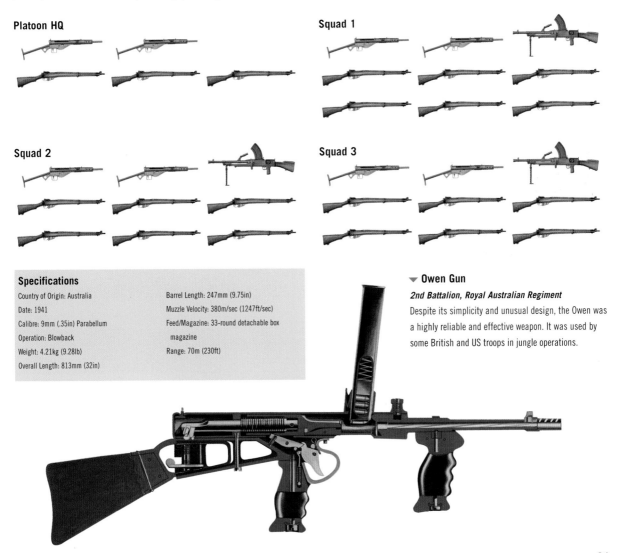

Platoon HQ

Squad 1

Squad 2

Squad 3

Specifications

Country of Origin: Australia
Date: 1941
Calibre: 9mm (.35in) Parabellum
Operation: Blowback
Weight: 4.21kg (9.28lb)
Overall Length: 813mm (32in)

Barrel Length: 247mm (9.75in)
Muzzle Velocity: 380m/sec (1247ft/sec)
Feed/Magazine: 33-round detachable box
 magazine
Range: 70m (230ft)

▼ Owen Gun

2nd Battalion, Royal Australian Regiment

Despite its simplicity and unusual design, the Owen was a highly reliable and effective weapon. It was used by some British and US troops in jungle operations.

Chapter 2

Wars in Asia, 1947–89

Asia was the scene for enormous upheaval in
the years after World War II. Shifts in the worldwide power
balance and the weakening of traditional colonial powers in
the region coincided with the emergence of a newly unified
China. Thus began a clash of ideologies: independence
versus colonialism, Communism versus democracy.
Many conflicts saw extensive use of irregular forces and
asymmetric warfare techniques, countering the firepower of
the major armies with new tactics designed to nullify
their strengths. Wars in Asia thus tended to become
drawn-out affairs where a decisive victory
was seemingly impossible to achieve.

◀ **Weapons training**
A US Army advisor instructs a class of Army of the Republic of Vietnam (ARVN) soldiers in the workings
and construction of an M16 assault rifle.

Introduction

In the years immediately after World War II, conflicts in Asia demonstrated the truism that victory cannot be achieved solely by military means.

THE DEFEATS SUFFERED BY THE NETHERLANDS, Britain and France at the hands of the Axis powers early in World War II had lasting political implications worldwide. Not only did the colonial powers see a drastic reduction in their ability to deploy forces to their overseas possessions, but there was a shift in perception among the people of those areas. Independence movements began to emerge, and in some cases the pro-independence factions were willing to fight for their freedom.

The changed political climate also created opportunities for others to expand their influence. China, newly unified under a Communist regime, was willing and able to move into the power vacuum created by weakened Western powers. Thus emerged a complex politico-military situation in Asia, as the colonial powers sought to retain their hold on their possessions and other Western powers wanted to prevent the spread of Communism.

The Chinese Civil War produced large numbers of combat veterans and also political evangelists who were keen to spread Communism. This 'outreach' suited the purposes of the Chinese government, as it spread their influence wider. The war also displaced large numbers of people, who settled in areas such as Malaysia. There, they often lived in poverty in marginal areas. Deprivation made them receptive to the words of anyone who might be able to make things better.

Chinese influence was not a major factor in the Indonesian Revolution, which began in 1945, but displaced Chinese people and Communist Party officials played a major part in the Malayan Emergency which followed soon afterward. Meanwhile, France was drawn into a long conflict in what was then Indochina, beginning in 1946.

Indochina

French defeat in Indochina permitted the creation of a Communist state in North Vietnam, and the avowed intention of this state was to unify the whole of Vietnam under its rule. This objective, in turn, drew in the United States in an effort to prevent the spread of Communism. The conflicts in Malaysia, Indonesia and Indochina had involved colonial powers with a traditional interest in the region, but in Vietnam the Americans had a different goal.

The region had never been an American possession and the USA was not trying to make it one. The intent was to support the democratic state of South Vietnam and enable it to repel Communist encroachment. Perhaps there were echoes of Korea, where a Communist takeover had been prevented, but Vietnam was a different prospect. Indeed, the two sides were in many ways fighting quite different wars.

▲ **M79 grenade launcher**
A soldier from the Army of the Republic of Vietnam (ARVN) crouches with his M79 grenade launcher. The M79 proved to be an ideal squad support weapon during the Vietnam War.

▲ Dien Bien Phu

French legionnaires take a break during a patrol in northern Indochina during the fighting around Dien Bien Phu, 1954. All are armed with the French-made MAT 49 submachine gun, a versatile and hardy weapon that saw more than 30 years of service.

The USA and her allies sought a conventional military victory and were undeniably successful in military terms, but the North Vietnamese were applying the lessons of the Chinese Civil War and the Indochina conflict, and were fighting for a political victory. Thus, although undefeated in the field, the US was eventually forced to withdraw and leave South Vietnam to its fate.

Red Army in Afghanistan

The Soviet invasion of Afghanistan in 1979 resulted in a similar story. Although able to take control of the governmental structure and the key cities, the Soviet Union was unable to deal effectively with the insurgent groups that operated in the vast countryside of Afghanistan. Ambushes and raids took a steady toll on the Soviet occupation force and while huge reserves of manpower were available to replace casualties, the war ended up costing far too much and achieving far too little to be viable.

Ultimately, the Soviet Union was forced to withdraw from Afghanistan. Like the other conflicts in this chapter, the war could have been won if the Soviets were willing to pay the price. It was, however, simply not worth it. This has become a characteristic of modern warfare for insurgent groups – they may not be able to win in military terms, but if they can push up the price of continued involvement, a conventional army may decide to cut its losses and withdraw.

Malayan Emergency
1948–60

The conflict in Malaya was quite unlike the war the British Army had just fought, and required a wholly different strategy.

THE CHINESE CIVIL WAR displaced large numbers of people, many of whom settled in remote areas of Malaya. There, they lived in poverty for the most part, supporting themselves by subsistence agriculture. The Malayan Communist Party (MCP) found ready support among these people.

Before World War II, the MCP had little support in Malaya, but invasion by the Japanese allowed the MCP to rise to a leadership role within the less political Malayan People's Anti-Japanese Army (MPAJA). The MPAJA was anti-Japanese rather than affiliated to any political group, but the MCP played a prominent role and gained credibility in the struggle against occupation.

Weapons

The MPAJA was partly armed by weapons airdropped by the Allies during 1942–45, and was assisted by British officers assigned as advisors. Other weapons were scavenged from the battle sites of the 1942 invasion, in which British and Commonwealth troops unsuccessfully tried several times to halt the Japanese advance on their base at Singapore.

At the end of the war, British troops quickly arrived to retake control of Malaya and the MPAJA did not resist. In return for handing in weapons, the MCP received recognition as a legitimate political party. Support was still not strong, but the party had a following mainly among the Chinese segment of Malayan society.

MRLA forces began the conflict largely armed with weapons supplied during World War II for use against the Japanese occupiers. Although some of these had been handed in, large caches were hidden in the jungle for later use. These weapons were supplemented by arms brought in from China, many

◀ **Jungle patrol**
British special forces struggle through thick jungle somewhere in Malaya, 1957. The man in the foreground is armed with a Lee-Enfield No. 5 Mk 1 'Jungle Carbine', while his comrade behind carries an L1A1 SLR. In the background another soldier carries a Bren light machine gun.

of which were originally supplied to the Nationalist Chinese by the US.

Many British troops were armed with the Lee-Enfield No. 5 'Jungle Carbine', which had been developed for use in conditions much like those found in Malaya. A shortened and lightened version of the proven Lee-Enfield rifle, theoretically this was the ideal weapon for jungle fighting. In practice the Jungle Carbine underperformed sufficiently that production only lasted from 1944 to 1947, after which a replacement was sought. The main problems with the Jungle Carbine were excessive felt recoil, flash and noise. A rubber buttpad and large flash hider somewhat mitigated these faults but the weapon was soon phased out, with questions remaining about its accuracy.

After relying for a time on the rather better Lee-Enfield No. 4, British troops began receiving the L1A1 self-loading rifle. Whilst excellent for long-range marksmanship, the 'SLR' was less easy to handle in close jungle terrain. This limitation was offset by pairing it up with the Sterling submachine gun, which proved ideal for close-in fighting.

Emergency legislation

Tensions between the indigenous Malay population and the Chinese immigrants led to clashes in the 1945–48 period. The MCP championed the cause of the Chinese population, which gained it further support. Its power was sufficient that in 1948 the MCP launched an 'armed struggle' to take control of Malaya. At the same time, and not coincidentally,

Communist uprisings began in Burma, Indonesia and the Philippines.

Established by MCP personnel, former members of the MPAJA and disaffected segments of the population, the insurgents named themselves the Malayan People's Anti-British Army (MPABA) and began trying to take control of the country. The name was changed to Malayan Races' Liberation Army (MRLA) in 1949 even though only one in ten of its personnel were not of Chinese extraction.

With indigenous Malays as such a small minority, the MRLA did not gain significant support among the non-Chinese population. Nevertheless, the MPAJA was a formidable fighting force and had a network of supporters among the population who were willing to supply food and information.

The situation was not one that could be resolved by military force alone. There were no clear lines of battle and it was hard at times to tell innocent villagers from MRLA insurgents. Thus the measures adopted by the British were essentially political in nature, with the army deployed in force but as an aid to the civil power more than a warfighting force. Army units worked in conjunction with local police and civil authorities, and the intelligence services were effectively used to gather information on the insurgents' organization and operations.

The British response was to implement a set of emergency measures, starting in 1948. Suspects could be detained without trial, but cases were reviewed by non-government bodies to ensure fairness. Curfews and an identity card system were implemented, and

▲ **Lee-Enfield Rifle, No. 5 'Jungle Carbine'**
Royal West Kent Regiment, Kajang, 1952
The Rifle No. 5 was designed primarily for lightness. Unfortunately this low weight increased felt recoil considerably, but the weapon was still used successfully in Burma in World War II and later in Malaya during the Emergency.

Specifications

Country of Origin: United Kingdom	Barrel Length: 478mm (18.7in)
Date: 1944	Muzzle Velocity: 610m/sec (2000ft/sec)
Calibre: 7.7mm (.303in) British Service	Feed/Magazine: 10-round detachable box
Operation: Bolt action	magazine
Weight: 3.24kg (7.14lb)	Range: 1000m (3280ft)
Overall Length: 1000mm (39.37in)	

tied to an incentive scheme to encourage the population to look after their cards. Most importantly, perhaps, measures were taken to improve the loyal Malays' ability to defend themselves. While the Korean War was ongoing, British Army manpower in Malaya was limited. Great reliance was placed on local forces, which was a risky but ultimately rewarding strategy. The police force was expanded and rearmed, and Home Guards were created. These measures not only freed army units for operations against insurgent groups, but also demonstrated trust in the loyalist segment of the population. By giving the locals the strength to resist intimidation by the insurgents, the authorities denied the MRLA credibility and support.

The MRLA operated from bases in the jungle and with the support of the Chinese segment of the population, who mostly lived in remote areas. The major urban areas were secured by the authorities, but this did not prevent the MRLA from launching raids and ambushes in rural areas. European-owned property such as tin mines and rubber plantations were attacked, and in October 1951 the British High Commissioner was ambushed and killed.

Anti-guerrilla tactics

In 1950 the insurgents were able to operate in units of 100 or more, and were confident enough to attack police posts and other targets. A policy of aggressive response by mobile forces helped somewhat, but the situation was desperate for the authorities. Reacting to attacks was ineffective for the most part, and

operations against the guerrillas were problematic if their camps could not be found.

In a effort to deprive the guerrillas of support, the Chinese squatters, a prime recruiting ground for the MRLA, were relocated into 'new villages' and given land to farm. Most of these communities prospered; today the vast majority are thriving towns. In the shorter term, the new villages gave their inhabitants the chance of a better life. Most saw no point in fighting for what they were being given for free, and support for the MPLA dwindled.

Constant low-level patrolling and long-range missions by special forces units gathered information on the insurgents and inflicted a steady stream of casualties, driving down morale and providing prisoners who could be interrogated for information. A surprisingly large number were willing to lead the security forces to their former comrades in return for a pardon and a bounty.

The key to eventual victory was a combination of effective military operations and political measures. British, Gurkha and Malay units went into the jungle and fought the guerrillas in small-unit actions, keeping up constant pressure, while larger raids were launched when a camp was found. Meanwhile, the local population were given strong incentives not to support the insurgents.

Areas with significant guerrilla activity were subject to food rationing, curfews and other measures designed to make life hard for the guerrillas and their supporters. 'White' areas (those where there was little or no insurgent activity) had no such restrictions.

▲ L1A1 Self-Loading Rifle (SLR)
22 SAS, Ipoh, November 1954
From 1954 onwards the British Army began to be issued its first semi-automatic rifle, greatly increasing the firepower of the individual rifleman.

Specifications

Country of Origin: United Kingdom	Barrel Length: 535mm (21.1in)
Date: 1954	Muzzle Velocity: 853m/sec (2800ft/sec)
Calibre: 7.62mm (.3in) NATO	Feed/Magazine: 20-round detachable box
Operation: Gas, self-loading	magazine
Weight: 4.31kg (9.5lb)	Range: 800m (2625ft) +
Overall Length: 1055mm (41.5in)	

Protected by police and local Home Guard units, the people of these areas were strong enough to resist guerrilla attacks and had good reasons to want to keep them out of their territory.

Deprived of support and suffering constant casualties, the insurgents gradually lost heart, and many were willing to turn in their comrades. Some surrendered to avoid starvation, so successful were the measures to deprive them of support, and by the end of July 1960 the emergency was officially declared to be over. Although the military dimension was absolutely vital to victory in Malaya, the guerrillas were defeated in the hearts and minds of the local population. To this day the Malayan Emergency stands as a textbook example of how to conduct a counter-insurgency campaign.

▲ L4A1 Bren

3rd Battalion, Malay Regiment, Johore, 1960

The Malay Regiment was supplied with British-made weaponry such as the 7.62x51mm NATO conversion of the excellent Bren light machine gun.

Specifications

Country of Origin: United Kingdom	Barrel Length: 625mm (25in)
Date: 1958	Muzzle Velocity: 730m/sec (2400ft/sec)
Calibre: 7.62mm (.3in) NATO	Feed/Magazine: 30-round detachable box
Operation: Gas, air-cooled	magazine
Weight: 10.25kg (22.5lb)	Range: 1000m (3280ft) +
Overall Length: 1150mm (45.25in)	

Specifications

Country of Origin: United Kingdom	Barrel Length: 196mm (7.7in)
Date: 1951	Muzzle Velocity: 395m/sec (1295ft/sec)
Calibre: 9mm (.35in) Parabellum	Feed/Magazine: 34-round detachable box
Operation: Blowback	magazine
Weight: 2.7kg (5.9lb) empty	Range: 200m (656ft)
Overall Length: 686mm (27in) stock extended;	
481mm (18.9in) stock folded	

▲ Sterling L2A3

Royal Hampshire Regiment, Selangor, December 1955

Submachine guns proved their worth in vicious close-range firefights in the jungle, their high rate of fire increasing the chances of a hit on a fleetingly spotted human target.

Indochina
1946–54

After the end of World War II, a weakened France attempted to regain control of its South-East Asian territories.

FRANCE ACQUIRED SIGNIFICANT territories in South-East Asia in the latter half of the nineteenth century. Although nationalist movements did appear in the early years of the twentieth entury, French control was not seriously threatened until it was defeated by the Axis early in World War II. This left French colonial possessions vulnerable, and those in South-East Asia were overrun by Japanese forces.

The main force for national unity and independence in the region was the Indochina Communist Party, led by Ho Chi Minh. Under the title of Viet Nam Doc Lap Dong Minh Hoi (shortened to Viet Minh), the Communist Party organized resistance against the Japanese occupation. Its military chief was Vo Nguyen Giap.

Viet Minh control

Japanese defeat allowed the Viet Minh to take control of what is today northern Vietnam, with their capital at Hanoi in the region formerly known as Tongking. Communist support was strong in the north of the country but weaker in the south, where the United Party formed an administration.

The arrival of British troops soon after the end of the war resulted in the United Party losing control of the southern regions, with most towns and lines of

▲ **Squad machine gun**
French troops rest a Fusil Mitrailleur Mle 24/29 light machine gun on top of a US-made Garand M1 rifle, Indochina, 1952. The French Army in Indochina was armed with a lot of surplus American equipment.

FRENCH/VIET MINH BATTALION WEAPONS COMPARED, 1953*		
Armament	**French forces**	**Viet Minh**
Rifles	624	500
SMGs	133	200
LMGs	42	20
81mm (3.2in) mortars	4	8
60mm (2.4in) mortars	8	–
Recoilless rifles	3	–
Bazookas	–	3

*A comparison of the typical armament for French and VM battalions in 1953 was made by Capitaine Jacques Despuech (cited in Pierre Labrousse, *La Méthode Vietminh*).

communication soon firmly under British control. The Allies had decided at the Potsdam Conference in July 1945 that France would reclaim its former colonies, and in 1946 French troops began to take over from the British.

In the north, the French landed at Haiphong and pushed inland to Hanoi. However, the Viet Minh administration was left in place for the time being. Determined to fight for independence, the Viet Minh began to prepare for conflict. Their forces were marshalled in remote areas where the French had not yet penetrated, while guerrillas began attacking French outposts.

France
1946–54

France fielded a conventional army in Indochina, fighting a war that turned out to be anything but conventional.

FRANCE BEGAN THE POST-WAR PERIOD in considerable disarray. Recently liberated from German occupation, its armed forces had to be rebuilt from almost nothing. Reform required arming thousands of troops and providing artillery, vehicles and all other needs from whatever source presented itself. Quantities of French-made equipment were available from storage or new production, but this was not sufficient in the short term. Thus the French army was armed with large amounts of equipment donated by the other Allies, notably the USA.

Recent experience was of large-scale conventional conflict, and the army that France created was geared to fighting such a war. There really was no choice about this; France had been defeated and occupied by conventional means and its first priority was to prevent this defeat from happening again. However, a conventional army was not the ideal tool with which to tackle an insurrection in far-off colonies.

The force sent by France to her former colonies in Indochina was in many ways typical of the immediate post-World War II period. Primarily composed of infantry, who might be moved by truck or other vehicles but who fought in a traditional manner on foot, these forces were built around squads of riflemen supported by light machine guns.

The World War II-era rifle squad had proven effective in that conflict, but the jungle environment of Indochina was not ideal terrain for bolt-action rifles. Their long-range accuracy was wasted most of the time, and their slow rate of fire was a liability. Concentrated firepower was more effective when trying to repel an ambush or hit hostiles concealed by foliage. Rifle-calibre bullets did penetrate soft cover fairly well, whereas lighter rounds lost momentum fast when punching through the undergrowth.

Having been rebuilt almost from scratch after liberation during World War II, French forces were forced to use a mix of weaponry. Some came from pre-war stockpiles, while other weapons such as the M1 Garand were supplied by the United States. The new MAS-49 rifle became available during the conflict, and experience with it led to an updated MAS-49/56 model, which was introduced after the end of the war.

The French Army also made extensive use of submachine guns in Indochina. Although such weapons provided excellent close-range firepower,

▲ **M1A1 Carbine**

Far East Expeditionary Force / 1st Airborne Group, Mang Yang Pass, June 1954

The US-made M1A1 carbine was a popular weapon with airborne troops, combining lightness with a reasonable levels of power.

Specifications

Country of Origin: United States	Barrel Length: 457mm (18in)
Date: 1942	Muzzle Velocity: 595m/sec (1950ft/sec)
Calibre: 7.62mm (.3in) Carbine	Feed/Magazine: 15- or 30-round detachable box
Operation: Gas	magazine
Weight: 2.5kg (5.47lb)	Range: c.300m (984ft)
Overall Length: 905mm (35.7in)	

their pistol-calibre rounds were not always effective against hostiles behind even light cover. Something halfway between a full-bore battle rifle and a submachine gun was needed; a weapon firing high-velocity rounds rapidly using semi- or full-automatic fire. However, the French did not have access to the new generation of assault rifles then emerging, and largely had to make do with the bolt-action rifle/submachine-gun balance that had served many nations in World War II.

The most serious deficiencies were not in French equipment, however. What was most lacking was an understanding of the enemy and the nature of the war. In Europe, the recent conflict had been decided by control of cities and, to a lesser extent, the communications routes between them.

Indochina was a very different matter. Despite some guerrilla activity, the French seemed to be well in control of the country until February 1950, when Viet Minh forces overran a small position at Lao Kai in the very north of the region. Further attacks on thinly spread French outposts were successful, although a robust response drove off a major attack on Dong Khe in May. A second assault in September resulted in a Communist victory. Viet Minh forces ambushed the French relief operation and forced a retreat from Lang Son. Having fought a successful guerrilla war thus far, the Viet Minh went over to

▲ MAS Modèle 36 rifle

Far East Expeditionary Force / Mobile Group 2, Cho Ben Pass, November 1951

Although replacement of the MAS 1936 with a semi-automatic weapon began in 1949, it continued to serve with some units until the mid-1960s.

Specifications

Country of Origin: France
Date: 1936
Calibre: 7.5mm (.295in)
Operation: Bolt action
Weight: 3.7kg (4.1lb)
Overall Length: 1020mm (40in)

Barrel Length: 575mm (22.6in)
Muzzle Velocity: 853.6m/sec (2800ft/sec)
Feed/Magazine: 5-round internal box magazine, clip-fed
Range: 320–365m (1050–1198ft)

▲ Pistolet Mitrailleur MAS Modèle 38

Far East Expeditionary Force / 1st Foreign Airborne Battalion, Dien Bien Phu, November 1953

Although a well-made weapon, the MAS 38 fired a weak cartridge that limited its effectiveness. The bolt recoiled into a space in the stock, reducing overall length.

Specifications

Country of Origin: France
Date: 1938
Calibre: 7.65mm (.301in) Longue
Operation: Blowback
Weight: 4.1kg (9.1lb)

Overall Length: 832mm (32.75in)
Barrel Length: 247mm (9.75in)
Muzzle Velocity: 395m/sec (1300ft/sec)
Feed/Magazine: 32-round box magazine
Range: 70m (230ft))

more conventional tactics, launching repeated attempts to gain control of the area around Hanoi in early 1951.

Here, French weaponry and doctrine were well suited to the situation at hand, and Giap's forces were heavily defeated. The French then set up a defensive perimeter around Hanoi, with a mobile reserve to counter-attack any new offensive that the Viet Minh might mount. More confident now, the French made the decision to begin offensive operations against the Viet Minh bases; a strategy that would lead ultimately to defeat.

▲ MAT 49

Far East Expeditionary Force / 3rd Colonial Parachute Battalion, Red River Delta, October 1953

The MAT 49 submachine gun used a 9x19mm round and was consequently more potent than the MAS 38. Examples captured by the Viet Minh were often converted to 7.65x25mm to use readily available Soviet ammunition.

Specifications

Country of Origin: France
Date: 1949
Calibre: 9mm (.35in) Parabellum
Operation: Blowback
Weight: 3.5kg (7.72lb)
Overall Length: 720mm (28.35in)

Barrel Length: 228mm (8.98in)
Muzzle Velocity: 390m/sec (1280ft/sec)
Feed/Magazine: 20- or 32-round detachable box
    magazine
Range: 70m (230ft)

▲ Fusil Mitrailleur Mle 24/29

Far East Expeditionary Force / French Foreign Legion, Dong Khe, September 1950

The standard light support weapon of the French Army and colonial forces, the FM 24/29 remained in service with some reserve forces long after its official replacement in the 1960s.

Specifications

Country of Origin: France
Date: 1924
Calibre: 7.5mm (.295in) M29
Operation: Gas, air-cooled
Weight: 9.25kg (20.25lb)
Overall Length: 1080mm (42.5in)

Barrel Length: 500mm (19.75in)
Muzzle Velocity: 825m/sec (2707ft/sec)
Cyclic Rate: 500rpm
Feed/Magazine: 25-round detachable box
    magazine
Range:1000m (3280ft) +

Viet Minh
1946–54

The Viet Minh used tactics developed in the recent Chinese Civil War to offset the greater firepower of the French Army.

HAVING SUFFERED A SEVERE SETBACK before Hanoi, morale among the Viet Minh forces dropped sharply. The French, on the other hand, were determined to push through to victory and in November 1951 Hoa Binh was seized by paratroops, with mobile ground and riverine forces pushing through to join up with them.

The operation was intended to drive the Viet Minh out of their base areas, but instead it played into Giap's hands. Rather than attack the garrison at Hoa Binh, Viet Minh forces ambushed patrols and supply convoys using similar techniques to those of the Communist forces in northern China during the civil war. Although the French had a strong position at Hoa Binh, their forces were being slowly choked by pressure on the supply lines and were withdrawn in February 1952. A similar French operation in October 1952 ended the same way. Powerful conventional forces successfully drove off the Viet Minh from their bases at

Phu Doan and Phu Tho, but were unable to remain in possession of the area and were withdrawn some months later. The French were increasingly forced onto the defensive in the area around Hanoi, with the Viet Minh in control of the countryside.

However, there seemed to be a chance to win. The Viet Minh controlled the countryside but France had significant air transport assets which could be used to supply forward bases. Viet Minh attacks on well-defended areas were beaten off with heavy casualties. So, if the Viet Minh could be induced to attack such a target then they could be drawn out and defeated in open battle.

In November 1953, French paratroops seized Dien Bien Phu for use as a forward base. The aim was to disrupt Viet Minh operations by attacking their supply lines. This action, it was hoped, would draw an attack. Dien Bien Phu was fortified and supplies flown in, and the hoped-for assault began. However,

▲ **Maxim heavy machine gun**

Viet Minh / 308th Division / 36th Regiment, Chan Muong gorge,
November 1952

The Viet Minh were supplied with weapons which had, in some cases, changed hands several times during their long career. Although dated, the Maxim gun was still effective, though not very mobile.

Specifications

Country of Origin: Soviet Union	Barrell Length: 721mm (28.38in)
Date: 1910	Muzzel Velocity: 740/m/sec (2427.2ft/sec)
Calibre: 7.62mm (.3in)	Feed/Magazine: 25-round belt
Operation: Short recoil, toggle locked	Cycle Rate: 500rpm
Weight: 64.3kg (139.6lb)	Range: 1000m (3280ft)
Overall Length: 1067mm (42in)	

the Viet Minh proved more capable than expected. Surrounding the base with large numbers of troops, the Viet Minh brought up artillery and anti-aircraft guns, making resupply and reinforcement by air increasingly difficult. Supported by artillery, the Viet Minh slowly ground their way into the base by overrunning successive defensive posts until, after a 55-day siege, the remaining defenders surrendered.

Viet Minh weapons came from a variety of sources. Arms were supplied by the Western Allies during World War II, for use by anti-Japanese resistance forces, and these were augmented by former Nationalist Chinese equipment passed on by the friendly Communist regime in China. Large

quantities of Japanese equipment were captured at the end of World War II in both China and Vietnam, and this served to arm many of the early 'self defence groups' fielded by the Viet Minh.

French weapons also saw extensive use. Some were captured during the conflict, but most came from stockpiles held by the Japanese. These arms were taken originally following the Japanese occupation in 1941–42.

Weapons were also indigenously produced, in many cases in small workshops hidden in villages. Their products included copies of the British Sten gun as well as home-made versions of weapons supplied by China or taken from French forces.

Specifications

Country of Origin: USSR	Barrel Length: 254mm (10in)
Date: 1943	Muzzle Velocity: 500m/sec (1640ft/sec)
Calibre: 7.62mm (.3in) Soviet	Feed/Magazine: 35-round detachable box
Operation: Blowback	magazine
Weight: 3.36kg (7.4lb)	Cyclic Rate: 650rpm
Overall Length: 820mm (32.3in)	Range: 100m (328ft) +

▲ **PPS-43**

Viet Minh Guerrillas, North Vietnam, 1950

The cheap and simple PPS-43 was used to equip both regular troops and irregular militia of the Viet Minh. It was easy to maintain and highly effective in close assault operations.

Specifications

Country of Origin: USSR	Barrel Length: 605mm (23.8in)
Date: 1928	Muzzle Velocity: 840m/sec (2756ft/sec)
Calibre: 7.62mm (.3in) Soviet	Feed/Magazine: 47-round drum magazine
Operation: Gas, air-cooled	Cyclic Rate: 475rpm
Weight: 9.12kg (20.1lb)	Range: 1000m (3280ft)
Overall Length: 1290mm (50.8in)	

▲ **Degtyarev DP**

Viet Minh / 312th Division / 209th Regiment / Nghia Lo Valley, October 1951

Regular forces of the Viet Minh were organized in much the same way as Western armies, but with artillery, mortars and light support weapons supplied by Russia and China. Ammunition resupply came from the same sources.

The Vietnam War

The Geneva Accords of 1954 provided no long-term solution to political issues in Vietnam and soon a second, larger, conflict erupted.

THE GENEVA ACCORDS, which ended the Indochina War, were intended to pave the way for a permanent settlement, but this proved problematic. An initiative to recognize North and South Vietnam as separate nations foundered on the rocks of Cold War politics as the two halves of the region faced off over a Demilitarized Zone (DMZ) at the 17th Parallel. Refugees streamed south despite attempts by the North Vietnamese authorities to prevent the move; a rather smaller number went north to join the Communist state.

With US assistance, South Vietnam began to gain in economic and military strength, overcoming the problems caused by the influx of refugees and the difficulties of creating a state out of a former colonial territory. However, large numbers of former Viet Minh personnel still lived in South Vietnam and by 1959 they had begun waging a guerrilla war under

▲ **Squad capability**

A US Army squad prepares to move from cover somewhere in the Mekong Delta, 1967. The squad carries a Browning M1919 machine gun, while most of the riflemen are armed with either M1 carbines or M14 rifles – the standard infantry weapon until replaced by the M16 assault rifle from 1967.

the new banner of the Viet Cong, or Vietnamese Communists. The most effective response to the guerrilla threat came from small units of light infantry posted in villages, and the larger formations of the Civil Guard which responded to minor threats in their provinces. These forces did what they could, but were not equal to the task they faced. The Army of the Republic of Vietnam (ARVN) was not well suited to countering a guerrilla force. It had been built up along conventional lines to deal with an invasion across the Demilitarized Zone and was not trained for counter-insurgency warfare.

US intervention

With the situation deteriorating fast, American military aid was stepped up. Nevertheless, between 1959 and 1965 the Viet Cong gained in strength to the point where they could defeat ARVN units in conventional battle.

Meanwhile the South Vietnamese government was disintegrating. The US faced a choice between backing its anti-Communist stance with ground forces or pulling out entirely. The latter was not acceptable, so in February 1965 the first US combat units arrived to join the fighting.

US forces
1959–75

US forces began arriving in Vietnam in 1965. They faced an uphill struggle, entering a situation that was already almost beyond control.

WITH NORTH VIETNAMESE ARMY (NVA) units moving across the DMZ and the Viet Cong in the ascendant, the total collapse of South Vietnam seemed imminent as the first US troops arrived. Robust action was needed to remedy the situation, starting with the interdiction of North Vietnamese logistics routes. US combat aircraft attacked infrastructure, supply routes and supporting industry in North Vietnam, hoping to weaken the fighting power of the NVA.

However, the North Vietnamese were supplied by the Soviet Union and China, and the combat capability of the NVA was never seriously impaired. Attempts to prevent supplies from reaching the Viet Cong were similarly unsuccessful. Not only could they obtain support from local communities (not always willingly) but a major supply route, known as the Ho Chi Minh Trail, ran through Cambodia and Laos. This route was attacked from the air, which succeeded only in slowing the flow of supplies.

Conventional warfare

US forces were largely engaged in conventional operations against the NVA, which launched attacks across the DMZ and across the frontier from Cambodia and Laos. This strategy enabled NVA forces to retreat to a safe base if defeated; which they often were. US troops were better supported and had superior firepower, and could generally beat the NVA in the field without difficulty. Frequent victories led to false picture of success, with enemy withdrawals from the battle area and the infamous 'body count' coming out hugely in favour of the US forces. However, the strategic picture was quite different.

The conventional war was just a part of North Vietnamese strategy, which also relied upon gaining control of large areas of South Vietnam through insurgency warfare. Initially, it fell to South Vietnamese forces to counter the activities of the Viet Cong, a role to which they were poorly suited. Although political stability was somewhat rebuilt, the South Vietnamese government had little credibility in the rural areas.

US strategy was at first not overly concerned with building South Vietnam into a nation; it was more about the containment of Communism. It was originally hoped that by inflicting heavy casualties on the NVA and the Viet Cong, the US could force North Vietnam to pull out of the war. However, these measures were of little use to a high-population, totalitarian state that could keep putting men into the field to replace casualties.

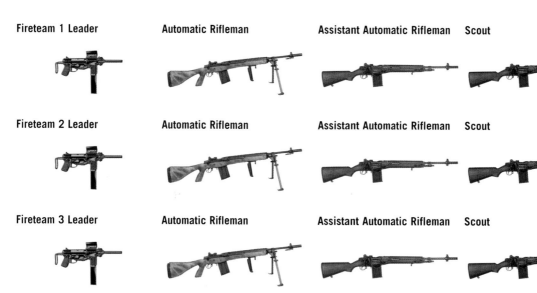

Fireteam 1 Leader   **Automatic Rifleman**   **Assistant Automatic Rifleman**   **Scout**

Fireteam 2 Leader   **Automatic Rifleman**   **Assistant Automatic Rifleman**   **Scout**

Fireteam 3 Leader   **Automatic Rifleman**   **Assistant Automatic Rifleman**   **Scout**

US Marine Rifle Squad, 1968

Each marine squad was broken down into three fireteams of four men. Each fireteam had an NCO as leader (armed with an M3A1 SMG), an automatic rifleman (M14 modified with bipod) and two riflemen (assistant automatic rifleman and scout), also armed with the standard M14. The modified M14 was used as an squad support weapon. All personnel were equipped with the M14 prior to 1968, after which the USMC were issued with the M16, though it was not uncommon for units to retain the modified M14s for extra firepower when necessary.

ORGANIZATION

Rifle Company
HQ

1 Rifle Platoon
HQ
1 2 3

2 Rifle Platoon
HQ
1 2 3

3 Rifle Platoon
HQ
1 2 3

Weapons Platoon
HQ

US MARINE CORPS RIFLE COMPANY: STRENGTH	
Personnel	Strength
Rifle platoons	3
Weapons platoon	1
Navy hospital corpsmen (one attached to each rifle platoon and the senior corpsman with the company headquarters)	4
Administrative clerk	1
Police sergeant (typically holding the rank of corporal or sergeant)	1
Training NCO	1
Company gunnery sergeant	1
First sergeant	1
Executive Officer (XO) typically a first lieutenant	1
Commanding officer (CO) typically a captain	1

US MARINE CORPS RIFLE PLATOON: STRENGTH	
Personnel	Strength
Platoon commander, usually a second lieutenant	1
Platoon sergeant (PSG), usually a staff sergeant	1
Platoon staff Radio-telephone operator (RTO) Forward observer (FO) FO's RTO Platoon medic	1 1 1 1
1 rifle squad	13
2 rifle squad	13
3 rifle squad	13
Total	45

▶ Browning High-Power pistol

Military Assistance Command, Vietnam – Studies and Observations Group

The 9mm (.35in) Browning was chosen as a sidearm by some members of US special forces acting as advisors to the South Vietnamese.

Specifications

Country of Origin: Belgium/United States

Date: 1935

Calibre: 9mm (.35in) Parabellum

Operation: Short recoil

Weight: .99kg (2.19lb)

Overall Length: 197mm (7.75in)

Barrel Length: 118mm (4.65in)

Muzzle Velocity: 335m/sec (1100ft/sec)

Feed/Magazine: 13-round detachable box
  magazine

Range: 30m (98ft)

◀ Smith & Wesson Model 10

1st Cavalry Division (Airmobile), Ia Drang Valley, November 1965

Revolvers were issued to helicopter pilots as emergency weapons only; pilots were not expected to have to engage hostiles under normal conditions.

Specifications

Country of Origin: United States

Date: 1899

Calibre: 9.6mm (.38in)

Operation: Double-action revolver

Weight: .51kg (1.1lb)

Overall Length: 190mm (7.5in)

Barrel Length: 83mm (3.27in)

Muzzle Velocity: 190m/sec (625ft/sec)

Feed/Magazine: 5-round cylinder

Range: 20m (66ft)

▲ Ithaca Model 37 M

1st Infantry Division / 28th Infantry Regiment, Bonh Duong Province, October 1967

Shotguns were extensively used by 'point men' leading patrols during search-and-destroy missions, enabling a fast response to any sudden threat or ambush.

Specifications

Country of Origin: United States

Date: 1970

Gauge/Calibre: 12-, 16-, 20- or 28-gauge

Operation: Pump action

Weight: Variable

Overall Length: Variable

Barrel Length: 330–762mm (13–30in)

Muzzle Velocity: Variable, depending on type of
  ammunition

Feed/Magazine: 4-round integral tubular
  magazine

Range: 100m (328ft)

Firebases

US tactics revolved around the application of heavy firepower. Heavily protected bases were used along the DMZ frontier, often in an interlocking pattern of 'firebases' from which artillery could support other fortified areas or fire on targets identified by ground or air reconnaissance.

These bases, and also supply bases located in what might otherwise have been considered rear areas, were the subject of constant harassment and occasional large-scale attack. To a great extent they suited US purposes; by drawing concentrated enemy forces onto their defences, the US forces could bring firepower to bear on their own terms while the enemy struggled through minefields and barbed wire.

The fire and support bases had to be resupplied, necessitating constant patrols along supply routes and the surrounding jungle. Response forces were dispatched from their base whenever an ambush or a patrol contact occurred, but were not always successful in bringing the enemy to battle. Sometimes the response force itself was ambushed en route or had to fight through a blocking force to assist the original victims.

Specifications

Country of Origin: United States	Barrel Length: 558mm (22in)
Date: 1957	Muzzle Velocity: 595m/sec (1950ft/sec)
Calibre: 7.62mm (.3in) NATO	Feed/Magazine: 20-round detachable box
Operation: Gas	magazine
Weight: 3.88kg (8.55lb)	Range: 800m (2625ft) +
Overall Length: 1117mm (44in)	

▲ M14 rifle

1st Infantry Division / 173rd Airborne Brigade, Operation Crimp, January 1966

The M14 was the standard US infantry rifle until replaced by the M16. It was effective in both small-scale patrol actions and divisional-level operations.

▲ M16A1 assault rifle

101st Airborne Division / 3rd Brigade, Firebase Ripcord, July 1970

The individual firepower offered by the fully automatic M16A1 was instrumental in the defence of Firebase Ripcord, the last major US ground engagement of the war.

Specifications

Country of Origin: United States	Barrel Length: 508mm (20in)
Date: 1963	Muzzle Velocity: 1000m/sec (3280ft/sec)
Calibre: 5.56mm (.219in) M193	Feed/Magazine: 30-round detachable box
Operation: Gas	magazine
Weight: 2.86kg (6.3lb)	Range: 500m (1640ft) +
Overall Length: 990mm (39in)	

Helicopter mobility was a key US asset in Vietnam, allowing troops to be deployed quickly, supported in the field and withdrawn. Helicopters were also extensively used for casualty evacuation and fire support. They gave rise to a new style of warfare, in which airmobile infantry were supported by relatively distant artillery at the firebases, and by helicopter gunships giving close support. Other aircraft, ranging from conventional fighter-bombers to converted cargo planes serving as gunships, also provided heavy fire support.

Air mobility allowed the US to put a lot of troops quickly into an area and to set up ambushes across the retreat routes of enemy forces. This tactic was at times highly effective, and the US won all the significant battles it fought. However, in order to gain control over the countryside it was necessary to send patrols into the jungle and fight the insurgents wherever they could be found.

Sniper war

Snipers played a significant part in this kind of operation, not only as shooters but also as observers. A two-man sniper team could disrupt a large enemy force by killing officers, pinning down the force as a whole, and calling in artillery or air support to inflict

▲ M21 sniper rifle

9th Infantry Division / 60th Infantry Regiment, Ben Tre, February 1969

Derived from the M14 rifle, the M21 sniper rifle could carry a telescopic sight, or a light-intensifying 'starlight scope' to assist in finding targets at night.

Specifications

Country of Origin: United States	Barrel Length: 559mm (22in)
Date: 1969	Muzzle Velocity: 853m/sec (2798ft/sec)
Calibre: 7.62mm (.3in) NATO	Feed/Magazine: 20-round detachable box
Operation: Gas	magazine
Weight: 5.55kg (12.24lb)	Range: 800m (2625ft) +
Overall Length: 1120mm (44.09in)	

Specifications

Country of Origin: United States	Barrel Length: 610mm (24in)
Date: 1966	Muzzle Velocity: 777m/sec (2550ft/sec)
Calibre: 7.62mm (.3in) NATO	Feed/Magazine: 5-round integral box magazine
Operation: Bolt action	Range: 800m (2625ft) +
Weight: 6.57kg (14.48lb)	
Overall Length: 1117mm (43.98in)	

▲ M40A1 sniper rifle

5th Marine Regiment, Sgt 'Chuck' Mawhinney, 1968–70

In the hands of a skilled sniper, a bolt-action rifle could inflict serious casualties on the enemy. Sergeant Mawhinney achieved more than 100 confirmed kills in his 16-month tour.

heavy casualties. Their skills in moving unseen through the jungle were critical to their effectiveness; a detected sniper team could be overwhelmed by enemy fire.

The sniper version of the M14 rifle, designated the M21, proved extremely effective. Its 20-round capacity and semi-automatic mechanism allowed a sniper to shoot repeatedly at targets who might take cover while he worked the action of a bolt-action weapon. The M21 also made a good battle rifle if the

sniper team became caught in a close-range firefight. Using a suppressor, the M21 made it hard for hostiles to locate the sniper, which improved survivability.

Infantry weapons and tactics

The standard US infantry platoon during the war was composed primarily of riflemen, with some specialists. 'Point men', who led patrols, were often armed with shotguns. While lacking range and penetration, the shotgun allowed a fast response to an

▲ M3A1 'Grease Gun'

9th Infantry Division / 47th Mechanized Infantry, Bin Phuoc, March 1970

The M3A1, an improved version of the original M3, was issued to vehicle crews and rear-echelon personnel as a self-defence weapon that could be stowed conveniently aboard a vehicle.

Specifications

Country of Origin: United States
Date: 1944
Calibre: 9mm (.35in) Parabellum or 11.4mm (.45in) .45 ACP
Operation: Blowback
Weight: 3.7kg (8.15lb)
Overall Length: 762mm (30in)
Barrel Length: 203mm (8in)
Muzzle Velocity: 275m/sec (900ft/sec)
Feed/Magazine: 30-round detachable box magazine
Range: 50m (164ft)

▲ M60 general-purpose machine gun

9th Infantry Division / 31st Infantry Regiment, Ben Luc, April 1969

Despite a tendency to malfunction or become damaged, the M60 was valued for its sustained-fire capability. The Stellite-lined bore permitted firing even when the barrel was white-hot.

Specifications

Country of Origin: United States
Date: 1960
Calibre: 7.62mm (.3in) NATO
Operation: Gas, air-cooled
Weight: 10.4kg (23lb)
Overall Length: 1110mm (43.75in)
Barrel Length: 560mm (22.05in)
Muzzle Velocity: 855m/sec (2805ft/sec)
Feed/Magazine: Belt-fed
Cyclic Rate: 600rpm
Range: 1000m (3280ft) +

▶ **Jungle firefight**
A US Marine recon squad aim an M60 machine gun into long grass during a patrol near Con Thien, 1969.

ambush or fleeting target and made a hit more likely.

Fire support was provided by a general-purpose machine gun, usually an M60. This weapon was effective when it worked properly but it was heavy and had so many problems that it was nicknamed 'the pig' by soldiers. Nevertheless the M60 could lay down effective suppressing fire and could be 'walked' onto a target. Its heavy 7.62x51mm rounds penetrated far into the jungle; the sound of bullets smashing into branches and through leaves could induce many hostiles to disengage or seek better cover.

Grenade launchers were also widely used. The M79 'thump gun' in skilled hands could put an explosive grenade into a target the size of a building window at 100–150m (328–492ft). Specialist ammunition such as 'multiple projectile' – essentially a giant 40mm shotgun shell – made the M79 more versatile, but the grenadier was issued a pistol for self-defence; alone the M79 was not an all-round weapon.

The standard US infantry rifle at the beginning of the war was the M14, a 7.62x51mm automatic rifle. It was potent but had significant drawbacks. Its 20-round magazine was quickly emptied when using automatic fire, which limited effectiveness compared with the 30-round capacity of the opposing AK-47. The M14 was hard to control under automatic fire, which further wasted ammunition. Most M14s were converted to semi-automatic fire, and an accurized version was produced to arm snipers.

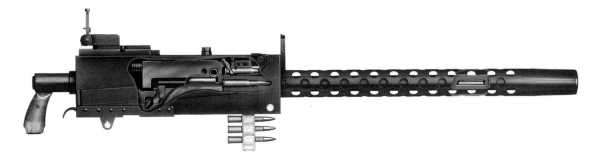

Specifications	
Country of Origin: United States	Barrel Length: 610mm (24in)
Date: 1936	Muzzle Velocity: 853m/sec (2800ft/sec)
Calibre: 7.62mm (.3in) Browning	Feed/Magazine: 250-round belt
Operation: Recoil, air cooled	Cyclic Rate: 400–600rpm
Weight: 15.05kg (31lb)	Range: 2000m (6560ft) +
Overall Length: 1041mm (41in)	

▲ **Browning M1919A4**

Mobile Riverine Force / River Assault Squadron 13, Mekong Delta, December 1968

Specialist forces patrolled the waterways of the Mekong Delta aboard heavily armed boats equipped with .30- and .50-calibre Browning machineguns, 20mm cannon and grenade launchers.

M16 arrives

From 1968 onwards, the M16 rifle began to become available. It first went to some special operations units before becoming standard issue. However, the original model had some serious flaws, notably a tendency to jam when exposed to the filthy conditions of the Vietnamese jungle. Some potential users viewed the M16 with suspicion, calling it a 'toy rifle', which referred to both its plastic components and its small calibre. Whatever faults weapons such as the M14 may have had, they fired a powerful 7.62mm (.3in) cartridge. The lighter 5.56mm (.21in) round had not proven its effectiveness in action, and there was an intuitive connection between a smaller bullet and lessened stopping power which concerned many users. It might be satisfactory for the needs of the first service to adopt it, the US Air Force, but combat troops had their doubts about the new weapon.

A chief concern was that the M16 might fail to fire at all. Despite being billed as a wonder rifle that never needed cleaning, it fouled quickly. This problem was compounded by a lack of cleaning kits. The fault did not, in truth, lie entirely with the weapon. The decision to dispense with cleaning kits was a cost-saving measure, compounded by a switch to cheaper ammunition whose propellant caused serious fouling.

These problems were gradually ironed out, creating the M16A1 model that included a cleaning kit carried in the stock and a forward assist to enable the bolt to be closed on even a badly fouled chamber. The M16A1 was altogether better, providing every US infantryman with the capability to lay down controllable suppressing fire. However, this firepower did lead to a tendency to 'spray and pray', resulting in enormous ammunition expenditure in return for relatively few hits.

Submachine guns and heavy weapons

Submachine guns were extensively issued in Vietnam, mainly to artillery and vehicle crews who needed a means of self-defence but were not intended to engage the enemy directly. The standard-issue US SMG was the M3 'Grease Gun', which had started out as a World War II expedient weapon but was produced in such numbers as to ensure longevity in military service.

Submachine guns had in the past been used for counter-ambush techniques, but automatic rifles took over this role. An assault rifle could lay down the same volume of fire as an SMG and in addition had longer range and better penetration. While some troops were issued shotguns for the point-man role, there was no need to deprive the squad of several riflemen to create a specialist close-range high-firepower capability.

Thus submachine guns played a relatively small part in combat initiated by the US forces. They were rarely deployed with troops going in search of the enemy, but when the Viet Cong or NVA ambushed a convoy or attacked a firebase, the firepower of multiple submachine guns was a welcome addition to the defensive effort. Repelling a convoy ambush or a base assault was often a close-quarters scramble,

Specifications	
Country of Origin: United States	Overall Length: 783mm (29in)
Date: 1961	Barrel Length: 357mm (14in)
Calibre: 40mm (1.57in)	Muzzle Velocity: 75m/sec (245ft/sec)
Operation: Breech-loaded	Feed/Magazine: Single shot
Weight: 2.95kg (6.5lb) loaded	Range: 150m (492ft)

▲ **M79 grenade launcher**

199th Infantry Brigade / 7th Infantry Regiment, Long Binh, January 1968

The M79 'Thump Gun' provided infantry platoons with the capability to deliver indirect fire on enemy positions. Its break-open breech-loading action resulted in a low rate of fire, and the grenadier could not also carry a rifle.

sometimes in the dark, where long-range fire might be impossible. Here, the submachine gun was extremely potent.

Heavier weapons were generally used from fixed defensive positions or aboard vehicles, helicopters and river patrol boats. The venerable Browning M1919 and its water-cooled M1917 cousin served in the fire-support role with US and ARVN forces, where they proved themselves as effective as ever.

'Vietnamization'

A shift in US strategic perspective occurred in 1969, with the emphasis moving more towards 'Vietnamization'; taking control of the countryside back from the Viet Cong and developing the ability of South Vietnam to stand against the North as a united nation. US forces were reduced to appease the anti-war movement, and negotiations with the North were opened in the hope of finding a settlement.

By 1972 the Viet Cong, already depleted by the 1968 Tet Offensive, had lost control over much of countryside. The NVA responded with a conventional offensive, which was exactly what the US forces were best at dealing with. However, despite a victory the USA had problems at home, and internal pressure eventually forced a decision to pull out. The USA took steps to enable South Vietnam to defend itself, but these eventually proved inadequate in the face of an overwhelming Northern invasion. By then, however, US involvement in Vietnam was over.

▶ M26 fragmentation grenade

1st Marine Regiment, Hue, February 1968

The city of Hue was the site of the only real Communist success in the NVA Tet Offensive, and even that didn't last. Bitter urban fighting went on for a month before the city was retaken by US and ARVN forces. Fragmentation grenades proved especially lethal in confined spaces.

Specifications

Country of Origin: United States	Diameter: 57mm (2.24in)
Date: 1950s	Detonation Mechanism: Timed friction fuse
Type: Fragmentation	Filling: Composition B
Weight: .454kg (1lb)	Lethal radius:15m (49ft)
Height: 99mm (3.89in)	

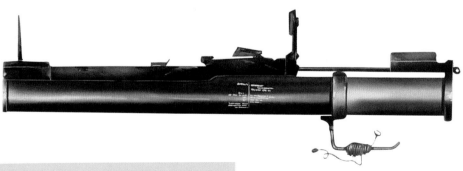

Specifications

Country of Origin: United States	Overall Length: 950mm (37.4in)
Date: 1963	Muzzle Velocity: 145m/sec (475ft/sec)
Calibre: 66mm (2.6in)	Feed/Magazine: Single-shot, muzzle-loaded
Operation: Rocket motor	Range: c.200m (650ft)
Weight: 2.5kg (5.5lb)	

▲ M72 LAW

196th Infantry Brigade / Operation Cedar Falls, January 1967

The M72 Light Anti-Tank Weapon was used in Vietnam primarily against bunkers and other fortified positions, as NVA tanks were rarely encountered.

US special forces
1967–75

A variety of special operations forces took part in the Vietnam conflict. They were given considerable latitude in choosing their weaponry.

THE US SENT MILITARY ADVISORS to South Vietnam long before its conventional forces became involved in the conflict. Increasing numbers of special forces personnel were deployed as the war went on, undertaking a wide variety of operations.

During World War II, special forces units had served mainly as covert raiding forces, but by 1960 they were heavily involved in training local personnel. The beneficiaries included the South Vietnamese regular army, as well as local defence units and irregulars recruited from indigenous peoples living in remote areas of Vietnam. Contacted and befriended by special operations groups, they were given training and weapons and fought against the Communists under US special forces leadership.

From 1960 to 1965 the US special forces learned their new role and developed their techniques to suit. The situation in Vietnam was novel, and beyond the existing experience of the US military, so a trial-and-error approach had to be used. Gradually, a body of knowledge was developed which could be applied to the unique demands of the situation. One key role of the special forces was reduction of Viet Cong

▲ **Advisory role**
A US special forces advisor accompanies two south Vietnamese irregulars. He is armed with a Colt Commando, a weapon issued primarily to US special forces.

influence by helping local communities defend themselves. Collectively known as the Civilian Irregular Defense Group (CIDG), this organization used special forces personnel to train local militias in weapons handling and small-unit tactics, and give

▲ **Heckler & Koch HK33**
5th Special Forces Group, Thong Binh, January 1968
The HK33 was used in very limited numbers by US special forces personnel, especially the US Navy SEALs, who prized its accuracy and reliability under difficult conditions.

Specifications

Country of Origin: West Germany	Barrel Length: 332mm (13.1in)
Date: 1968	Muzzle Velocity: 880m/sec (2887ft/sec)
Calibre: 7.62mm (.3in) NATO	Feed/Magazine: 20-round detachable box
Operation: Delayed blowback	magazine
Weight: 4.4kg (9.7lb)	Range: 500m (1640ft) +
Overall Length: 940mm (37in)	

them the confidence to defy the Viet Cong. CIDG was generally successful, and eventually CIDG personnel were able to go over from local defence duties to engaging the Viet Cong actively wherever they could be found.

Special forces personnel also engaged in more conventional operations, such as long-range reconnaissance and intelligence-gathering, ambushes, and rescues of personnel who had been captured or cut off. They had a range of weaponry at their disposal for these missions. The choice was usually high-firepower weapons that enabled the inevitably outnumbered special forces personnel to level the odds in an engagement.

Special forces units made extensive use of suppressed versions of standard firearms, which were highly useful in eliminating sentries or isolated personnel without alerting their comrades. Light, handy weapons such as submachine guns or the Colt Commando – a shortened version of the M16 rifle – were also popular. Weapons were selected to suit each mission; there was no standard issue.

Many weapons were 'sanitized', i.e. they had their serial numbers removed to prevent identification of the personnel involved in an incident. Some special forces troopers even favoured enemy equipment, making it easy to obtain ammunition during a long mission.

▲ **Ingram MAC 10**

CIA Operatives, Laos, 1971

The small size of the MAC 10 and its ability to use a suppressor made it an ideal weapon for covert operatives, whose mission might be compromised by even a victorious firefight.

Specifications

Country of Origin: United States	Overall Length: 548mm (21.57in)
Date: 1970	Barrel Length: 146mm (5.75in)
Calibre: 11.4mm (.45in)/45 ACP;	Muzzle Velocity: 366m/sec (1200ft/sec)
9mm (.35in) Parabellum	Feed/Magazine: 32-round detachable box
Operation: Blowback	magazine
Weight: 2.84kg (6.25lb)	Range: 70m (230ft)

▲ **Colt Commando**

US NAVY SEAL Teams / Mekong Delta, March 1970

The US Navy's Sea-Air-Land (SEAL) teams were active in Vietnam throughout the war, notably in operations to deny the enemy the use of waterways for logistics and troop movements.

Specifications

Country of Origin: United States	Overall Length: 780mm (30.7in)
Date: 1967	Barrel Length: 290mm (11.5in)
Calibre: 5.56mm (.219in) NATO	Muzzle Velocity: 796m/sec (2611ft/sec)
Operation: Gas	Feed/Magazine: 30-round box magazine
Weight: 2.44kg (5.38lb)	Range: 400m (1312ft)

Stoner Weapon System
1963–67

The Stoner Weapon System was built around a common receiver; it could be configured as a rifle, a carbine or a light machine gun.

EUGENE STONER designed the AR-15 rifle, which became the M16 in US military service, as well as several other weapons. His vision for the 'Stoner Weapon System' was to create a weapon that could be rapidly reconfigured to suit changing needs by fitting different barrels, feed mechanisms and stocks to a common receiver.

Evaluation

After experimenting with 7.62x51mm calibre, Stoner settled on 5.56x45mm and developed a prototype for military evaluation. Examples were deployed to Vietnam with special forces and some US Marine Corps units. There, the weapon system was found to be overcomplex and difficult to maintain in the field, though small numbers remained in use with the US Navy's SEAL teams for some years.

The Stoner receiver could be fed from a 20- or 30-round box magazine, a 100-round drum or a 100- or 150-round belt. The belt could be carried in a box or drum, allowing the weapon to be used as an assault rifle with huge ammunition capacity. The drum configuration proved to be the most popular of the possible options with US special forces, largely for this reason.

Barrels were designed for quick interchangeability, which also allowed a hot machine gun barrel to be rapidly swapped under sustained-fire use. A

▲ M63 tripod-mounted machine gun
US Navy SEALS (location unknown)
Mounted on a tripod, the Stoner M63 could fulfil a sustained-fire role for defence of a base or installation. It was still closer to a light machine gun than a general-purpose machine gun, however.

Specifications

Country of Origin: United States

Date: 1963

Calibre: 5.56mm (.219in)

Operation: Gas, air-cooled

Weight: 5.3kg (11.68lb)

Overall Length: 1022mm (40.25in) standard barrel

Barrel Length: 508mm (20in) standard; 399mm (15.7in) short

Muzzle Velocity: 1000m/sec (3280ft/sec)

Feed/Magazine: 150-round disintegrating-link boxed belt or a detachable box magazine

Cyclic Rate: 700–1000rpm

Range: 1000m (3280ft)

detachable bipod was often used in the light machine gun role, but could be removed or replaced with a tripod mount.

Different configurations

The weapon could be configured with a standard or folding stock and different barrels, and set up to fire from a closed or open bolt depending on its intended role. The carbine version, with a short barrel and folding stock, did not prove popular for various reasons. Notably, it was heavy for a weapon of its type. The assault rifle version fared little better, for much the same reasons.

As a light machine gun, the Stoner weapon system was a modest success. US special forces liked it, especially in 'Commando' configuration. This was a drum-fed variant of the LMG, which was light enough to be used as a rifle.

▲ M63 assault rifle

1st Marine Division / 1st Marine Regiment (location unknown), 1967

USMC units trialled the Stoner Weapon System in rifle configuration during 1967, but did not recommend it for adoption as a service weapon.

Specifications

Country of Origin: United States
Date: 1963
Calibre: 5.56mm (.219in)
Operation: Gas, rotating bolt
Weight: 5.3kg (11.68lb)
Overall Length: 1022mm (40.25in)

Barrel Length: 508mm (20in)
Muzzle Velocity: 3250ft/sec (991m/sec)
Feed/Magazine: 30-round detachable box magazine
Range: 200–1000m (656–3280ft)

Specifications

Country of Origin: United States
Date: 1963
Calibre: 5.56mm (.219in)
Operation: Gas, air-cooled
Weight: 5.3kg (11.68lb)
Overall Length: 1022mm (40.25in) standard barrel

Barrel Length: 508mm (20in) standard; 399mm (15.7in) short·
Muzzle Velocity: 1000m/sec (3280ft/sec)
Feed/Magazine: 150-round disintegrating-link boxed belt or a detachable box magazine
Range: 1000m (3280ft)

▲ M63 light machinegun

US Navy SEALs (location unknown)

The light machine gun version was used by some Navy SEAL teams. Its chief advantage was a huge ammunition capacity in a weapon not much heavier than a standard assault rifle.

AVRN forces
1959–75

The Army of the Republic of Vietnam (ARVN) was created with US assistance, and was armed and equipped along American lines.

AFTER THE INDOCHINA WAR ENDED, it was necessary to help South Vietnam create a military capable of defending against the Communist threat from the north. The recent Korean conflict shaped the thinking of US advisors sent to train the new force, and the strategists who decided what form it would take.

In Korea, the threat was a massive conventional attack by hordes of infantry and possibly tanks. The conventional force fielded by the USA and other nations, based on World War II experience, had proved effective against this threat, and so it was logical to build the ARVN along those lines.

This policy turned out to be a mistake. The ARVN lacked the training and confidence to deal with a mass insurgent campaign of the sort waged by the Viet Cong. It might possibly have handled a conventional invasion, but as post-US

▲ 'Tommy Gun'

US Army special advisors instruct South Vietnamese militia in the use of the Thompson submachine gun. 'Tommy Guns' were widely used by South Vietnamese army troops and security forces.

▲ M14A1 squad support weapon

25th ARVN Division / 50th ARVN Infantry Regiment, An Loc, April 1972

The M14 was not a huge success as an automatic rifle, and many examples were converted to squad-level support weapons, with a modified handgrip and stock. Ammunition supply and the lack of a quick-change barrel limited sustained-fire capability.

Specifications

Country of Origin: United States	Barrel Length: 558mm (22in)
Date: 1963	Muzzle Velocity: 595m/sec (1950ft/sec)
Calibre: 7.62mm (.3in) NATO	Feed/Magazine: 20-round detachable box
Operation: Gas	magazine
Weight: 3.88kg (8.55lb)	Range: 800m (2625ft) +
Overall Length: 1117mm (44in)	

withdrawal events showed, it could well have been as overmatched by the conventional forces of the NVA in 1959 as it was in 1975.

Imported weaponry

There was nothing wrong with the weaponry of the ARVN units. Much of it was perhaps obsolescent, such as the Thompson submachine gun, but it was still effective. Indeed, Thompsons were still being issued to some US troops due to insufficient numbers of the 'official' submachine gun, the M3 'Grease Gun'.

Significant amounts of ARVN equipment was bought overseas with US dollars, such as the Danish Madsen submachine gun. Other weapons were handed over as they became obsolete in US service. As the M14 rifle was replaced by the M16, quantities became available for other purposes. Some (in semi-automatic and full-automatic configurations) went to ARVN units, while others were converted to squad support weapons as the M14A1. Whilst not ideal for the role, the M14A1 did provide reasonable squad-level automatic fire support.

▲ Thompson Model 1928

25th ARVN Division / 25th Recon Battalion, An Loc, April 1972

Although its range was limited, the Thompson's reliability and good stopping power made it popular with reconnaissance and 'point' troops who might have to respond to a sudden contact or an ambush.

Specifications

Country of Origin: United States	Barrel Length: 266mm (10.5in)
Date: 1928	Muzzle Velocity: 280m/sec (920ft/sec)
Calibre: 11.4mm (.45in) M1911	Feed/Magazine: 18-, 20- or 30-round detachable
Operation: Delayed blowback	box magazine
Weight: 4.88kg (10.75lb)	Range: 120m (394ft)
Overall Length: 857mm (33.75in)	

Specifications

Country of Origin: Denmark	530mm (20.85in) stock folded
Date: 1950	Barrel Length: 197mm (7.75in)
Calibre: 9mm (.35in) Parabellum	Muzzle Velocity: 380m/sec (1274ft/sec)
Operation: Blowback	Feed/Magazine: 32-round detachable box
Weight: 3.17kg (6.99lb)	magazine
Overall Length: 800mm (31.5in) stock extended;	Range: 150m (492ft) +

▲ Madsen M50

1st ARVN Airborne Task Force, Hue, February 1968

The Madsen M50 had the unusual feature of a safety lever located just behind the magazine well, which functioned as a foregrip. If the weapon was not securely held in both hands, it could not fire.

Overall, the equipment of ARVN units was generally somewhat inferior to that of US forces, but not by such a great margin that they were massively outgunned by the NVA and Viet Cong. Indeed, the Communist forces were often using their own versions of the same weapons.

The main factors limiting the effectiveness of ARVN units were strategic, based on misconceptions about the nature of the war they were to fight, plus a lack of training and skilled leadership. Nevertheless, ARVN formations could and did fight well in the right circumstances.

▶ **Weapons training**

A US Army advisor trains ARVN irregulars in the use of a mortar. Most of the ARVN soldiers are armed with M1 carbines, although one can be seen holding a Thompson submachine gun.

Specifications

Country of Origin: United States	Barrel Length: 610mm (24in)
Date: 1918	Muzzle Velocity: 850m/sec (2800ft/sec)
Calibre: 7.62mm (.3in)	Feed/Magazine: Belt-fed
Operation: Recoil, water-cooled	Cyclic Rate: 600rpm
Weight: 15kg (32.75lb)	Range: 2000m (6560ft) +
Overall Length: 980mm (38.5in)	

▼ **Browning M1917**

7th Infantry Division / 11th Infantry Regiment, Ap Bac, January 1963

The water-cooled M1917, predecessor to the highly successful M1919, was primarily useful for defensive operations. Heavy and bulky, it required a steady supply of water for the cooling jacket.

Australian/NZ forces
1962–73

Both Australia and New Zealand deployed significant numbers of troops to Vietnam, and both suffered anti-war protests as a result.

CONCERNED ABOUT THE RISE OF COMMUNISM in nearby South-East Asia, Australia began sending military advisors to South Vietnam from 1962 onwards. New Zealand also sent military personnel, but these assisted in civilian construction and medical projects. From 1965, the New Zealand contribution included combat troops in the form of artillery and infantry, which were integrated into a joint Australian/New Zealander (ANZAC) battalion.

The Australian contribution was rather larger, creating an all-arms force which at first assisted US troops and then began to undertake operations within its own area of responsibility. The Australian units included special forces personnel and tanks as well as tactical air support elements.

The ANZAC forces proved to be extremely good jungle fighters, drawing on expertise gained in World War II, the Malayan Emergency and in Indonesia. They were capable in both small-scale patrol actions and larger battles, inflicting heavy casualties in defence of their bases. In 1968 the ANZAC force took part in resisting the Tet Offensive, with many troops established in blocking or ambush positions to prevent NVA infiltration.

Cordon-and-search operations

Most commonly, ANZAC forces were involved in typical cordon-and-search operations of a sort used by the British in dealing with many insurgencies. An area would be cordoned off and then systematically combed for hostiles and weapons caches. Those who tried to escape the encirclement were dealt with by the cordoning troops. Although slow and manpower-intensive, these operations were successful in reducing the enemy's ability to operate in the countryside.

Cordon-and-search operations, and patrols in the jungle, required good leadership at junior levels, skill and patience. ANZAC operations were often very methodical, reducing the chances of being ambushed but inviting criticism from US commanders who

favoured a firepower-and-aggression approach to driving the enemy from his hiding places.

Although the ANZAC contingent did have armoured, air and artillery support, it was rifle squads that fought the bulk of actions. Whereas the US policy was to call in air and artillery support to inflict casualties on the enemy wherever possible, the ANZAC force preferred to use small-unit tactics and to stay in contact with a withdrawing enemy. Small units would be used to locate and track the enemy, with larger forces then brought up for an attack.

Artillery or air bombardment would have forced friendly ground troops to halt out of the danger zone and allowed enemy survivors a chance to disengage, but by relying only on their squad weapons the ANZAC infantry could maintain a close pursuit and deny the guerrillas their primary advantage – the ability to break contact and disappear.

▲ **Anti-guerrilla operations**
Armed with trusty L1A1 SLR rifles, Australian troops exchange fire with Communist forces somewhere in Vietnam.

The primary infantry weapon of Australian and New Zealander forces was the FN FAL/L1A1 rifle, chambered for 7.62x51mm ammunition. In the hands of troops whose training emphasized individual marksmanship over suppressive fire, this was an effective weapon, although its long-range accuracy was somewhat wasted in jungle engagements. For high firepower at close range, Australian troops favoured the indigenous F1 submachine gun. Although a curious top-loading design it proved reliable and easy to handle, and less prone to stoppages than many other contemporary submachine gun designs.

Overall, the ANZAC forces fought their part of the war on a small scale, using similar tactics to the guerrillas they hunted, and they were feared by their opponents. However, increasing opposition to the war and a lack of confidence in the US commitment to it after 1968 led to a gradual reduction in commitment and a complete withdrawal in 1973.

Specifications

Country of Origin: Belgium	Barrel Length: 533mm (21in)
Date: 1954	Muzzle Velocity: 853m/sec (2800ft/sec)
Calibre: 7.62mm (.3in) NATO	Feed/Magazine: 20-round detachable box
Operation: Gas, self-loading	magazine
Weight: 4.31kg (9.5lb)	Range: 800m (2625ft) +
Overall Length: 1053mm (41.46in)	

▲ FN FAL/L1A1

1st Australian Task Force / 6th Battalion, Royal Australian Regiment, Long Tan, August 1966

The 7.62x51mm L1A1 (the British and Australian version of the Belgian FN FAL) was best suited to actions in the open at medium to long range, where its user's marksmanship was a big advantage. At closer range it was arguably outgunned by assault rifles like the AK-47.

Specifications

Country of Origin: Australia	Overall Length: 715mm (28.1in)
Date: 1963	Barrel Length: 203mm (8in)
Calibre: 9mm (.35in)	Muzzle Velocity: 365m/sec (1200ft/sec)
Operation: Blowback	Feed/Magazine: 34-round magazine
Weight: 3.26kg (7.1lb)	Range: 100–200m (328–656ft)

▲ F1 submachine gun

173rd Airborne Brigade (US) / 1st Royal Australian Regiment, Gang Toi, November 1965

The F1 submachine gun favoured by Australian forces used a two-stage trigger for fire selection; halfway for single shots and a full trigger pull for automatic fire.

Specifications

Country of Origin: United Kingdom	660mm (26in) stock folded
Date: 1967	Barrel Length: 198mm (7.8in)
Calibre: 9mm (.35in) Parabellum	Muzzle Velocity: 300m/sec (984ft/sec)
Operation: Blowback	Feed/Magazine: 34-round detachable box
Weight: 3.6kg (7.94lb)	magazine
Overall Length: 864mm (34in) stock extended;	Range: 120m (394ft)

▲ **L34A1 Sterling**

1st Australian Task Force / Special Air Service Regiment, Suoi Pha Chau, August 1967

The Australian SAS made extensive use of the suppressed Sterling L34A1 during reconnaissance patrols and covert operations.

NVA/Vietcong Forces
1959–75

The North Vietnamese Army (NVA) and Viet Cong were separate forces operating in different ways towards a common political goal.

THE NORTH VIETNAMESE ARMY was a conventionally equipped force capable of undertaking large-scale operations in the field. Although it was also entirely able of carrying out small-scale guerrilla actions, its main role was that of any regular army – the defeat of the enemy's major forces and the capture of their bases.

The Viet Cong, on the other hand, was a guerrilla force unsuited to major conventional actions. Its personnel were equipped with a variety of armament and, usually, little in the way of support weapons. The Viet Cong was well suited to contesting control of the countryside. Its units needed little in the way of resupply; food, clothing and ammunition were all that was required and much of this could be extorted from villages or scavenged from enemy casualties.

Weapons

NVA and Viet Cong forces inherited a large quantity of arms left over from the previous war against France. This was augmented by locally produced weapons based on Soviet designs or near-identical copies of them, and examples of the original weapons

themselves supplied by the Soviet Union and China. Viet Cong units often had to make do with whatever weapons were left over after equipping NVA infantry units, and so were issued a wide range of equipment. This included obsolete but effective weapons such as unlicensed Chinese copies of the Mauser C/96 pistol and other European weapons. Other, near-identical, weapons were originals supplied for use in earlier conflicts.

Regular NVA units were equipped as uniformly as possible and with the best weapons available. These included the Soviet AK-47 and the Chinese Type 56, which was a direct copy. Although lacking the long-range accuracy of Western rifles, the AK-47 was robust, easy to maintain and reliable even in jungle conditions. Its 30-round magazine and powerful round gave greater and more controllable firepower than US M14 rifle, while the M16 was (at least at first) far less reliable than its less advanced opponent.

Viet Cong capabilities

The Viet Cong did have considerable popular support in many areas, though this tended to vary according to how effectively the government's counter-insurgency measures were working. Genuine supporters were greatly outnumbered by those who could be swayed by a show of strength, and as the Viet Cong's power in the south waned, so did the degree of support it received.

However, the Viet Cong also received support via the Ho Chi Minh Trail through Laos and Cambodia, despite US efforts to interdict the flow of supplies. Thus many of its units were armed with Chinese, Soviet or North Korean weapons, while others had to make do with whatever could be scavenged.

Some personnel were armed with extremely outdated equipment, though this did not equate to ineffectiveness in combat. Like all successful guerrillas, the Viet Cong were skilled at striking and then disappearing into the countryside or hiding among the general populace. Here again, the relative power of the Viet Cong in a region would often determine how willing the local population would be to hide guerrillas from the authorities.

In the early years of the conflict, the Viet Cong were the main instrument used by the Communists, and up until 1965 they were successful enough that political collapse in South Vietnam seemed likely. Lightly-equipped NVA units were slipped into South

▶ Mauser C96

Viet Cong / 514th Battalion, Ap Bac, January 1963

Chinese copies of the venerable Mauser C96 were supplied to Viet Cong fighters along with thousands of other weapons made available by the end of the Chinese Civil War.

Specifications

Country of Origin: Germany	Barrel Length: 140mm (5.51in)
Date: 1896	Muzzle Velocity: 305m/sec (1000ft/sec)
Calibre: 7.63mm (.3in)	Feed/Magazine: 6- or 10-round integral or
Operation: Short recoil	detachable box magazine
Weight: 1.045kg (2.3lb)	Range: 100m (328ft)
Overall Length: 295mm (11.6in)	

Specifications

Country of Origin: USSR	Barrel Length: 415mm (16.34in)
Date: 1959	Muzzle Velocity: 600m/sec (2350ft/sec)
Calibre: 7.62mm (.3in) Soviet M1943	Feed/Magazine: 30-round detachable box
Operation: Gas	magazine
Weight: 4.3kg (9.48lb)	Range: 400m (1312ft)
Overall Length: 880mm (34.65in)	

▲ AKM assault rifle

North Vietnamese Army / 325th Division, A Shau, March 1966

The NVA equipped many of its units with an updated version of the AK-47 designated AKM, supplied in large numbers by the Soviet Union. The AKM was introduced into Soviet Army service in 1959, and became the most ubiquitous variant of the entire AK series.

Vietnam in 1964 in anticipation; once in place they would be quickly able to restore order and install the Communist regime in a unified country.

However, instead of accepting victory, the NVA formations found themselves deep in enemy territory as the US intervention began. Unable to take on the Americans directly, many units dispersed to add to the strength of the Viet Cong. Although casualties were high in the clashes that followed, they never exceeded half the birth rate and were acceptable to the leaders and population of North Vietnam.

The NVA faced major US formations across the DMZ, exchanging artillery fire and engaging in near-constant skirmishing. Its forces also operated out of Laos and Cambodia, launching attacks into South Vietnam and then withdrawing to safety. Meanwhile, other elements were engaged in defensive operations in North Vietnam itself. The possibility of a US invasion was never ruled out, and the NVA had to be ready to respond at any time.

The Viet Cong, meanwhile, launched ambushes and attacked outposts throughout South Vietnam. One tactic was to attack an isolated post and then ambush the relief force, which of course had to proceed along a predictable route. The main role of the Viet Cong, however, was political rather than military. The casualties it inflicted on the US forces would have been acceptable in a major conflict like World War II or even Korea, but by the mid 1960s the mood 'back home' had changed and even

relatively low casualties provoked a negative response. The Viet Cong not only inflicted a steady stream of casualties but also drained US and South Vietnamese resources. Bridges, roads and towns had to be guarded; movement in many areas was only possible in heavily escorted convoys. Artillery firebases and supply bases were constantly harassed, tying down yet more resources. The Viet Cong also exerted strong influence over the population of the countryside, who lost faith in a government that seemed unable to protect them.

By 1968, the conflict had settled into a fairly steady pattern. The NVA tied up large-scale US formations and the Viet Cong wore down the political will of, and support for, the US and South Vietnamese governments. Nowhere in South Vietnam was entirely safe from guerrilla attacks and larger NVA offensives were capable of reaching areas a considerable distance from the Laotian or Cambodian border. The US forces had reason to believe that they were winning the war, however. Body counts were massively in favour of the USA and every major battle against the NVA had been won.

Tet Offensive

In January 1968, the North launched an operation that became known as the Tet Offensive, named after the period of the Vietnamese calendar in which it occurred. Attacks were coordinated between the NVA and the Viet Cong, which committed its entire

Specifications

Country of Origin: China	Barrel Length: 415mm (16.34in)
Date: 1956	Muzzle Velocity: 600mps (1969ft/sec)
Calibre: 7.62mm (.3in) Soviet M1943	Feed/Magazine: 30-round detachable box
Operation: Gas	magazine
Weight: 4.3kg (9.48lb)	Range: 400m (1312ft)
Overall Length: 880mm (34.65in)	

▲ Chinese Type 56 assault rifle

NVA 2nd Corps / 304th Division, Hue, March 1975

The Type 56 rifle supplied by China to many NVA units was distinguishable from the AK-47, of which it was a copy, mainly by the folding bayonet, though not all Type 56 rifles had this feature.

strength. More than 50 provincial capitals were attacked as well as outposts, bases and towns all over the country.

Tet was a failure for the North Vietnamese. It took a month to clear NVA forces from the ancient city of Hue, but most other objectives were either successfully defended or were cleared within a few days. The Viet Cong suffered such a mauling that it ceased to be much of a factor after Tet.

Connected with the Tet offensive was the siege of Khe Sanh, a major US base close to the border. Although there were fears that the North Vietnamese might succeed in turning Khe Sanh into another Dien Bien Phu, the base was never seriously threatened and the siege was called off after heavy fighting once the failure of Tet made it irrelevant.

The attacks on Khe Sanh were conventional infantry assaults with artillery support, carried out by regular troops. Although some assaults were successful, the US forces within the base were able to hold their perimeter and were eventually relieved by a ground and airmobile advance. After the Tet Offensive, the power of the Viet Cong was broken and the NVA carried on the war. It attempted to wage a guerrilla campaign in the south but was not very successful, and gradually the military balance tipped towards the US and South Vietnam. However, Tet had shaken the confidence of the USA to win the war, and prompted ever more intense anti-war sentiment. Despite being a military failure, Tet was a war-winning political success for the North.

Re-equipped

As the US tried to strengthen South Vietnam so that it could extricate itself from the conflict, the North attempted another major offensive in 1972. Re-

◀ Tula-Tokarev TT-33

Viet Cong / 186th Battalion, Mekong Delta, January 1965

The Soviet-supplied Tokarev handgun fired a weak cartridge but was reliable in combat. It was used more for intimidation purposes or covert attacks than as a serious combat weapon.

Specifications

Country of Origin: USSR	Barrel Length: 116mm (4.57in)
Date: 1933	Muzzle Velocity: 415m/sec (1362ft/sec)
Calibre: 7.62mm (.3in) Soviet	Feed/Magazine: 8-round detachable box
Operation: Short recoil	magazine
Weight: .83kg (1.83lb)	Range: 30m (98ft)
Overall Length: 194mm (7.6in)	

▲ Simonov SKS

Viet Cong / 275th Regiment, Long Tan, August 1966

Fed by an internal 10-round magazine, the SKS belonged to an earlier generation of rifles but remained effective in the hands of concealed guerrilla marksmen.

Specifications

Country of Origin: China/USSR	Overall Length: 1021mm (40.2in)
Date: 1945	Barrel Length: 521mm (20.5in)
Calibre: 7.62mm (.3in)	Muzzle Velocity: 735m/sec (2411ft/sec)
Operation: Gas short-stroke piston	Feed/Magazine: 10-round integral box magazine
Weight: 3.85kg (8.49lb)	Range: 400m (1312ft)

equipped with armament supplied by the Soviet Union, the NVA could field 130mm (5.1in) artillery and T54 tanks. Small arms included AK-47s from the Soviet Union and Type 56 rifles from China, which was more or less a direct copy. Some units still had to make do with what weapons they could get but on the whole the NVA was well equipped as a modern fighting force, and was quite capable of taking on ARVN formations equipped in the US style.

Advances were made into the north of the country from Laos and across the DMZ, while other NVA forces attacked towards Saigon from bases in Cambodia. The offensive was initially successful, defeating many ARVN formations in conventional battle, but gradually stalled in the face of stiffening resistance and US air support. Logistical difficulties plagued the NVA forces, along with a lack of experience at coordinating all arms in large-scale mobile operations. After years of relatively subtle guerrilla warfare, the NVA commanders resorted to frontal assaults against prepared positions, and their forces suffered accordingly.

The 1972 spring offensive collapsed so decisively that the NVA desperately needed time to reorganize and bring its depleted units up to strength. Negotiations were opened to stall for time, preventing a counter-offensive by ARVN forces, and over the next months the NVA rebuilt its strength.

Specifications

Country of Origin: Germany	Barrel Length: 418mm (16.5in)
Date: 1944	Muzzle Velocity: 700m/sec (2300ft/sec)
Calibre: 7.92mm (.312in) Kurz	Feed/Magazine: 30-round detachable box
Operation: Gas	magazine
Weight: 5.1kg (11.24lb)	Range: c.400m (1312ft)
Overall Length: 940mm (37in)	

▲ **Sturmgewehr 44**

Viet Cong Irregulars, Mekong Delta, April 1962

The StG44 was the world's first true assault rifle. Examples generally found their way into Viet Cong hands by way of the Soviet Union, which had captured large numbers during the invasion of Germany at the end of World War II.

Specifications

Country of Origin: USSR	Barrel Length: 520mm (20.5in)
Date: 1962	Muzzle Velocity: 735m/sec (2410ft/sec)
Calibre: 7.62mm (.3in) M1943	Feed/Magazine: 100-round belt contained in
Operation: Gas, air-cooled	drum
Weight: 7kg (15.43lb)	Cyclic Rate: 700rpm
Overall Length: 1041mm (41in)	Range: 900m (2953ft)

▲ **RPD light machine gun**

North Vietnamese Army / 304th Division / 66th Regiment, Khe Sanh, January 1968

The Soviet-supplied RPD was essentially an overgrown Kalashnikov rifle fed by a 100-round belt carried in a drum. It offered heavy squad-level firepower using the same ammunition as the surrounding riflemen.

US departure

US forces in South Vietnam were gradually reduced, with the last ground formations leaving in 1973. They left behind a situation that seemed generally positive despite continued NVA attacks. The ARVN had a numerical superiority over its opponents and was well equipped with artillery and armoured vehicles. However, the NVA had learned from its disastrous offensive in 1972 and had been extensively rearmed. By early 1974 it once again outnumbered its opponent, not least due to force reductions in South Vietnam after the withdrawal of US military aid. No longer needing to worry about the possibility of a US invasion, the NVA could commit its whole strength to a new offensive, and could concentrate at a point of its choosing. The whole eastern frontier of South Vietnam was open to attack, along with the obvious route across the DMZ from the north.

▲ **CZ Model 25**

North Vietnamese Army, 1970

The CZ Model 25 was the best known of a series of Czechoslovak-designed submachine guns introduced in 1948. After the Model 25 was declared obsolete in 1968, many of the 9mm (.35in) weapons were sold around the world. The surplus weapons were exported to other Communist countries, including North Vietnam.

Specifications

Country of Origin: Czechoslovakia	Overall Length: 686mm (27in)
Date: 1948	Barrell Length: 284mm (11.18in)
Calibre: 7.62mm (.3in); 9mm (.35in)	Muzzel Velocity: not known
Operation: Blowback	Feed/Magazine: 24- or 40-round box magazine
Weight: 3.27kg (7.20lb)	Range: 100–200m (328 feet to 656 feet)

Specifications

Country of Origin: USSR	Barrel Length: 1066mm (42in)
Date: 1938	Muzzle Velocity: 850m/sec (2788ft/sec)
Calibre: 12.7mm (.5in) Soviet	Feed/Magazine: 50-round belt
Operation: Gas, air-cooled	Cyclic Rate: 550rpm
Weight: 35.5kg (78.5lb)	Range: 2000m (6560ft) +
Overall Length: 1586mm (62.5in)	

▲ **DShK heavy machine gun**

North Vietnamese Army / 304th Division / 24th Regiment, Lang Vei, January 1968

The DShK machine gun was used in an infantry support role and also as an anti-aircraft weapon. Some examples in NVA service came from the Soviet Union; others were near-identical Chinese copies.

Afghanistan
1979–89

Intervention by the Soviet Union in Afghanistan led to a drawn-out counter-insurgent war that has been called 'The Soviet Vietnam'.

RUSSIA, AND LATER THE SOVIET UNION, had a long-standing interest in Afghanistan, dating from the middle of the nineteenth century. In the 1950s, Afghanistan requested financial aid from both the USA and the Soviet Union, which was granted for political reasons. For some years the country benefited from the superpowers competing for influence, but US aid was curtailed in the 1960s. Although still officially independent, Afghanistan was now firmly in the Soviet sphere of influence and reliant on financial aid from Moscow.

Turbulent Afghan politics produced a revolution in 1973 and a counter-revolution in 1978. The new government, with Soviet assistance, pushed through a number of reforms which alarmed traditionalists within Afghan society. Rebellion followed, spreading out from the Kunar Valley into most of Afghanistan's provinces.

The Soviet Union was concerned at this threat to its influence in Afghanistan and supplied modern weaponry to the Afghan Army, along with advisors to improve training standards. It also advised the Afghan government to slow down the pace of reforms and also to negotiate with the rebels, actions that caused a split in the Afghan government and an attempted coup.

With matters getting out of hand, the Soviet Union reluctantly decided upon a full-scale intervention. The incursion was presented as assistance to the Afghan government rather than an invasion, but all the same it provoked international sanctions and fierce resistance from Afghan rebels.

With advisors in place, gathering intelligence was not a problem for the Soviet forces, but the units that carried out the invasion were on the whole inexperienced. Many formations were composed of reservists who had been activated for the operation. There were some high-quality units involved, however, such as the Guards Airborne Division, which secured Bagram airbase in order to permit reinforcements to be flown in directly.

The Afghan response was derailed partly by deception. Many units were told by their advisors that their vehicles were to be upgraded or replaced; they were actually taken out of service by their own maintenance crews. At Bagram, Soviet troops were expected. They were supposedly coming to help with the security situation, which was at least partially true. Much of the Afghan army was disarmed and disbanded after the Soviets secured themselves in the country. A significant proportion of these troops joined the rebels – the real struggle was beginning.

▶ **Makarov PM pistol**

Soviet advisors to the Afghan Army, December 1979

The standard Soviet military handgun, the Pistolet Makarova (PM), fired a 9x18mm round that was incompatible with 9mm weapons used in the rest of the world.

Specifications

Country of Origin: USSR	Barrel Length: 91mm (3.5in)
Date: 1951	Muzzle Velocity: 315m/sec (1033ft/sec)
Calibre: 9mm (.35in) Makarov	Feed/Magazine: 8-round detachable box
Operation: Blowback	magazine
Weight: .66kg (1.46lb)	Range: 40m (131ft)
Overall Length: 160mm (6.3in)	

Soviet forces
1979–89

Soviet forces brought decent weapon systems to the war in Afghanistan, although as events demonstrated these could not compensate for poor training.

THE SOVIET ARMY that entered Afghanistan was shaped by the needs of the Cold War and the unique circumstances of the Soviet Union and its Warsaw Pact allies. With enormous manpower available, the Soviet Union relied on a short-service conscript army backed up by reserve units that could be filled out to full strength as needed. As a result, training levels were not high and most tactics were simple. The vast number of men fielded by the Soviet Union meant that the cost of equipment was critical. It also had to be simple and rugged; as 'soldier-proof' as possible to survive in the hands of relatively unskilled conscripts. This did not make Soviet equipment ineffective; large amounts of adequate weaponry may in some circumstances be more useful than smaller quantities of more advanced equipment.

The standard rifle used by the Soviet forces, the AK-74, was first and foremost easy to use and maintain, and extremely tolerant of abuse. It was developed from the AK-47 through the improved AKM and used the same basic mechanism. However,

it fired a lighter 5.45x39mm round and thus produced less recoil.

Range limits

Like all assault rifles, the AK-74 was primarily designed for combat at 200–300m (656–984ft) ranges or closer, and was less accurate at longer ranges than the M16. Its capabilities could be a limiting factor in Afghanistan, where combat ranges might be several hundred metres, but in any case the average conscript lacked the marksmanship skills to shoot effectively at such ranges. Where the AK-74 excelled was in delivering mass suppressive fire at moderate range, which suited the Soviet way of fighting.

The limited effective range of the AK-74 was somewhat offset by the inclusion in each platoon of a designated marksman armed with a Dragunov SVD rifle. These men were not snipers as such; their role was essentially that of a long-range marksman within the 'ordinary' infantry formations. While others delivered suppressive fire, the marksman was to pick off high-

▲ **Kalashnikov AK-74**

Soviet 40th Army / 5th Guards Division, Kandahar, January 1979

The AK-74 used a lighter round than the AK-47. The round reduced the gun's felt recoil and made the weapon more controllable to fire in both automatic and semi-automatic modes.

Specifications

Country of Origin: USSR	Barrel Length: 400mm (15.8in)
Date: 1974	Muzzle Velocity: 900m/sec (2952ft/sec)
Calibre: 5.45mm (.215in) M74	Feed/Magazine: 30-round detachable box
Operation: Gas	magazine
Weight: 3.6kg (7.94lb)	Range: 300m (984ft)
Overall Length: 943mm (37.1in)	

value targets such as officers and radio men. In Afghanistan this role was usually modified to one of engaging long-range or difficult targets, such as enemy riflemen hidden in high rocks during an ambush.

Fire support

Fire support was provided by RPK-74 and PKM machine guns, which had slightly different roles. The RPK-74 was essentially an AK-74 with a larger magazine capacity and a heavy barrel to dissipate heat. For squad-level light support it was effective, but it was not capable of sustained fire in the manner of a 'true' machine gun, due to ammunition capacity and overheating. It was lighter and more mobile however, which made it a useful weapon when operating in the difficult terrain of Afghanistan's mountains.

The PKM was a true machine gun, capable of sustained fire. Versions were used for infantry support and mounted on armoured vehicles. The BMP armoured personnel carrier used by the Soviet Army generally carried a pintle-mounted PKM, which could be used to support the infantry when dismounted.

Some Soviet units were issued the AKS-74, a version of the standard AK-74 with a folding stock. This was useful for troops who moved in and out of vehicles a lot, but was otherwise similar to the standard infantry rifle. The AKS-74U was a shortened carbine version of the AK-74 with a folding stock. It was largely used by airborne troops and special forces, as well as being issued to vehicle and artillery crews.

Uncoventional enemy

The Soviet forces that entered Afghanistan were well suited to conventional action against a clear enemy, and at first this is what they encountered. Some elements of the Afghan Army tried to oppose the intervention. In open battle they were no match for the Soviets, who had good air and artillery support. Popular uprisings in some urban centres were also relatively easy to put down.

The Soviet Army thus found it relatively straightforward to occupy and secure the cities of Afghanistan, but provincial areas were more of a problem. Most of the country was outside government control, and Soviet forces initially concentrated on securing the main communications

RED ARMY MOTORIZED RIFLE COMPANY, HQ EQUIPMENT	
Personnel	Equipment
Company HQ	BMP
Company Commander	PM (Makarov pistol)
Deputy Commander/Political Officer	PM
Senior Technician	PM
First Sergeant	AK-74
BMP Commander/Gunner	PM
BMP Driver/Mechanic	PM

RED ARMY MOTORIZED RIFLE COMPANY, PLATOON EQUIPMENT	
Personnel	Equipment
Platoon HQ	3 x BMPs
Platoon Leader	PM
Assistant Platoon Leader	AK-74

RED ARMY MOTORIZED RIFLE COMPANY, SQUAD EQUIPMENT	
Personnel	Equipment
Squad	BMP
Squad Leader/BMP Commander	AK-74
Assistant Squad Leader/BMP Gunner	AK-74
BMP Driver/Mechanic	PM
Machine Gunner	RPK-74
Machine Gunner	RPK-74
Grenadier	RPG-16/PM
Senior Rifleman	AK-74
Rifleman/Assistant Grenadier	AK-74
Rifleman	AK-74

One squad in each platoon was equipped with an SVD sniper rifle, in addition to the weapons listed above.

routes. Once established, and with a pro-Soviet Afghan government in place, the army began to launch operations against the rebels, or Mujahadeen.

Government installations in many of the provinces were in a state of virtual siege, and a major goal of operations against the insurgents was to break up or at least drive off nearby rebel groups, allowing the government apparatus to function as it was supposed to. This strategy was successful for a time after each operation, but control of most regions was lost soon after the troops returned to base.

Initially, the Soviets hoped to take a supporting role, assisting the Afghan Army in clearing the insurgents. Low morale, massive desertion and inadequate training made the Afghan Army ineffective in this role, and it was not greatly helped by a Soviet strategy that was interpreted as hiding behind the Afghan troops. Soviet personnel took on specialist roles such as artillery, armoured and air support while the bulk of the infantry work, and therefore casualties, fell on the Afghans. This situations caused resentment and drove down morale.

Unable to rely on the personnel they were ostensibly helping, the Soviets were forced to undertake operations on their own. Search-and-destroy operations were common, not unlike those used by the Americans in Vietnam. Ground troops were used to locate insurgent groups, which were then attacked by helicopter gunships and infantry with armoured vehicles in support.

Other measures included air attacks on villages suspected of offering support to the Mujahadeen, in the hope of depriving the insurgents of some of their bases of operations. Covert operations by Soviet special forces and infiltration by Afghan agents were also somewhat successful in reducing the effectiveness of the Mujahadeen in some areas.

However, the Mujahadeen were still able to attack installations, from public buildings to pipelines and power stations. They assassinated government figures, contested control over the countryside, and ambushed Soviet patrols or military convoys wherever they could.

There are few routes suitable for military convoys in the entire country, and these often run through mountainous areas full of excellent ambush spots. The Afghan tribes have a long tradition of resisting foreign invaders, and at times attacked Soviet convoys at points that had been used to ambush British troops a century before. Attacks ranged from harassment by the occasional sniper high up in the rocks beside the road to full-scale assaults with the intent of overrunning a convoy or part of it. Afterward, the insurgents withdrew into the mountainous terrain and broke contact.

One solution to the problem of ambushes along the mountain roads was to use airmobile forces to occupy high ground ahead of the convoy, picking up troops after the convoy had passed and moving them forward to the next overwatch point. This method was an extremely expensive and resource-intensive way to provide security, but it did prove effective. Helicopter gunships were also used against insurgent groups and were often successful in dispersing their attacks.

▲ **AKS-74**

Soviet 40th Army / 201st Motor Rifle Division, Kunduz, April 1979

The AKS-74 had a folding stock, which made it convenient for troops using motorized transport. It could be fired with reasonable short-range accuracy with the stock folded.

Specifications

Country of Origin: USSR	Barrel Length: 400mm (15.8in)
Date: 1974	Muzzle Velocity: 900m/sec (2952ft/sec)
Calibre: 5.45mm (.215in) M74	Feed/Magazine: 30-round detachable box
Operation: Gas	magazine
Weight: 3.6kg (7.94lb)	Range: 300m (984ft)
Overall Length: 943mm (37.1in) stock extended;	
690mm (27.2in) stock folded	

Up until 1985, the Soviets tried to defeat the insurgency by bringing the Mujahadeen to action and defeating them in the field. If enough bases could be destroyed, the insurgents could be driven from a region and the government could take control. Also, if enough casualties could be inflicted, the rebels might lose heart. However, despite successes in action, the Soviet Army was primarily engaged in holding onto its position in Afghanistan rather than making any real headway against the Mujahadeen.

The Soviet Army was generally effective in direct combat against the Mujahadeen forces, and could bring much greater numbers to bear at any given point than most insurgent bands. Yet it could only exert control over a region by direct action. Once the Soviet troops moved on, the insurgents came out of hiding or returned from other regions. Only by strengthening the control of the Afghan government could the insurgency be defeated.

To this end, attempts were made to build up the Afghan Army along Soviet lines. Provided with good, modern weapons and properly trained, the Afghan Army might be able to take over the fight against the Mujahadeen. After 1985, this effort was more about ending the Soviet involvement in Afghanistan than winning the fight. The cost of remaining in Afghanistan was becoming too high, in terms of casualties, money and also international politics.

▶ **AKS-74U**

Soviet 40th Army / 70th Separate Motor Rifle Brigade, Laghman Province, February 1983

A specially created counter-insurgency formation, the 70th Motor Rifle Brigade combined mobile ground troops with an air assault formation. The small AKS-74U was widely issued to heliborne troops.

Specifications

Country of Origin: USSR	Barrel Length: 390mm (15.3in)
Date: 1974	Muzzle Velocity: 900m/sec (2952ft/sec)
Calibre: 5.45mm (.215in) M74	Feed/Magazine: 30-round detachable box
Operation: Gas	magazine
Weight: 3.2kg (7lb)	Range: 300m (984ft)
Overall Length: 730mm (28in)	

Specifications

Country of Origin: USSR	Barrel Length: 610mm (24in)
Date: 1963	Muzzle Velocity: 828m/sec (2720ft/sec)
Calibre: 7.62mm (.3in) Soviet	Feed/Magazine: 10-round detachable box
Operation: Gas	magazine
Weight: 4.31kg (9.5lb)	Range: 1000m (3280ft)
Overall Length: 1225mm (48.2in)	

▲ **Dragunov SVD**

Soviet 40th Army / 108th Motor Rifle Brigade, Jalalabad, March 1989

The Dragunov SVD provided infantry platoons with long-range firepower, extending the effective engagement range out to about 600m (1970ft). Its users were not snipers in the conventional sense, but infantry marksmen who were integrated with the rest of the unit.

▲ **PKM general-purpose machine gun**

Soviet 40th Army / 5th Guards Motor Rifle Division / 68th Guards Separate
Engineer Battalion, Adraskan, July 1984

The PKM machine gun was a workhorse that could be used for infantry support or
to create defended positions in a secured base area. It was fed by 25-round belts,
several of which could be linked together to create a longer belt.

Specifications

Country of Origin: USSR	Barrel Length: 658mm (25.9in)
Date: 1969	Muzzle Velocity: 800m/sec (2600ft/sec)
Calibre: 7.62mm (.3in) M1943	Feed/Magazine: Belt-fed (belts contained in
Operation: Gas, air-cooled	boxes)
Weight: 9kg (19.84lb)	Cyclic Rate: 710rpm
Overall Length: 1160mm (45.67in)	Range: 2000m (6560ft) +

This investment in the Afghan Army was partially successful, but the Afghan force was still prone to high levels of desertion. In some cases this was deliberate; insurgents would join in the hope of obtaining training, weaponry and information about government operations, then return to their comrades in arms. Sometimes they were able to take Soviet-supplied weapons with them.

The Soviets returned to a policy of using Afghan troops for the majority of infantry operations, with Soviet personnel in support. By this time the Mujahadeen were sufficiently powerful that they would sometimes contest a region rather than dispersing when large government forces moved in, and though the Afghan Army achieved some successes they came at the cost of serious casualties.

Despite the fact that the Afghan Army was not confident enough, nor capable enough, to take on the insurgents alone, the Soviets began a withdrawal from Afghanistan in 1987. This was in part to extricate itself from an impossible and costly situation, and partly driven by politics. Under new leadership, the Soviet Union was seeking better relations with the rest of the world, and ending the contentious involvement in Afghanistan removed a significant bone of contention.

Towards the end of their involvement in Afghanistan, Soviet forces were limited to self-defence and limited local operations to ensure the security of their supply lines. In 1989, Soviet forces made their withdrawal from Afghanistan. Negotiations with the Mujahadeen were generally successful in permitting a bloodless pullout in most areas, but a major clash occurred in the Panjshir valley. Soviet forces declined to close with the enemy but instead used air power and artillery to inflict casualties from a distance.

After the Soviet withdrawal, the Afghan Army abandoned some regions where the Mujahadeen were considered too strong to take on, but had victories in other engagements. The situation in Afghanistan did not greatly change in the immediate aftermath of the Soviet withdrawal. However, the government was still reliant on Soviet financial support. Economic troubles in the Soviet Union reduced the funds available for assistance, and the Afghan government could not maintain its forces in the field.

The defection of previously pro-government militias to the Mujahadeen sealed the fate of the government, which collapsed into factional infighting. Mujahadeen forces entered Kabul in 1992 and, after fighting among themselves for control of the capital, succeeded in creating the Islamic State of Afghanistan. This was toppled in 1996 by the

▲ **Basic army**
Armed with a variety of Soviet-made small arms, Afghan Army soldiers pose during the Soviet withdrawal from Kabul. 1989.

forces of the Taliban, which set up the Islamic Emirate of Afghanistan.

The Taliban government received little international recognition and was frequently condemned for its disregard of human rights. In 2001 it was removed from power by another invasion, this time by Western forces. By then, however, the Soviet Union had ceased to exist and its successor states showed little interest in further involvement with Afghanistan.

Specifications	
Country of Origin: USSR	Barrel Length: 658mm (25.9in)
Date: 1974	Muzzle Velocity: 800m/sec (2600ft/sec)
Calibre: 5.45mm (.215in) M74	Feed/Magazine: 30- or 45-round detachable
Operation: Gas, air-cooled	box magazine
Weight: 9kg (19.84lb)	Range: 2000m (6560ft) +
Overall Length: 1160mm (45.67in)	

▲ **RPK-74 light support weapon**
Soviet 40th Army / 201st Motor Rifle Division / 149th Motor Rifle Regiment, Takhar Province, January 1984
The RPK light support weapon was issued with 45-round magazines, though it could also take 30-round AK-74 magazines if needed. It was operated almost exactly the same way as an AK-74, allowing any squad member to take over the gun in an emergency.

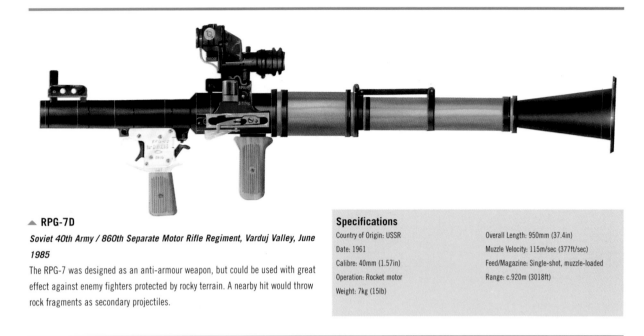

▲ **RPG-7D**

Soviet 40th Army / 860th Separate Motor Rifle Regiment, Varduj Valley, June 1985

The RPG-7 was designed as an anti-armour weapon, but could be used with great effect against enemy fighters protected by rocky terrain. A nearby hit would throw rock fragments as secondary projectiles.

Specifications

Country of Origin: USSR	Overall Length: 950mm (37.4in)
Date: 1961	Muzzle Velocity: 115m/sec (377ft/sec)
Calibre: 40mm (1.57in)	Feed/Magazine: Single-shot, muzzle-loaded
Operation: Rocket motor	Range: c.920m (3018ft)
Weight: 7kg (15lb)	

Mujahadeen
1979–89

The Mujahadeen was an alliance of several factions, all opposed to the pro-Soviet Afghan government. Its forces became more organized as the conflict went on.

RESISTANCE TO THE SOVIET OCCUPATION came primarily from tribal groups loosely aligned with regional warlords. These groups were effective guerrilla fighters from the start, drawing upon the experience of previous generations who had opposed other foreigners. The Mujahadeen were not strong enough to take on the Soviets directly, and were too disjointed to put together a sufficiently large force, but each group did what it could in isolation or, sometimes, in loose cooperation with others.

The result was to turn the areas controlled by the Afghan government and the Soviet armed forces into islands in a hostile sea, and even the islands were not safe. Mujahadeen personnel ambushed lone Soviet soldiers or small groups and carried out a campaign of sabotage and defiance in the cities.

Initially, the Mujahadeen were equipped with whatever weapons they had possessed before the conflict. These added up to a significant amount of small arms, as weapons ownership was a strong tradition in many tribes. Additional weaponry was captured from Afghan or Soviet army units, or stolen from armouries. The weapons were generally Soviet types, notably AK-47s, or identical Chinese copies that used the same ammunition. Heavier weapons such as Stinger anti-aircraft missiles were also supplied via the CIA. Foreign aid also provided large quantities of arms. The US provided significant numbers of Stinger missiles to permit the insurgents to fight back against Soviet helicopter gunships, and to attack transport aircraft. These were delivered to the Mujahadeen via neighbouring Pakistan.

This external support provided the Mujahadeen with equivalent firepower to their opponents in some cases. However, their fighting methods were based around individuals and small groups, with few commanders able to field more than 200–300 men. Tactics generally revolved around ambushes or hit-and-run raids, avoiding stand-up fights which the Soviet Army was almost certain to win.

The most prized personal weapons among the Mujahadeen were assault rifles of the AK series. AK-47s and more modern AK-74s were popular for their reliability and ease of use. The effectiveness of these weapons depended very much on the user; most Mujahadeen fighters were individually courageous but lacked skills in fighting as a unit.

Older weapons such as bolt-action rifles were widely used, and could be deadly in the hands of a marksman concealed in the rocks above a road or outpost. One common Mujahadeen tactic was to harass an outpost with sniper fire at night, denying the troops posted there proper rest. There was no way to know whether the sniper was alone or an ambush force was waiting to attack a patrol sent out to deal with the sniper. The Mujahadeen also possessed quantities of captured heavy weapons and machine guns, but ammunition supply was always a limiting factor in their use. Even when the Mujahadeen groups became more organized and were able to field larger forces they remained essentially militias rather than trained and organized military forces, and lacked the logistical 'tail' required to keep the fighting 'teeth' supplied with much more than food and small-arms ammunition. Thus even the capture of the Afghan government's tanks and aircraft at Kabul did not change the essential character of the Mujahadeen as a guerrilla force.

▲ **Short Magazine Lee-Enfield (SMLE) Rifle No. 1 Mk III**

Mujahadeen Insurgents, Kunar Province, May 1979

The Mujahadeen possessed many weapons left over from previous conflicts. The British Lee-Enfield rifle was accurate and reliable, making it deadly in the hands of a gunman concealed in the rocks above a road.

Specifications

Country of Origin: United Kingdom	Barrel Length: 640mm (25.2in)
Date: 1906	Muzzle Velocity: 751m/sec (2465ft/sec)
Calibre: 7.7mm (.303in)	Feed/Magazine: 10-round box, loaded with 5-
Operation: Bolt action	round charger clips
Weight: 4.14kg (9.125lb)	Range: 500m (1640ft)
Overall Length: 1129mm (44.4in)	

Specifications

Country of Origin: USSR	Barrel Length: 415mm (16.34in)
Date: 1947	Muzzle Velocity: 600m/sec (1969ft/sec)
Calibre: 7.62mm (.3in) Soviet M1943	Feed/Magazine: 30-round detachable box
Operation: Gas-operated	magazine
Weight: 4.3kg (9.48lb)	Range: 400m (1312ft)
Overall Length: 880mm (34.65in)	

▲ **AK-47 assault rifle**

Mujahadeen Insurgents, Helmand Province, September 1986

AK rifles, and Type 56 Chinese copies, were supplied to the Mujahadeen in large quantities by other nations. Several Islamic nations, and also the United States, supported the Mujahadeen with funds and arms.

Chapter 3

Middle East and Africa, 1950–2000

The collapse of European colonial empires
in Africa created a volatile situation, as new states and
factions arose to seek a national identity. Some conflicts in
the region have roots going back centuries; others are
relatively new. Many African conflicts in the latter half of the
twentieth century pitted ill-armed militias against one
another or against European-equipped forces.
In the Middle East, a series of wars were fought between
Israel and its Arab neighbours. These conflicts were more
conventional in nature than the majority of African wars, and
were characterized by armoured warfare supported by air
power. However, in the final analysis it was infantry
equipped with small arms who took and held ground.

◀ **Congo force**
May 1978: Zairean Army troops strike an aggressive pose for photographers at Kolwezi Airport after they
recaptured it from the Katangan rebels after fierce fighting. Most are armed with FN FAL rifles.

Introduction

World War II itself had relatively little effect on the Middle East and sub-Saharan Africa, though the consequences of the war were far-reaching.

T HE COASTAL STRIP along the Mediterranean coast was the scene of heavy fighting, but elsewhere, World War II did not much affect the people of the region. Similarly, the Middle East was the scene of relatively limited action; the main contest for ownership of the Middle Eastern oil fields was played out along the north coast of Africa.

After the war, its political consequences were felt throughout the region. Perhaps the greatest upheaval was the creation of a Jewish state. Jews and Arabs had lived, peaceably for the most part, in the region that is now Israel for centuries. The creation of a Jewish homeland and the arrival of thousands of European Jews, whose culture was radically different from that of those they came to join, caused massive upheaval and a violent backlash. The early history of Israel was troubled, and in 1956 Egypt implemented a blockade that resulted in an Israeli invasion of the Sinai Peninsula, timed to coincide with an Anglo-French attempt to capture the Suez Canal. Although the Suez affair was something of a fiasco for the British and French, it did establish Israel's reputation for military effectiveness, and secured Israel a strong bargaining position in the subsequent ceasefire negotiations.

With the blockade lifted, Israel once again had access to overseas trade. However, enmity between the new Jewish state and its neighbours continued to grow. Many Arab nations had expelled their Jewish population, or discriminated against them, and many of these dispossessed Jews settled in Israel. Meanwhile, many non-Jewish residents of the new Israel were opposed to the Jewish state. Many hundreds of thousands had left or been driven out, and later returned. There was no clear-cut solution

▲ **Freedom fighters**

Guerrilla fighters from the Liberation Front of Mozambique (FRELIMO) listen as their leader Samora Machel addresses them in a jungle camp in Mozambique, 1975. They are armed with a mixture of Portuguese and other European-made rifles and submachine guns.

▲ **Overwatch duties**

A US Marine mans an M60 general purpose machine gun during peacekeeping operations in the Lebanese capital Beirut, 1982.

and internal troubles were common. External influences exacerbated this situation, with neighbouring Arab countries backing insurgents against the Israeli government. In 1964 the Palestine Liberation Organization (PLO) was formed with the express intent of destroying Israel. Surrounding nations made no secret that this was also their goal. The result was that Israel became an armed camp, surrounded on all sides by enemies. A large proportion of the population were reservists in a military system designed to be rapidly activated. Rapid response was a stark necessity; Israel's borders are in some places just hours from the capital as the tank drives.

Decolonization

Meanwhile, European nations were losing their colonial possessions in Africa. Some tried to hold onto them. Others, like Britain, made a conscious choice to divest themselves of colonies that had become a burden. The 'retreat from Empire' that ensued was characterized by what became known as 'brushfire wars'. These were often complex affairs, with numerous factions fighting one another as well as the former colonial powers.

The small wars became, in many cases, proxy conflicts for the Cold War. The Soviet Union was willing to provide arms, funding and advisors to pro-Communist forces. Western powers felt compelled to counter with assistance to anti-Communist factions,

leading to Western support for highly dubious factions. A similar situation occurred in the 1980s, after the overthrow of the Shah of Iran by fundamentalist Muslim forces. The main enemy of the newly Theocratic Iran was Iraq, ruled by the brutal but at least not anti-Western regime of Saddam Hussein.

Fearing a fundamentalist takeover of the critical oil-producing Persian Gulf region, Western nations supported Saddam Hussein and turned a blind eye to his internal repression and use of chemical weapons against the Iranians. This necessary evil led to the Gulf War, after the end of the Iran–Iraq War in 1988.

Faced with crippling debt to neighbours such as Kuwait, who had supported the war against Iran, Iraq found a twofold solution to the problem. An invasion and annexation of Kuwait would not only remove the necessity to repay the debt, but would also give access to Kuwait's massive oil reserves, which could be used to rebuild the Iraqi economy.

The invasion was easy enough to accomplish, as Kuwait's armed forces were massively overmatched. The result, however, was an international coalition to remove Iraqi forces from Kuwait, which brought the world's most advanced military forces into conflict with the huge Iraqi Army.

Revolt in Algeria
1954–62

Military success against the Algerian insurgency was ultimately nullified by a changed political stance that was unacceptable to many within the French Army.

ALTHOUGH ALGERIA was recognized as part of metropolitan France, the political situation was typical of a colonial possession; a small minority of white settlers held political and economic power while a much larger Muslim population got by as best it could. The desire for independence and self-rule had always existed, but by 1954 it was being expressed in violence against the white settlers and French government possessions. The organization responsible was the FLN, or Front de Liberation Nationale. The FLN was a Muslim group which represented a large segment of the population through a number of popular leaders. Its opponents, the French government and the white settlers, were often at odds with one another, which complicated the situation significantly.

The French Army was effective in countering the early attacks, despite its recent humiliation in Indochina, and by early 1955 several key FLN leaders were either dead or imprisoned. The FLN was reduced to ineffectiveness, but even as the French government tried to win over the Muslim population with measures that were viewed with mistrust by the white settlers, the FLN was rebuilding its strength.

Violence erupted again, with massacres and revenge attacks launched by both the FLN and the settler militias. Operating from bases in newly-independent Tunisia and Morocco, the FLN launched attacks and terrorist operations, targeting in particular the capital, Algiers.

Army intervention

With the situation in Algiers out of control, the French Army was given a free hand to restore the situation, ordered only to do whatever was necessary to deal with the FLN. The city was subdivided by checkpoints and searches were conducted, but these measures were only partially successful. Without good intelligence about the FLN it was hard to find them, unless they revealed themselves in an attack.

Much of the army's work was routine: patrolling and standing guard or carrying out cordon-and-search operations. However, firefights with the FLN were not uncommon, as were sniper attacks on army personnel. Arrest operations were also carried out against targets suspected by the police of being FLN sympathizers or members. These people were interrogated, sometimes under torture, and yielded

▶ **MAS Mle 1950**

10th Parachute Division, Algiers, January 1957

The MAS 1950 was a robust weapon popular with its users. French paratroops searching houses for FLN personnel and weaponry found handguns more easily manoeuvrable than their rifles, especially when detaining suspects at gunpoint.

Specifications

Country of Origin: France	Overall Length: 195mm (7.7in)
Date: 1950	Barrel Length: 111mm (4.4in)
Calibre: 9mm (.35in) Parabellum	Muzzle Velocity: 315m/sec (1033ft/sec)
Operation: Short recoil, locked-breech	Feed/Magazine: 9-round detachable box
Weight: .86kg (1.8lb)	magazine

enough information to eventually cripple the FLN in Algiers.

Meanwhile, support for the FLN from outside the country was impeded by the 'Morice Line', an electrified fence and minefield along the Tunisian border. The line was patrolled constantly and breaches in the fence set off alarms that would trigger a response ranging from artillery bombardment to the deployment of tank, helicopter and mobile infantry forces to oppose any large-scale incursion.

French Army forces also took the offensive against FLN 'safe areas' in the countryside, and were generally very effective. Yet with the insurgents all but defeated, the French government changed its stance towards Algerian independence. Despite the revolt of elements within the French Army who found Algerian independence unacceptable after the sacrifices they had made fighting the insurgents, France pulled out and Algerian independence was declared in 1962.

▲ **Fusil Mitrailleur Modele 49 (MAS 49)**

25th Parachute Division, Algiers, January 1960

Re-arming after World War II, France sought to replace the assortment of older weapons then in service with a new semi-automatic rifle. The resulting MAS 49 was highly reliable and chambered a 7.5mm (.295in) round instead of the NATO standard 7.62mm (.3in) ammunition. .

Specifications

Country of Origin: France	Overall Length: 1010mm (39.7in)
Date: 1949	Barrel Length: 521mm (20.51in)
Calibre: 7.5mm (.295in)	Muzzle Velocity: 817m/sec (2680ft/sec)
Operation: Gas	Feed/Magazine: 10-round fixed box magazine
Weight: 3.9kg (8.6lb)	Range: 500m (1640ft)

Specifications

Country of Origin: France	Barrel Length: 600mm (23.62in)
Date: 1952	Muzzle Velocity: 840m/sec (2756ft/sec)
Calibre: 7.5mm (.295in)	Cyclic Rate: 700rpm
Operation: Lever-delayed blowback	Feed/Magazine: 50-round metal-link belt
Weight: 10.6kg (23.37lb)	Range: 1200m (3937ft)
Overall Length: 1080mm (42.5in)	

▲ **MAS AAT-52**

10th Parachute Division, Algiers, April 1955

Designed for mass production, the MAS AAT-52 used simple stamped and welded components. Static checkpoints allowed the French Army to restrict the movements of FLN personnel. Protected by sandbagged machine guns, these positions were usually strong enough to deter attack.

Arab–Israeli wars
1948–2000

Surrounded by nations intent on its destruction, Israel has fought several wars for survival; sometimes on the defensive and at times as the aggressor.

THE MODERN NATION OF ISRAEL was founded in 1948, in a region that has historical significance for both Arabs and Jews. Conflict was perhaps inevitable, and even before the United Nations had agreed on the creation of a new state, Jewish and Arab militias were fighting for control of the territories they claimed. It is not always possible to separate Israel's internal and external conflicts; both were aspects of the complex political situation in the troubled region.

On the day that Israel declared its independence, 14 May 1948, it was in control of strategic territories within its claimed borders, but was immediately invaded by forces from the surrounding Arab nations. A successful defence and counter-attack led to Israel's borders actually expanding as a result of this first war of survival.

The first major test for the Israel Defense Forces (IDF) was the 1956 invasion of Sinai, in response to the Egyptian blockade and closing of the Suez Canal. Skirmishing on the border and externally sponsored insurgency within Israel had been near-constant, but in October 1956 the nations of Egypt, Jordan and Syria openly declared their intent to launch a joint destruction of Israel under Egyptian command. The 1956 Israeli campaign into Sinai was to a great extent the only option available; a pre-emptive

strike whose success bought Israel 11 years of relative security. Then, in 1967, Egypt re-implemented the blockade of Israel and openly made preparations for invasion. Another pre-emptive strike derailed this plan, but the Arab leaders continued to express their intent to destroy Israel. In 1973, it was the Arabs that struck first, inflicting severe losses on the unprepared Israeli forces before being driven back by a desperate counter-attack.

Tensions subsided somewhat after 1973, with peace treaties signed between Israel and some Arab countries, notably Egypt. The PLO continued to attack Israel, sometimes with Syrian assistance. This prolonged campaign led to an Israeli invasion of Lebanon in 1978 to drive out the PLO and eliminate Syrian missiles based there. Political initiatives have attempted to reduce the level of conflict between the PLO and Israel itself, with some success. However, terrorist attacks from the likes of Hamas and Hezbollah and aggressive Israeli responses still continue.

▶ **Militia fighters**
Armed with a variety of weapons, including FN FAL rifles, AK-47s, RPGs and M16 assault rifles, members of the Army of South Lebanon (ASL), a Christian militia, pose for the camera, Lebanon 1985.

Israel Defense Forces
1956–2000

The Israel Defense Forces (IDF) were initially armed with World War II-era equipment, but experience in action resulted in the development of weaponry and systems better tailored to the Israeli needs.

ONE EXAMPLE IS THE MERKAVA TANK, a uniquely Israeli design with the engine at the front. This gives the crew additional protection and leaves room for a compartment at the rear that can be used to transport infantry or supplies. Other success stories to come out of the Israeli arms industry are the Galil rifle series and the Uzi submachine gun. Early models of the Uzi were fitted with a fixed wooden stock, but soon a folding stock became available. This made the Uzi an ideal weapon for issue to vehicle crews and other personnel who might need a high-firepower self-defence capability, but could not carry a full-sized rifle. The Uzi was also issued to special forces and paratroop units, who prized its lightness, small size and deadly firepower.

Development of the Galil

Israel's Arab opponents were chiefly armed with Soviet weapons, including the ubiquitous AK-47 assault rifle. This weapon sufficiently impressed the Israelis that they decided to create an assault rifle of their own – the Galil – based on the Kalashnikov's mechanism. As other militaries discovered, the combination of a semi-automatic battle rifle and a submachine gun (the FN FAL and Uzi in the case of

the Israeli Defence Force) was effective in some ways but limited in others. At long ranges, only rifle-armed troops could engage, while in close combat the FAL was less effective than Arab assault rifles. The adoption of the Galil enabled every Israeli soldier to engage at all ranges, increasing the overall effectiveness of the force. The Galil was every bit as rugged as the AK-47, and was overall a better rifle, giving the Israelis a man-for-man advantage in later conflicts which was beneficial to a nation whose forces were always outnumbered.

The Galil rifle made use of the extremely robust Kalashnikov rifle mechanism, but was constructed to a much higher standard than most AK rifles. The result was a highly effective assault rifle that has been gradually updated over the years. The 7.62mm (.3in) and 5.56mm (.219in) versions, configured as carbines, assault rifles and light support weapons, were an export as well as domestic success.

The Galil Sniper variant demonstrates the Israeli attitude to weaponry. It is essentially a very accurate semi-automatic version of the Galil. As such, it is not as accurate as a dedicated sniper weapon and has a shorter effective range. However, it is very tough and tolerant of arduous desert conditions. The Israeli

▶ **Beretta M1951**

IDF / 27th Armoured Brigade, Rafah, November 1956

The 9mm Beretta M1951 was used by both Arab and Israeli forces as a sidearm for officers and vehicle crews. It proved reliable and popular with its users.

Specifications

Country of Origin: Italy	Barrel Length: 114mm (4.5in)
Date: 1951	Muzzle Velocity: 350m/sec (1148ft/sec)
Calibre: 9mm (.35in) Parabellum	Feed/Magazine: 8-round detachable box
Operation: Short recoil, locked-breech	magazine
Weight: .87kg (1.92lb) empty	Range: 50m (164ft)
Overall Length: 203mm (8in)	

military believes that it is better to deploy a robust weapon that will continue to function under almost all circumstances than a sophisticated one that may not be available due to failure in field service.

Campaigns

In 1956, the Israeli units that took part in the offensive into the Sinai were largely composed of reservists called up for the conflict. The plan emphasized speed and aggression as there was little room for subtlety in the Sinai desert. Paratroops dropped in front of a rapid advance across the peninsula and southwards towards the Egyptian base at Sharm el Sheikh. The first Uzis saw combat during the Suez campaign, and proved useful for mechanized infantry needing a compact weapon, and for infantry units clearing bunkers and other confined spaces.

The Egyptian Army had significant forces deployed close to the Israeli border, but few reserves on the eastern side of the Suez Canal, and once the outer positions were cracked the Egyptians were unable to recover enough to mount an effective defence in most areas. This problem was compounded by the Anglo-French invasion of Suez, which forced the Egyptians to pull back from the Sinai in order to defend more critical territory.

▲ Uzi

IDF / 7th Armoured Brigade, Valley of Tears, October 1973

The Uzi saw action in 1956 in its original form with a fixed wooden stock. It was later issued with a folding metal stock and featured in virtually every Israeli conflict of the twentieth century. Handy, reliable and accurate, it was popular with vehicle crews and security forces.

Specifications

Country of Origin: Israel	Barrel Length: 260mm (10.23in)
Date: 1953	Muzzle Velocity: 400m/sec (1312ft/sec)
Calibre: 9mm (.35in) Parabellum	Feed/Magazine: 25- or 32-round detachable
Operation: Blowback	box magazine
Weight: 3.7kg (8.15lb)	Range: 120m (394ft)
Overall Length: 650mm (25.6in)	

▶ Mini Uzi

Israeli Special Forces, Lebanon, June 1982

The Mini-Uzi is well suited to use by special forces personnel operating in the close urban terrain of a city such as Beirut.

Specifications

Country of Origin: Israel	Barrel Length: 197mm (7.76in)
Date: 1980	Muzzle Velocity: 352m/sec (1155ft/sec)
Calibre: 9mm (.35in) Parabellum	Feed/Magazine: 20-, 25- or 32-round detachable
Operation: Blowback	box magazine
Weight: 2.7kg (5.95lb)	Range: 50m (164ft)
Overall Length: 600mm (23.62in)	

Israel Defense Forces Platoon, 1956

The Israel Defense Forces were initially equipped with weapons left over from World War II. Some of these came from stocks captured or confiscated from Germany by the Allies at the end of the war. This equipment was gradually replaced by home-produced weaponry.

Platoon HQ (6 x Uzis, 2 x Mauser Kar 98 rifles, 1 x Bazooka)

Rifle Squad 1 (1 x Uzi, 1 x Bren LMG, 8 x Mauser Kar 98 rifles)

Rifle Squad 2 (1 x Uzi, 1 x Bren LMG, 8 x Mauser Kar 98 rifles)

Rifle Squad 3 (1 x Uzi, 1 x Bren LMG, 8 x Mauser Kar 98 rifles)

Specifications

Country of Origin: Israel

Date: 1972

Calibre: 5.56mm (.219in) NATO

Operation: Gas

Weight: 4.35kg (9.59lb)

Overall Length: 979mm (38.54in)

Barrel Length: 460mm (18.11in)

Muzzle Velocity: 990m/sec (3250ft/sec)

Feed/Magazine: 35- or 50-round detachable box magazine

Range: 800m (2625ft) +

▲ **Galil**

IDF / 91st Division, Southern Lebanon, August 1982

Based on the ever-popular AK-47, the Galil was introduced to replace the FN FAL in Israeli service. The Galil is unusual in that it uses a 35-round magazine instead of the more typical 30 rounds. The long magazine can make firing from a prone position awkward.

The conflict ended with a UN-supervised Israeli withdrawal and the capture of large amounts of Egyptian vehicles and equipment. Some of this was pressed into service in other wars. Meanwhile, other Israeli forces pushed into Gaza, where there was fighting against Palestinian forces.

The 1956 campaign demonstrated the effectiveness of the tank to the IDF. Thus far the main arm had been infantry, with tanks and weapons mounted on light vehicles used for support. After 1956 the emphasis was placed on armoured forces, to the point where other arms received perhaps too little attention. Other lessons were learned but perhaps too well. Initiative and aggression rather than careful cooperation and mutual support had permitted a rapid advance and a successful campaign. The victory led to the belief that a headlong armoured charge would carry all before it, which created the potential for disaster as well as excellent success.

By 1967, Israel once again faced an imminent threat and responded with a pre-emptive strike. The conflict that became known as the Six-Day War opened with an all-out attack by the Israeli Air Force (IAF) against the air forces of its enemies. The first strikes were against Egyptian targets, but by the end of the first day the air forces of Jordan, Iraq and Syria had also been shattered.

The offensive against Egypt took the form of armoured thrusts along much the same routes as the 1956 attacks had followed. Surprise and sheer aggression allowed the leading armoured units to punch holes in the defence and overrun unprepared units. However, the Egyptian forces put up a stubborn resistance and held up the advance at several points. Total Israeli air superiority allowed heavy air attacks that broke numerous positions and allowed the advance to continue, and air power allowed a daring raid by helicopter-borne troops on a major Egyptian artillery concentration. As the Egyptian army disintegrated, both sides raced for the Suez Canal. The Israelis were able to trap large Egyptian forces on the western size, eliminating most of the Egyptians' armoured strength.

Meanwhile, other elements of the IDF attacked Syria and Jordan. Jordanian forces fought bravely but were no match for the better-equipped IDF. In Syria, the Israeli goal was to capture the Golan Heights, which would serve as a defensive barrier against future threats. By the end of the war Israel had expanded its borders out to natural barriers: the Golan Heights, the River Jordan and the Suez Canal. However, the IDF had acquired a dangerous level of overconfidence which would cost it dear in action six years later.

Specifications

Country of Origin: Israel	Barrel Length: 508mm (20in)
Date: 1972	Muzzle Velocity: 815m/sec (2675ft/sec)
Calibre: 7.62mm (.3in) NATO	Feed/Magazine: 20-round detachable box
Operation: Gas, self-loading	magazine
Weight: 6.4kg (14.11lb)	Range: 800m (2625ft) +
Overall Length: 1115mm (43.89in)	

▲ **Galil AR sniper**

IDF / Golani Brigade, Siege of Beirut, August 1982

The Galil Sniper is more accurately described as a 'designated marksman rifle' than a sniper weapon. It gives infantry formations additional long-range firepower.

In 1973, the Arab nations struck first, attacking on the Israeli holy day of Yom Kippur. Syrian armoured forces pushed into the Golan Heights while the Egyptians used Soviet river-crossing techniques to make an assault across the Suez Canal.

The IDF responded aggressively but in an uncoordinated fashion. This played into the Egyptians' hands; tank forces attacked without support and ran into new anti-armour weapons supplied by the Soviet Union. Despite heavy losses

the IDF was able to seize the initiative and bring about the sort of mobile battle it was best suited for, driving back the Egyptians to the Suez Canal. Meanwhile the Syrian armoured thrusts had been narrowly defeated and a successful counter-attack was in progress. Diplomatic pressure secured a ceasefire, leading to more permanent treaties. For the IDF, the lesson learned was that all-arms cooperation was necessary, returning infantry and artillery to a more prominent role.

▲ IMI Negev

IDF / Givati Brigade, Gaza Strip, 2000

Designed as a multi-purpose weapon, the Negev machine gun can be fed using a 150-round belt or Galil rifle magazines. With the assistance of an adapter it can take standard M16 magazines.

Specifications

Country of Origin: Israel	Barrell Length: 460mm (18.1in)
Date: 1997	Muzzle Velocity: 915m/sec (3,002ft/sec)
Calibre: 5.56mm (0.21in)	Feed/Magazine: 150 round amunition belt or
Operation: Gas, rotating bolt	35-round box magazine
Weight: 7.40kg (16.31lb)	Range: 300–1000m (984–3280ft)
Overall Length: 1020mm (40in)	

▲ IMI Tavor TAR 21

IDF / Golani Brigade, Operation Defensive Shield, Jenin, 2002

The TAR 21 is the IDF's latest servce weapon. It follows a general trend towards 'bullpup' configuration weapons (the action set behind the pistol grip), which are easy to handle in the confined spaces of urban combat.

Specifications

Country of Origin: Israel	Overall Length: 720mm (28.3in)
Date: 2001	Barrel Length: 460mm (18.1in)
Calibre: 5.56mm (.219in) NATO	Muzzle Velocity: 910m/sec (2986ft/sec)
Operation: Gas, rotating bolt	Feed/Magazine: Various STANAG magazines
Weight: 3.27kg (7.21lb)	Range: 550m (1804ft)

Arab forces
1956–82

While there has always been conflict among the people of the Middle East, clashes between Arabs and Jews became much more prevalent in the 1920s.

JEWS BEGAN TO SETTLE in what is now Israel in order to escape Nazi persecution, and there is strong evidence that some anti-Jewish activity in the Middle East was funded by the Nazi Party. Whatever the root cause, conflict gradually intensified. Even when Israel was not engaged in hostilities with her neighbouring countries, insurgent forces were at work within the state. Conflict over disputed territories such as the Gaza Strip created an endless cycle of attack and retribution, with Jewish irregular forces carrying on their own local wars even when the IDF was not involved.

The creation of the PLO in 1964 represented a serious threat to Israel's internal and international security. The PLO received support from neighbouring Arab countries and could field well-armed fighters who had, in some cases, received formal training from overseas advisors.

The main threat to Israel's existence, however, was from Egypt and her allies. Largely equipped with Soviet-supplied weaponry or locally made derivatives, Egypt's military was, on the whole, willing and able to fight but poorly led. In particular, officers and enlisted men tended to come from entirely different social classes and lacked confidence in one another. Thus Egyptian formations proved brittle in some actions. Egyptian forces were relatively poor in fluid combat, largely because their armoured forces were inadequately trained for the complex nature of mobile warfare. The infantry and artillery, whose operations were not so complex, tended to perform better. Thus the Egyptians were at their best in static defensive operations. At times, Egyptian defensive positions were breached by Israeli armour, which then raced on to new objectives leaving its supporting arms unable to push through the battered but stubborn defence.

However, extensively equipped with the AK-47 assault rifle, Arab forces enjoyed a significant firepower advantage over their Israeli opponents at all ranges. Each soldier could deliver suppressing fire, making fire-and-manoeuvre tactics more effective. When aimed fire was more appropriate, the AK-47 was accurate out to a reasonable distance; at least as far as the typical soldier can shoot effectively. Although the AK-47's performance dropped off after around 300-400 metres (950–1300 feet), this was not a significant disadvantage, especially during fighting on the relatively cluttered terrain of the Golan Heights.

▶ **Tokagypt 58**

Palestinian Irregulars, Gaza Strip, June 1967

An export version of the Tokarev semi-automatic pistol, the 'Tokagypt' was intended for army use but was adopted by the Egyptian police instead. Some examples of the weapon found their way into the hands of Egyptian-supported Palestinian militias.

Specifications

Country of Origin: Egypt/Hungary	Barrel Length: 114mm (4.5in)
Date: 1958	Muzzle Velocity: 350m/sec (1150ft/sec)
Calibre: 9mm (.35in) Parabellum	Feed/Magazine: 7-round detachable box
Operation: Short recoil	magazine
Weight: .91kg (2.01lb)	Range: 30m (98ft)
Overall Length: 194mm (7.65in)	

▶ Helwan pistol

Egyptian Army / 3rd Armoured Battalion, El Arish, October 1956

The 'Helwan' pistol was an Egyptian copy of the Beretta M1951, which was used under its own name by the Israeli forces.

Specifications

Country of Origin: Egypt	Barrel Length: 114mm (4.5in)
Date: 1955	Muzzle Velocity: 350m/sec (1148ft/sec)
Calibre: 9mm (.35in) Parabellum	Feed/Magazine: 8-round detachable box
Operation: Short recoil	magazine
Weight: .89kg (1.96lb)	Range: 50m (164ft)
Overall Length: 203mm (8in)	

Specifications

Country of Origin: Egypt	Barrell Length: 638mm (25.1in)
Date: Early 1950s	Muzzel Velocity: 853.44m/sec (2800ft/sec)
Calibre: 7.62mm (.3in)	Feed/Magazine: 10-round box magazine
Operation: Gas, tilting bolt	Range: 457m (1500ft)
Weight: 4.4kg (9.7lb)	
Overall Length: 1216mm (25.1in)	

▲ Hakim rifle

Egyptian Army / 5th Brigade, Rafah, October 1956

The Hakim rifle was derived from a Swedish weapon and fired a full-power battle rifle cartridge. It was replaced in service by the AK series, but many examples remained in reserve.

Improved training

With assistance from Soviet advisors, the standard of Egyptian training and combat doctrine improved considerably. After the crushing defeat of 1967, the IDF became complacent, while the Egyptian Army was rebuilt and retrained with the lessons of the Six-Day War in mind. In 1973, the Egyptian Army proved that it could not only conduct a river crossing in the Soviet style, but could adapt and innovate to meet the unique challenges of crossing the Suez Canal.

While greatly improved, the Egyptian armoured forces were still not a match for the Israelis, at least not tank for tank. This disadvantage was offset by the use of new Soviet-supplied guided anti-tank weapons and better tactics. Where possible the Egyptians halted and allowed the Israelis to launch their customary headlong armoured counter-attack. This allowed the (often unsupported) tanks to be engaged by both the tank guns of Egyptian armoured forces but also by infantry firing large numbers of guided missiles.

The Israelis learned to support their tanks properly, and to counter the Egyptians' wire-guided missiles by hosing the crews' suspected location with machine-gun fire. If the operator was forced to take cover, the missile could not be successfully guided. Nevertheless, the Egyptian Army inflicted heavy losses on the Israelis before being driven back across the canal by a counter-attack.

Syria, too, increased in capability. In 1967, the Israeli advance into the Golan Heights was contested by only part of the Syrian Army, and without great determination. In 1973, the Syrian Army made a massive effort in the Golan Heights and almost succeeded in breaking the Israeli resistance. The assault was made on a broad front by infantry divisions, each of which had some tanks, while the two Syrian armoured divisions were held in reserve to make a breakthrough or exploit an opportunity that might arise.

In the first two days of fighting the Israeli forces holding the heights suffered massive casualties, but managed to cling to their positions long enough for reinforcements to arrive. That scratch Israeli forces, thrown together from whatever tanks and troops could be assembled, were able to delay the Syrian advance owes much to Israeli superiority of equipment.

However, the Israelis had been planning to fight a defensive action on the heights since 1967, and wrung the absolute maximum value out of each scrap of defensive terrain. Against such a strong defence any army would have been sorely tested.

▲ **Rasheed carbine**

Egyptian Army / 9th Reserve Brigade, Umm Ketef – Abu Aelia Defensive Perimeter, October 1956

The Rasheed carbine was derived from the Hakim rifle, but was issued only in small numbers before being phased out in favour of the AK series assault rifle.

Specifications

Country of Origin: Egypt	Barrel Length: 520mm (20.5in)
Date: 1960	Muzzle Velocity: Not known
Calibre: 7.62mm (.3in)	Feed/Magazine: 10-round detachable box
Operation: Gas	magazine
Weight: 4.19kg (9.25lb)	Range: 300m (984ft)
Overall Length: 1035mm (40.75in)	

Specifications

Country of Origin: USSR	Barrel Length: 415mm (16.34in)
Date: 1947	Muzzle Velocity: 600m/sec (1969ft/sec)
Calibre: 7.62mm (.3in) Soviet M1943	Feed/Magazine: 30-round detachable box
Operation: Gas	magazine
Weight: 4.3kg (9.48lb)	Range: 400m (1312ft)
Overall Length: 880mm (34.65in)	

▲ **AK-47**

Egyptian Army / 2nd Infantry Division, Sinai, October 1973

Having obtained advisors and weaponry from several sources at times, the Egyptian Army was re-equipped in the Soviet style after 1967. In 1973 it proved to be a much more effective fighting force than previously.

Civil wars and revolutions

1960–PRESENT

In a continent the size of Africa, it is inevitable that there will be conflict ongoing somewhere at any given time. Some of these conflicts have origins going back to colonial intervention by European powers or the power vacuum left by their withdrawal.

IN 1960, THE CONGO became independent from Belgium and immediately descended into civil war. As is common in civil strife, there were no 'frontlines' as such, though some areas were recognized as the territory of one faction or another. Operations were launched by organized forces, but for the most part the conflict was one of low-level skirmishes between bands of 50–100 gunmen or soldiers. Massacres were common, and foreign troops were not exempt from being the victims of atrocities.

The Congo conflict was characterized by the use of European mercenaries. They trained local forces, protected white citizens who were being victimized by various factions, and took part in combat operations. Later in the conflict, mercenaries were involved in revolts and coup attempts. In 1971 the country was renamed Zaire, by which time the conflict was over.

The Portuguese withdrawal from their holdings in Africa (Angola, Guinea and Mozambique) was also very troubled. In each of these territories, the small Portuguese garrisons were caught unprepared by revolts and forced to fight increasingly large guerrilla

forces. The conflicts were influenced by the insurgents' use of bases in other countries; many of the guerrillas fighting in Angola were based out of Zaire, while those operating in Mozambique could take refuge in Tanzania or Zambia where the Portuguese could not pursue them.

The Portuguese forces used a combination of concessions, improvements in conditions for the local population, and military force to combat the insurgents. Extensive use was made of trainer aircraft converted to the light strike role and acting in conjunction with ground units. Horsed cavalry was deployed in areas impassable to motor vehicles, and much of the infantry was from high-quality units such as marines and paratroops. However, lack of support for the war eventually caused the Portuguese to withdraw,

The insurgents' arsenal was augmented by foreign powers, enabling the guerrillas in Angola to make extensive use of mines. Among the insurgents, mine injuries were more common than wounds sustained from direct combat. Most insurgent groups were small, but as the conflict progressed the average

▶ **Vigneron M2**

Belgian Parachute Commando Regiment, Stanleyville, November 1964

Belgian paratroops were deployed to the Congo to rescue civilians trapped by the fighting. Their light, high-firepower weapons were well suited to rapid operations but limited in protracted fighting

Specifications

Country of Origin: Belgium	705mm (27.75in) stock folded
Date: 1952	Barrel Length: 305mm (12in)
Calibre: 9mm (.35in) Parabellum	Muzzle Velocity: 365m/sec (1200ft/sec)
Operation: Blowback	Feed/Magazine: 32-round detachable box
Weight: 3.29kg (7.25lb)	magazine
Overall Length: 890mm (35in) stock extended;	Range: 200m (656ft) +

formation went from about 20 men armed with an assortment of weapons to 100–150 equipped with AK-series assault rifles. Mortars, rocket launchers and artillery were deployed by the rebels at times, with ground-to-air missiles appearing from about 1973.

International intervention was also a critical factor in the Nigerian Civil War. At the beginning of the conflict in 1967, the Nigerian military was equipped with World War II armaments, mostly of British origin, as were the forces of newly independent Biafra. As the conflict continued, various nations sent aid to one side or the other, ranging from small arms

to jet fighters. The Biafran revolt was crushed, largely by the small Nigerian armoured force, and Biafra was reintegrated into Nigeria.

Ethiopia is one of the poorest regions in the world, and has been troubled for much of its history. In 1974, conflict in the breakaway region of Eritrea was compounded by a revolution in Ethiopia. The revolution was followed by further coup attempts and widespread use of terror tactics. Support came from the Soviet Union, whose relations with neighbouring Somalia were cooling rapidly. Meanwhile Somalia, which had been trying to wrest the province of

Specifications

Country of Origin: USSR	Barrel Length: 520mm (20.5in)
Date: 1962	Muzzle Velocity: 735m/sec (2410ft/sec)
Calibre: 7.62mm (.3in) M1943	Feed/Magazine: 100-round belt contained in
Operation: Gas, air-cooled	a drum
Weight: 7kg (15.43lb)	Cyclic Rate: 700rpm
Overall Length: 1041mm (41in)	Range: 900m (2953ft)

▲ RPD

Guerrilla Forces, Angola, September 1969

Although dated, the RPD was an effective weapon that combined mobility with firepower. Using the same cartridge as Soviet-supplied rifles simplified the supply situation for the rebel groups.

Specifications

Country of Origin: Spain	Barrel Length: 450mm (17.72in)
Date: 1958	Muzzle Velocity: 800m/sec (2625ft/sec)
Calibre: 7.62mm (.3in) NATO	Feed/Magazine: 20- or 30-round detachable box
Operation: Delayed blowback	magazine
Weight: 4.4kg (9.7lb)	Range: 500m (1640ft) +
Overall Length: 1015mm (40in)	

▲ CETME assault rifle

Portuguese Paratroop Battalion No 31, Mozambique, 1972

Developed in Spain by a German team continuing their wartime work on the StG45 project, the CETME was a simple and easy-to-use assault rifle. The CETME assault rifle was the basis for the H&K G3, and was developed into a family of assault rifles in 5.56 and 7.62mm calibres.

Ogaden from Ethiopia using small-scale guerrilla forces, took advantage of the situation and invaded. Both sides largely used Soviet-supplied equipment, but the decisive factor was direct Soviet intervention on the Ethiopian side.

Ethiopian forces, which included tanks and aircraft, were able to inflict heavy losses on Eritrean insurgents and weakened their control of many areas, but this success was illusory. Heavy-handedness on the part of the Ethiopians caused recruits to flock to the cause of Eritrean independence, and along with a reduction in Soviet assistance this situation denied Ethiopia the clear victory to which it aspired. Eritrea was granted independence in 1993, but this did not end either internal conflict or clashes with Ethiopia. Disputes over territory led to a renewed war in 1998–2000, along with intermittent clashes between militias in the border areas.

Meanwhile, Somalia also descended into civil war, beginning in 1991. This conflict started as a factional dispute, but gradually changed in character. Today, there is a great deal of militant Islamic involvement in the war which, despite United Nations' efforts, remains ongoing.

▲ PPSh-41

Ethiopian People's Militia, Addis Ababa, 1977

The Soviet Union supplied large quantities of arms to various factional and government forces in Africa. Some weapons, like the PPSh-41, were of World War II vintage but were still highly effective.

Specifications

Country of Origin: USSR	Barrel Length: 266mm (10.5in)
Date: 1941	Muzzle Velocity: 490m/sec (1600ft/sec)
Calibre: 7.62mm (.3in) Soviet	Feed/Magazine: 35-round box magazine or 71-
Operation: Blowback	round drum magazine
Weight: 3.64kg (8lb)	Range: 120m (394ft)
Overall Length: 838mm (33in)	

Specifications

Country of Origin: Sweden	Barrel Length: 213mm (8.38in)
Date: 1945	Muzzle Velocity: 410m/sec (1345ft/sec)
Calibre: 9mm (.35in) Parabellum	Feed/Magazine: 36-round detachable box
Operation: Blowback	magazine
Weight: 3.9kg (8.6lb)	Range: 120m (394ft)
Overall Length: 808mm (31.81in)	

▲ Carl Gustav 45

Somalian Pirates, Horn of Africa, October 2009

An assortment of weapons from the Somalian and Ethiopian conflicts found their way into the hands of gunmen and pirates operating along the Somali coast. The seas off the Horn of Africa are among the worst of the world's piracy hotspots.

▲ SKS carbine

Guerrilla Forces, Guinea, August 1971

The SKS rifle, supplied by the Soviet Union, was a typical personal weapon among the guerrilla forces. Some fighters managed to obtain AK-47s instead.

Specifications

Country of Origin: USSR

Date: 1945

Calibre: 7.62mm (.3in)

Operation: Gas short-stroke piston

Weight: 3.85kg (8.49lb)

Overall Length: 1021mm (40.2in)

Barrel Length: 521mm (20.5in)

Muzzle Velocity: 735m/sec (2411ft/sec)

Feed/Magazine: 10-round integral box magazine

Range: 400m (1312ft)

▲ FN FAL

Nigerian Federal Forces, March 1970

Britain contributed quantities of small arms to the Nigerian government, largely as a counter to Soviet influence. Poor training levels reduced the effectiveness of these weapons in federal hands.

Specifications

Country of Origin: Belgium/UK

Date: 1954

Calibre: 7.62mm (.3in) NATO

Operation: Gas, self-loading

Weight: 4.31kg (9.5lb)

Overall Length: 1053mm (41.46in)

Barrel Length: 533mm (21in)

Muzzle Velocity: 853m/sec (2800ft/sec)

Feed/Magazine: 20-round detachable box magazine

Range: 800m (2625ft) +

▲ FBP submachine gun

Portuguese Paratrooper Battalion No. 21, Angola, 1961

The FBP was primarily issued to officers and NCOs, giving them greater firepower than a sidearm without the weight of a rifle. It was phased out in favour of the Uzi submachine gun.

Specifications

Country of Origin: Portugal

Date: 1948

Calibre: 9mm (0.35in)

Operation: Blowback

Weight: 3.77kg (8.31lb)

Overall Length: 807mm (31.8in)

Barrell Length: Not known

Muzzle Velocity: 390m/sec (1280ft/sec)

Feed/Magazine: 21- or 32-round detachable box magazine

Range: Not known

South African security forces
1970–90

The legacy of European colonialism resulted in conflict in southern Africa as new national identities were forged.

IN 1970, BOTH SOUTH AFRICA and Rhodesia were ruled by a white minority, with the much larger black population as second-class citizens. Naturally, there was resentment against this system and this anger bubbled over into conflict. In addition, other clashes occurred along tribal lines or arose out of factional differences. The security forces of South Africa and Rhodesia attempted to maintain the status quo, which meant operating both in urban areas and over vast distances in the bush.

After a series of political organizations were banned in the 1960s in Rhodesia, guerrilla forces began to appear. These cooperated with South African insurgents, leading to joint operations between South African and Rhodesian security formations. The early guerrilla groups were poorly armed and disorganized, and were easily broken up.

From 1976 onwards, a new wave of insurgent activity began, inspired in part by the Portuguese withdrawal from neighbouring Mozambique. Attempts to find a peaceful solution failed, while guerrilla activity increased in both effectiveness and intensity. By the late 1970s large areas of Rhodesia were effectively under guerrilla control.

To counter the guerrillas, the government of Rhodesia could field a conventional infantry-based force backed up by an armoured car regiment, plus special security forces. These included the Rhodesian Special Air Service (which was essentially an elite counter-insurgency force at this point), the Selous Scouts and a mounted unit named Grey's Scouts, which operated over long distances in the bush.

The counter-insurgency forces specialized in tracking and ambushing guerrilla units, using hunting skills. They operated without the usual helicopter and ground vehicle support that might tip off guerrillas that security forces were in the area. Some operations were carried out by the elite units themselves; at other times they passed information to the regular forces, which could then launch a conventional operation. Despite the successes of these units, the guerrillas were able to force the ruling elite to the negotiating table and in 1980 Rhodesia became Zimbabwe under a new government.

The South African apartheid system, under which the black and white populations were segregated, had long been the subject of internal and external opposition. South Africa was the subject of an arms embargo and so developed its own armament industry. A number of small arms and heavier weapons systems were created, which were uniquely suited to the needs of the South African forces.

◀ **BXP submachine gun**
South African Security Forces, 1980–present
The BXP was designed for both military and security applications. It can be fired one-handed with reasonable effectiveness, and can launch rifle grenades from a muzzle adapter.

Specifications

Country of Origin: South Africa	Barrel Length: 208mm (8.2in)
Date: 1980	Muzzle Velocity: 370m/sec (1214ft/sec)
Calibre: 9mm (.35in) Parabellum	Feed/Magazine: 22- or 32-round detachable
Operation: Blowback	box magazine
Weight: 2.5kg (5.5lb)	Range: 100m (328ft) +
Overall Length: 607mm (23.9in)	

Security forces were at times involved in wider conflicts but also struggled to keep order within South Africa's borders. Attempts to train guerrillas to fight against the government were made prior to 1970, but the guerrilla groups were largely broken up and their parent organizations destroyed or driven underground. Nevertheless, a low-level resistance continued in the countryside, with occasional riots in the cities. These were dealt with using very heavy-handed methods, often sparking further violence.

Insurgent groups attempted to disrupt the national infrastructure with attacks on power stations and other services, The security forces also had to deal with serious levels of violent crime and gang wars within the cities, as well as terrorist attacks. In addition, it was necessary to conduct operations over large areas of the countryside

Externally, South African forces made forays into neighbouring states. After the departure of the Portuguese, South African forces moved into Angola and Mozambique to oppose the South-West African People's Organization (SWAPO), which was already fighting against South African troops in Namibia. Other forces assisted the Rhodesian government in resisting internal insurgency, until the 1980 elections changed the political landscape completely. Eventually, political change in South Africa created an entirely new situation, with the scrapping of apartheid and the creation of a state that was acceptable to the wider world.

Specifications

Country of Origin: South Africa	Barrel Length: 460mm (18.11in)
Date: 1982	Muzzle Velocity: 980m/sec (3215ft/sec)
Calibre: 5.56mm (.219in) M193	Feed/Magazine: 35- or 50-round detachable
Operation: Gas	box magazine
Weight: 4.3kg (9.48lb)	Range: 500m (1640ft)
Overall Length: 1005mm (35.97in)	

▲ **Vektor R4**

South African Security Forces, Angola, 1986

The Vektor assault rifle was derived from the Israeli Galil. A very robust and reliable rifle, it was issued to infantry while vehicle crews received a shortened carbine variant designated R5.

▲ **Striker shotgun**

South African Security Forces, 1990

The Striker solved the problem of limited ammunition capacity in a shotgun by using a revolving drum. However, reloading is slow, as each round must be separately loaded through a gate.

Specifications

Country of Origin: South Africa	Barrel Length: 304mm (12in) or 457mm (18in)
Date: 1985	Muzzle Velocity: Variable
Gauge/Calibre: 12-gauge	Feed/Magazine: 12- or 20-round revolving
Operation: Rotary cylinder	magazine
Weight: 4.2kg (9.25lb)	Range: 100m (328ft)
Overall Length: 792mm (31.18in)	

▲ Milcor MGL

South African Army, 1995

The MGL (Multiple Grenade Launcher) is a lightweight 40mm (1.57in) semi-automatic grenade launcher. The MGL allows six grenades to be fired in rapid succession. It can be used as a battlefield support weapon or for security applications, firing less-lethal ammunition directly at a target.

Specifications

Country of Origin: South Africa	Barrel Length: 300mm (11.8in)
Date: 1983	Muzzle Velocity: 76m/sec (249ft/sec)
Calibre: 40mm (1.57in)	Feed/Magazine: 6-round rotating swing-out-type
Operation: Double-action	cylinder
Weight: 5.3kg (11.68lb)	Range: 400m (1312ft)
Overall Length: 778mm (30.6in)	

Gulf War: Coalition forces
1991

The 1991 Gulf War pitted a coalition of nations against the large but obsolescent army of Iraq, which was defeated after 100 hours of high-tempo ground operations.

TENSIONS HAD ALWAYS BEEN HIGH between Iran and Iraq, and after the revolution which deposed the Shah and did away with Iranian monarchy, Iraq invaded the country. Iran possessed significant quantities of modern military equipment, but the revolutionary state lacked the skilled personnel to make good use of it. The war gradually became one between the modern, Soviet-equipped forces of Iraq and the massed infantry mobs of Iran. Despite an enormous casualty rate, stalemate resulted and by 1988 a ceasefire brought the Iran–Iraq War to an end.

At the end of the Iran–Iraq War, Iraq's economy was badly damaged and vast sums were owed to Kuwait and Saudi Arabia to repay war loans. Demands by Iraq to write off the debt were declined, so Iraqi President Saddam Hussein decided to solve the problem by military force. Invading Kuwait would not only eliminate the debt but also increase Iraq's oil reserves and further strengthen the country.

The invasion began on 2 August 1990. At this time the Iraqi Army was one of the largest in the world, and had little difficulty in overrunning Kuwait. It seemed entirely possible that Iraq might move on Saudi Arabia next. The United Nations issued a resolution demanding withdrawal, and economic sanctions were imposed. Iraq refused to withdraw unless various concessions, unacceptable to other nations, were made. The UN response was to set a deadline for withdrawal – 15 January 1991 – after which military action would be taken to remove the Iraqi presence from Kuwait.

Desert Shield/Storm

Thus began Operation *Desert Shield*, a massive build-up of forces from many nations. The main contributions were from the United States and Britain, but they were part of a huge international coalition, including many Arab nations. The build-

US INFANTRY PLATOON, 1991	
Unit	**Strength**
Platoon HQ	
Platoon leader	1
Platoon sergeant	1
Platoon RATELO	1
Machine gunners	2
Assistant machine gunners	2
Rifle Squad 1	
Squad leader	1
Fireteam (x 2)	
Team leader	1
Rifleman	1
Automatic rifleman	1
Grenadier	1
Rifle Squad 2	
Squad leader	1
Fireteam (x 2)	
Team leader	1
Rifleman	1
Automatic rifleman	1
Grenadier	1
Rifle Squad 3	
Squad leader	1
Fireteam (x 2)	
Team leader	1
Rifleman	1
Automatic rifleman	1
Grenadier	1

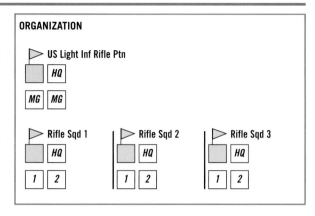

ORGANIZATION

US Light Inf Rifle Ptn — HQ — MG MG — Rifle Sqd 1 (HQ, 1, 2) — Rifle Sqd 2 (HQ, 1, 2) — Rifle Sqd 3 (HQ, 1, 2)

▲ **Training exercise**
Marines from the 22nd Marine Expeditionary Unit train during preparations for
Operation *Desert Storm*. The Marine in the foreground is armed with an
M16A2/M203 grenade launcher.

up would take time, and during this period preparations for eventual ground operations began with air attacks. The intent was to weaken Iraq's ability to fight by crippling its infrastructure as well as launching direct strikes on command posts and troop concentrations. The codename for active operations against Iraqi forces was Operation *Desert Storm*.

The Coalition forces were limited by their UN remit, which was to expel the Iraqis from Kuwait. An advance into Iraq to depose Saddam Hussein's regime seemed desirable to many, but it was not UN-sanctioned and could not be considered. This did not rule out incursions into Iraq of course.

Special forces patrols were inserted to gain intelligence and to locate the launchers for Iraq's mobile SCUD missiles. Special forces patrols were lightly equipped, as they often had to move on foot, but still carried considerable firepower. Light machine guns and assault rifles, sometimes with an under-barrel grenade launchers, were typical weapons. Although the patrols had relatively similar weaponry to the Iraqi forces they encountered, their high levels of skill, aggression and confidence multiplied their weapons' effectiveness. The special forces troops were also able to call on air support from helicopters and fast jets, often using laser-designated bombs to eliminate targets found by the ground troops.

Sniper weapons

Snipers played an important part in the ground campaign as well. Not only could they shoot high-value personnel such as officers and radio operators, but snipers armed with heavy anti-materiel rifles such as the M82A1 could destroy equipment. Primary targets included communications and radar

▲ M16A2

US 101st Airborne Division, Forward Operations Base Cobra, February 1991

The M16A2 was developed from earlier versions of the weapon. Rather than being capable of full-automatic fire it featured a burst limiter, allowing the choice of single shots or three-round bursts.

Specifications

Country of Origin: United States
Date: 1984
Calibre: 5.56mm (.219in) M193
Operation: Gas
Weight: 2.86kg (6.3lb)
Overall Length: 990mm (39in)

Barrel Length: 508mm (20in)
Muzzle Velocity: 1000m/sec (3280ft/sec)
Feed/Magazine: 30-round detachable box
 magazine
Range: 500m (1640ft) +

▲ M21 sniper rifle

US 24th Infantry Division, Jalibah Airfield, February 1991

The M21 sniper rifle proved highly effective in eliminating well-dug-in support weapon positions that were resistant to less precise small-arms fire.

Specifications

Country of Origin: United States
Date: 1969
Calibre: 7.62mm (.3in) NATO
Operation: Gas, self-loading
Weight: 5.55kg (12.24lb)
Overall Length: 1120mm (44.09in)

Barrel Length: 559mm (22in)
Muzzle Velocity: 853m/sec (2798ft/sec)
Feed/Magazine: 20-round detachable box
 magazine
Range: 800m (2625ft) +

Specifications

Country of Origin: United States
Date: 1983
Calibre: 12.7mm (.5in) / 50 BMG
Operation: Short recoil, semi-automatic
Weight: 14.7kg (32.41lb)
Overall Length: 1549mm (60.98in)

Barrel Length: 838mm (33in)
Muzzle Velocity: 843m/sec (2800ft/sec)
Feed/Magazine: 11-round detachable box
 magazine
Range: 1000m (3280ft) +

▲ Barrett M82A1 anti-materiel rifle

US Special Forces, Southern Iraq, February 1991

Anti-materiel sniper rifles were used to eliminate enemy command and control facilities and light vehicles, adding to the confusion and command paralysis when the ground offensive began.

equipment, but vehicle engines and even heavy weapons could be rendered useless by a well-aimed shot. If a machine-gunner were killed by a sniper, another man could take his place. An armour-piercing round through the receiver of the weapon would render it useless in anyone's hands.

Conventional ground combat took place mainly at the end of the campaign, during the Coalition attack

<table>
<tr><th colspan="2">Specifications</th></tr>
</table>

Country of Origin: Belgium	Barrel Length: 466mm (18.34in)
Date: 1982	Muzzle Velocity: 915m/sec (3000ft/sec)
Calibre: 5.56mm (.219in) NATO	Feed/Magazine: 30-round STANAG magazine or
Operation: Gas, air-cooled	100-round belt
Weight: 6.83kg (15.05lb)	Cyclic Rate: 750–1100rpm
Overall Length: 1040mm (40.56lb)	Range: 2000m (6560ft) +

▲ **FN Minimi**

US 1st Marine Division, Kuwait City, February 1991

Designated M249 in US military service, the FN Minimi saw action as a squad support weapon, mounted aboard vehicles, and also in defensive positions, undertaking the general-purpose machine gun role.

▲ **L85A1 (SA80)**

British 1st Armoured Division / 4th Mechanized Brigade, Southern Iraq, February 1991

Significantly improved over the original L85, the L85A1's short length was an advantage for mechanized troops who might have to dismount and remount their vehicles rapidly during fluid mobile operations. The optical sight attached to most L85 rifles is extremely useful as a surveillance tool, effectively giving every soldier a telescope to monitor the situation at a safe distance.

<table>
<tr><th colspan="2">Specifications</th></tr>
</table>

Country of Origin: United Kingdom	Barrel Length: 442mm (17.4in)
Date: 1985	Muzzle Velocity: 940m/sec (3084ft/sec)
Calibre: 5.56mm (.219in) NATO	Feed/Magazine: 30-round detachable box
Operation: Gas	magazine
Weight: 3.71kg (8.1lb)	Range: 500m (1640ft)
Overall Length: 709mm (27.9in)	

on Iraqi forces. There were clashes before this, however. The city of Khafji in Saudi Arabia was attacked in late January. The attack was initially successful against light resistance, but a counter-attack by mainly Saudi and US Marine Corps forces drove the Iraqis out of the city.

Ground campaign

The ground campaign to liberate Kuwait began on 23 February 1991 and was characterized by a short but tremendously intense period of mobile armoured warfare. The Coalition advance was spearheaded by US and British armoured units, whose tanks were a generation more advanced than the T-72s of the Iraqi army. More importantly, the Coalition armoured forces were better trained and had the advantage of total air superiority.

The result was a classic armoured breakthrough, followed by a 'rolling up' of the Iraqi defensive line by the armoured forces. Mechanized infantry, supported by armoured vehicles, was able to advance rapidly and attack unprepared enemy units. Artillery, command and logistics formations, thinking themselves safe in the rear, were quickly overrun, while even dug-in infantry and armoured units were flanked or punched out of their positions.

The rapid collapse of the Iraqi Army was followed by a precipitate flight northwards, pursued by Coalition ground forces and attacked from the air. Huge numbers of armoured vehicles were lost and it is not likely that the Iraqis could have stopped an advance on Baghdad. However, this was beyond the scope of the operation at hand, and the Saddam Hussein regime survived.

Alongside the main armoured thrusts were other operations. US and Arab troops, including a large US Marine contingent, pushed into Kuwait City while airborne forces seized air bases. In some cases these attacks were supported by a mechanized advance; in others they were an airborne infantry affair.

The ground offensive was halted after 100 hours of extremely intense combat, with the Iraqi Army in full flight and Kuwait liberated. The ceasefire that followed became permanent, allowing Saddam Hussein to deal brutally with uprisings that followed his defeat in Kuwait. At the time, there were those who predicted that they 'were going to have to do it again', i.e. fight Iraq once more at some point in the future. In 2003, that prediction came true.

BRITISH INFANTRY PLATOON (MECHANIZED), 1991		
Unit	Equipment	Strength
Platoon	Warrior	1
Commander	SA80	1
Sergeant	SA80	1
Radio operator	SA80	1
Mortar operator	51mm mortar	1
Section 1	432 AIFV	1
Fireteam 1		
Comd Cpl	SA80	1
Rifleman	SA80	1
Rifleman	SA80	1
LMG gunner	LMG	1
Fireteam 2		
2 i/c Comd LCpl	SA80	1
Rifleman	SA80	1
Rifleman	SA80	1
LMG gunner	LMG	1
Section 2	432 AIFV	1
Fireteam 1		
Comd	SA80	1
Rifleman	SA80	1
Rifleman	SA80	1
LMG gunner	LMG	1
Fireteam 2		
2 i/c Comd	SA80	1
Rifleman	SA80	1
Rifleman	SA80	1
LMG gunner	LMG	1
Section 3	432 AIFV	1
Fireteam 1		
Comd	SA80	1
Rifleman	SA80	1
Rifleman	SA80	1
LMG gunner	LMG	1
Fireteam 2		
2 i/c Comd	SA80	1
Rifleman	SA80	1
Rifleman	SA80	1
LMG gunner	LMG	1

L85 in combat

The Gulf War was the first major conflict fought by the British using their new L85 assault rifle. Various problems with early models of this weapon were exacerbated by the harsh desert conditions, with weapon malfunctions being unacceptably common. The L85 was difficult to maintain properly in an environment where sand and dust were prevalent. Experience in action prompted a set of revisions and upgrades to the weapon, eventually resulting in the A2 version, which was available in time for the Iraq War in 2003.

British Army Infantry Platoon (Mechanized), 1991

The organization of a platoon into three sections, each with its own support weapons, allows for a great deal of tactical flexibility. The classic 'two up, one back' arrangement keeps a section in reserve while the others alternate fire and manoeuvre, and is the basis of infantry tactics used by many nations.

Platoon HQ (3 x L85A1, 1 x 50mm mortar)

Section 1 (6 x L85A1, 2 x L86A1 LSW)

Section 2 (6 x L85A1, 2 x L86A1 LSW)

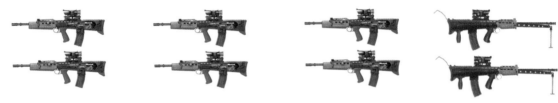

Section 3 (6 x L85A1, 2 x L86A1 LSW)

Specifications

Country of Origin: United Kingdom

Date: 1985

Calibre: 7.62mm (.3in) NATO and others

Operation: Bolt action

Weight: 6.2kg (13.68lb)

Overall Length: 1163mm (45in)

Barrel Length: 654mm (26in)

Muzzle Velocity: 840m/sec (2830ft/sec)

Feed/Magazine: 10-round detachable box
  magazine

Range: 1000m (3280ft)

▲ L96A1 sniper rifle

British 22 SAS, Iraq, February 1991

The L96A1 was adopted for British Army service in 1982. Its long-range accuracy proved to be an asset in open desert terrain. The sniper rifle has seen service in every conflict involving British forces since the mid 1980s.

Believing that there was no such thing as too much firepower, the US Army had made a more or less off-the-shelf purchase of the FN Minimi light support weapon, introducing it as the M249 Squad Automatic Weapon (SAW). Unlike the rifle-based light support weapons deployed by some nations, the M249 was a true light machinegun with a quick-change barrel and large ammunition capacity provided by belt feed. Like most other weapons, the M249 suffered from occasional malfunctions in the desert, but most troops developed a positive impression of its firepower, lightness and reliability.

▲ L86A1 LSW

British Royal Regiment of Fusiliers, Wadi Al Batin, February 1991

The L86 is a heavy-barrel version of the L85 assault rifle. It is accurate and can be used by any infantryman, but lacks the sustained firepower of a true general-purpose machine gun.

Specifications

Country of Origin: United Kingdom	Barrel Length: 646mm (25.43in)
Date: 1985	Muzzle Velocity: 970m/sec (3182ft/sec)
Calibre: 5.56mm (.219in) NATO	Feed/Magazine: 30-round detachable box
Operation: Gas, air-cooled	magazine
Weight: 5.4kg (11.9lb)	Range: 1000m (3280ft)
Overall Length: 900mm (35.43in)	

▲ L7A1/A2 (FN MAG)

British King's Own Scottish Borderers, Southern Iraq, February 1991

Although officially replaced by the L86A1 LSW as the standard light support weapon of the British Army, a large number of FN MAG machine guns (designated L7 in British service) reappeared in time to deploy to the Gulf.

Specifications

Country of Origin: Belgium	Barrel Length: 546mm (21.5in)
Date: 1955	Muzzle Velocity: 853m/sec (2800ft/sec)
Calibre: 7.62mm (.3in) NATO	Feed/Magazine: Belt-fed
Operation: Gas, air-cooled	Cyclic Rate: 600–1000rpm
Weight: 10.15kg (22.25lb)	Range: 3000m (9842ft)
Overall Length: 1250mm (49.2in)	

Gulf War: Iraqi forces
1991

The Iraqi Army of 1991 was one of the largest in the world, with huge numbers of tanks. Its strength, however, was somewhat illusory.

THE IRAQI ARMY WAS CRIPPLED by a lack of initiative among its commanders and a habit of interference by political figures in Baghdad. These factors slowed reaction speeds at the best of times, and in an environment where command, control and communications had been severely disrupted by Coalition airstrikes it was a recipe for disaster. The communications issue ran both ways; the political leaders could not obtain a clear picture of the situation, and their orders were often out of date or lost in transmission.

The army was also beset by internal problems. The best units belonged to the Republican Guard, whose function was as much political as military. The Republican Guard received higher pay, greater benefits and much better equipment than the regular army, and was intended, among other things, to ensure the political reliability of the army.

The army itself was a conscript organization, poorly led and trained, and equipped with older weaponry. Its units were unenthusiastic at best, and prone to desertion. Doctrine, like equipment, was Soviet in origin, with some Chinese-supplied weaponry as well. The Iraqi Army was thus at a disadvantage when facing the cutting-edge military technology of US and British armoured forces.

The invasion of Kuwait was led by the Republican Guard, whose armoured forces were able to overrun the unprepared Kuwaitis. Commando formations launched an airmobile assault on Kuwait City as well as key military installations. Within two days resistance ended and the occupation began. A strangely hesitant foray into Saudi Arabia was defeated, after which the Iraqis showed no real inclination to go on the offensive.

As the Coalition build-up continued, Iraqi forces adopted a highly defensive deployment, digging in tanks as bunkers and establishing strong static positions. This tactic had worked well in the previous war, against ill-armed but fanatical Iranian infantry hordes, but against the Coalition they invited attack on the enemy's terms and therefore defeat.

With no effective counter to the Coalition air campaign, Iraqi forces were steadily worn down. Many units were badly shaken by air attack, especially carpet bombing by US B-52 bombers, and

▲ **AK-74**

Republican Guard / Medina Division, Medina Ridge, February 1991

The AK-74, which armed Republican Guard units, can be distinguished from AK-47 and AKM rifles (which use different ammunition) by the long groove in the gun's stock.

Specifications

Country of Origin: USSR	Barrel Length: 400mm (15.8in)
Date: 1974	Muzzle Velocity: 900m/sec (2952ft/sec)
Calibre: 5.45mm (.215in) M74	Feed/Magazine: 30-round detachable box
Operation: Gas	magazine
Weight: 3.6kg (7.94lb)	Range: 300m (984ft)
Overall Length: 943mm (37.1in)	

mass desertions were at times triggered by airdropped leaflets warning of an imminent bombing attack. Nevertheless, the Iraqi forces held their positions.

The Coalition ground offensive directed massive force at a few key points, and once breakthroughs were made the entire defensive line was compromised. The only real chance was an armoured counter-attack, but although some local offensives were made, in a piecemeal and disorganized manner, no serious counterthrust developed. This was in part due to successful Coalition deception about the location of the main attacks, and lack of initiative on the Iraqi side. Nevertheless, several stiff actions were fought. The Republican Guard demonstrated a greater tendency to hold its ground than the rest of the Iraqi Army, but was eventually broken by the relentless Coaltion pressure and driven northwards under heavy air attack.

In Kuwait City, most Iraqi forces put up a token resistance and then surrendered or tried to withdraw. The heaviest fighting took place for the airport, which was stubbornly defended against US Marines and Kuwaiti troops. Once this action ended, the Iraqi presence in Kuwait had been dislodged.

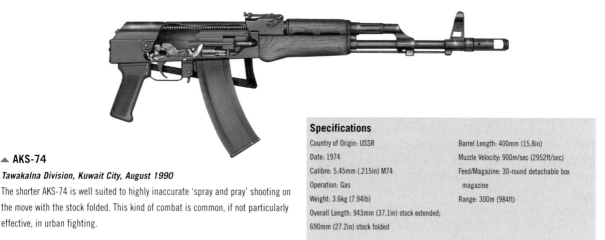

▲ AKS-74

Tawakalna Division, Kuwait City, August 1990

The shorter AKS-74 is well suited to highly inaccurate 'spray and pray' shooting on the move with the stock folded. This kind of combat is common, if not particularly effective, in urban fighting.

Specifications

Country of Origin: USSR	Barrel Length: 400mm (15.8in)
Date: 1974	Muzzle Velocity: 900m/sec (2952ft/sec)
Calibre: 5.45mm (.215in) M74	Feed/Magazine: 30-round detachable box
Operation: Gas	magazine
Weight: 3.6kg (7.94lb)	Range: 300m (984ft)
Overall Length: 943mm (37.1in) stock extended; 690mm (27.2in) stock folded	

Specifications

Country of Origin: USSR	Barrel Length: 658mm (25.9in)
Date: 1974	Muzzle Velocity: 800m/sec (2600ft/sec)
Calibre: 5.45mm (.215in) M74	Feed/Magazine: 30- or 45-round detachable box
Operation: Gas, air-cooled	magazine
Weight: 9kg (19.84lb)	Range: 2000m (6560ft) +
Overall Length: 1160mm (45.67in)	

▲ RPK-74

Hammurabi Armoured Division, Jal Atraf, Kuwait, August 1990

The RPK-74 is as easy to use and maintain as an AK-74. For an ill-trained army of conscripts this serviceability is a critical issue, as more sophisticated weapons may quickly become unworkable.

Peacekeeping forces, Africa
1990–2000s

Peacekeeping is one of the hardest tasks a military force can undertake. It requires patience and fortitude in a tense and hazardous environment.

THE ARMED FORCES of most nations are organized and trained for warfighting, i.e. engaging a major opposing force in conditions of open conflict. However, this state of conflict is relatively rare. In recent years it has been more common for armed forces to become involved in 'war-like situations' with no declared enemy, or in attempting to keep the peace in a troubled region. Such is a rather different challenge than warfighting, and cannot effectively be carried out by tanks and air power. Instead, the burden is carried by infantry and light vehicles equipped with small arms and support weapons.

Peacekeeping can be a matter of 'being seen to be there', with troops on the ground acting as a deterrent to conflict. In other cases, it is necessary to protect victims or refugees actively. Aid workers or the supplies they use are common targets for robbery and extortion, and also have to be guarded.

Peacekeeping is somewhat different to counter-insurgency warfare, though there is considerable overlap at times. Where the counter-insurgency force is primarily concerned with dealing with guerrillas or terrorists, peacekeepers are often constrained to fight only in self-defence. This situation can be intensely frustrating, with peacekeepers often attacked yet unable to retaliate or pre-empt the attack.

During the 1990s, peacekeeping forces under UN jurisdiction were deployed to Somalia in order to protect humanitarian aid workers there. Civil war and factional conflicts in an already desperately poor nation led to mass starvation, but assistance proved difficult to provide. Aid intended for needy refugees was stolen for sale on the black market, with the proceeds used to buy arms, or was taken to supply the militia of one faction or another. In this environment peacekeepers were tasked with protecting aid workers and non-combatants, as well as the supply lines to the civilian population.

After many years of effort, matters have improved in Somalia, and the suffering of innocents has been alleviated by international efforts. This would not have been possible without armed peacekeepers to

▲ **FR-F1**

United Nations Organization Stabilization Mission in the Democratic Republic of the Congo, Katanga Province, May 2005

The FR-F1 rifle is highly precise, which is of critical importance when non-combatant casualties must be avoided. Peacekeepers are often unable to shoot at obvious hostiles due to rules of engagement or the risk of collateral casualties.

Specifications

Country of Origin: France	Overall Length: 1138mm (44.8in)
Date: 1966	Barrel Length: 552mm (21.37in)
Calibre: 7.5mm (.295in)	Muzzle Velocity: 852m/sec (2795ft/sec)
Operation: Bolt action	Feed/Magazine: 10-round integral box magazine
Weight: 5.2kg (11.46lb)	Range: 800m (2625ft)

deter at least some of the violence and to ensure that aid reached those for whom it was intended.

Somalia is just one example of a situation that is all too common. Five years of war (1998–2003) in the Democratic Republic of the Congo caused thousands of deaths from secondary causes such as disease and starvation as well as directly in the violence. The United Nations deployed an international peacekeeping force in 2000 in order to support attempts to create a lasting ceasefire and, in 2003, the conflict was declared ended. As in many such regions, peace remains a fragile thing and is often maintained only if it is supported, ironically perhaps, by overt military force.

Specifications

Country of Origin: United Kingdom	Overall Length: 780mm (30in)
Date: 1985	Barrell Length: 518mm (20in)
Calibre: 5.56mm (0.219in) NATO	Muzzel Velocity: 940m/sec (3083ft/sec)
Operation: Gas, rotating bolt	Feed/Magazine: 30-round box magazine
Weight: 4.13kg (9.10lb)	Range: 500m (1640ft)

▲ L85A2
British Royal Marines, Somali Coast, November 2008

Magazines issued with the L85A1 were aluminium and not very robust. The L85A2 has three types of magazine, including the plastic Magpul EMAG. From 2007 an upgrade included Picatinny rails with optional hand grip.

▲ L110A1
Royal Irish Regiment, Sierra Leone, September 2000

A version of the FN Minimi used by the British Army, the L110 Para has a shortened barrel and sliding stock. It is deployed as a squad support weapon, giving greater firepower than the L86 LSW.

Specifications

Country of Origin: Belgium	Barrel Length: 466mm (18.34in)
Date: 1982	Muzzle Velocity: 915m/sec (3000ft/sec)
Calibre: 5.56mm (.219in) NATO	Feed/Magazine: 30-round STANAG magazine or
Operation: Gas, air-cooled	100-round belt
Weight: 6.83kg (15.05lb)	Cyclic Rate: 750–1100rpm
Overall Length: 1040mm (40.56in)	Range: 2000m (6560ft) +

Chapter 4

Latin America, 1950–Present

Many of the nations of Latin America were
originally European colonies, and began their nationhood in
revolution and civil war. Some achieved lasting stability, but
many areas of Latin America have a long history of internal
troubles or disputes with neighbours that have sometimes
boiled over into open warfare.

In the second half of the twentieth century,
Latin America was wracked by a series of revolutions that
threatened to replace the existing regimes with ones
sympathetic to or supported by the Communist bloc nations.
This situation was of grave concern to the United States,
which did not want a Communist foothold
in its 'backyard'.

◀ **Armed struggle**
Cuban revolutionary leader Fidel Castro (left, in spectacles) gives firing instructions to guerrilla fighters
who have come to join his armed forces in the Sierra Maestra, a mountainous region in the heart of Cuba,
January 1958.

Introduction

A successful revolution requires leaders, popular support and some source of equipment or funding. Where all three were available to rebels, governments are seriously threatened.

LATIN AMERICA'S PEOPLE are no more or less prone to revolution than anyone else. People everywhere tend to want, first and foremost, to be able to live their lives without undue disruption. An armed insurrection and the government measures required to oppose it will greatly affect the lives of ordinary people, and so for ordinary people to want a revolution, certain factors have to be present.

A revolution can be 'sold' to the people by popular leaders, at least to some extent. However, for the average person to be willing to risk the danger and disruption associated with a rebellion, the status quo must be unacceptable to them. The turning point can happen for many reasons; outrage at some event such as political arrests or blatant government corruption, desperation caused by starvation or impossible living conditions, or perhaps indoctrination into supporting a radical political or religious system.

With sufficient popular support, a revolutionary group can overcome government countermeasures and take power. Without it, all that is possible is to prolong the struggle long enough to obtain concessions at the negotiating table. Likewise, it is possible for a government to crush a rebellion simply through repression, but the hatred so caused can create another rebellion at a later date. Overall, in order to prevent revolution it is not necessary to please all of the people all of the time, nor in fact to please any of the people at any given moment. What

▼ **Sterling service**
British Royal Marine officers and men pose for the camera during the Falklands campaign, 1982. Many are armed with L2A3 Sterling submachine guns, issued to serving officers during the campaign. The Sterling was used by British armed forces from the Korean War until the Gulf War in 1991, with a total of 400,000 being manufactured over a 40-year period.

▲ **Loyal members**

Guatemalan government troops salute in the Quiche province of Guatemala, November 1982. They are armed with a mixture of small arms, including the Israeli-made Galil ARM assault rifle with its folding stock.

is necessary is to ensure that not too many of the people are angry at the same time. When this happens, governments fall.

The wave of Communist revolutions that swept through Latin America from 1959 onwards prompted US worries that each revolution would trigger others. This 'Domino Theory' suggested that a chain of successful revolutions might ripple through Latin America and create Communist-friendly regimes across the region. This did not occur. Only the Cuban revolution was a notable success.

Other revolts were put down or came to a negotiated settlement. Some continued at a level that permitted the country to continue functioning as such, but which caused severe economic damage and suffering to the population. The USA has intervened in several of these conflicts, for various reasons. The most obvious is the containment of Communism, but there have also been strong economic reasons for wishing to support a US-friendly government or rebel group.

Some US involvement has been overt, some less so. The global community does not, as a rule, approve of nations supporting rebel groups against the legitimate government of their country, no matter how corrupt and repressive that government may be. Covert or at least low-key support is usually the order of the day when working alongside rebels and revolutionaries – and there is always the chance that they will turn on their overseas supporters in the event of victory.

International struggles

Internal troubles were often a factor in external conflicts within Latin America. The 1982 invasion of the Falkland Islands by Argentina was part of an old dispute with Britain about ownership of the islands, but it also served to distract the Argentine public from internal problems and reduce opposition to the unpopular regime.

This is a common political gambit – attempting to create a popular cause such as an external war in order to rally support for an unpopular government. A real or claimed victory can pay dividends, but a lost war usually means even greater unpopularity and can lead to the fall of a government.

Cuban revolution
1956–59

Fidel Castro's revolution in Cuba was a startling success despite a near-fatal early setback. The key ingredient was lack of support for the government among the population.

GENERAL FULGENICO BATISTA was a dictator who came to power through a coup in 1952. His actions forestalled elections which, it had been hoped, would produce a government less corrupt than its predecessors. In the event Batista ran the country as little more than a money-making scheme for himself and his associates.

Batista's coup and subsequent government was opposed – at first through entirely legal channels – by, among others, a young politician named Fidel Castro. Unable to prevent Batista from taking power, Castro fled overseas and rallied support for what he viewed as a last resort – armed revolution.

Castro and his band of less than 100 followers landed in Cuba in December 1956, in a move designed to coincide with uprisings in various parts of the island. The revolts were put down by the security forces, and Castro's band was engaged by Cuban troops within days of landing. Scarcely more than a dozen survived the encounter. Fortunately for Castro, Batista's forces were not trained for counter-insurgency warfare and lacked any real loyalty to the government. Some elements within the army were opposed to Batista, and large segments of the population also disliked the regime. From these came new recruits for Castro's forces.

The revolutionaries had no real international backing, so were required to buy weapons on the black market. They armed themselves with whatever weapons they could obtain, many of which were of World War II vintage and came from Eastern Europe. Other equipment was captured from government forces, with the result that the revolutionaries became gradually better armed as the conflict went on.

Castro trod carefully, attacking 'soft' targets such as sugar mills owned by the rich elite. When the government forces responded, usually clumsily, Castro's men disengaged after inflicting a few casualties, deterring pursuit by using snipers to eliminate those who seemed too enthusiastic about chasing the rebels. By picking fights that he could win, Castro showed the people that his revolution

▲ **Thompson M1928**

Cuban Government Forces, Sierra Maestra, May 1956

The Thompson submachine gun was ideal for close-range ambushes in urban or overgrown terrain. A revolutionary could deliver withering firepower then make a quick escape while the survivors were still emerging from whatever cover they had found.

Specifications

Country of Origin: United States	Barrel Length: 266mm (10.5in)
Date: 1928	Muzzle Velocity: 280m/sec (920ft/sec)
Calibre: 11.4mm (.45in) M1911	Feed/Magazine: 18-, 20- or 30-round detachable
Operation: Delayed blowback	box magazine
Weight: 4.88kg (10.75lb)	Range: 120m (394ft)
Overall Length: 857mm (33.75in)	

▶ **People power**

Cuban revolutionaries attack a Nationalist army post at Camajuani during the battle for Santa Clara, Cuba, December 1958. The fighter in the centre appears to be resting a World War I-era Lewis Gun on a temporary barricade.

was worth backing. Meanwhile, Batista's troops responded with a campaign of more or less indiscriminate intimidation and repression. Opposition politicians who were against Batista, but nothing to do with the revolution, were murdered by the security forces.

Batista's brutal response alienated large segments of the population. Some were driven to join the rebels, though most just tried to stay out of the way and hoped that things would calm down. Even this passive opposition to the government worked against Batista, as it deprived him of sources of information among the general populace.

Government forces were largely armed with weapons of US origin, including Thompson submachine guns and M1 Garand rifles. Some of the latter had arrived by way of a convoluted deal that involved US arms dealers buying World War II lend-lease guns back from Britain, then supplying them to the Cuban armed forces.

By 1958, Castro was beginning to develop a large support base among the rural and urban populations. His forces achieved parity of numbers with the army, though the security forces were better equipped. In May, an attempt was made by the army to bring the rebels to action in Oriente province and defeat them.

The operation was a fiasco, with government forces ambushed or driven off with losses despite air support. This victory prompted Castro to launch a more general offensive all over the island, seizing his moment of opportunity. The Cuban Army was severely demoralized by its recent defeat, and fought poorly in the clashes that followed. These were small-scale affairs and were quite within the capabilities of Batista's army to cope with, but the troops were prone to panic and were repeatedly defeated. The result was a further drop in morale, which was not helped by Batista's orders to have an aircraft loaded with gold and money ready for him to escape.

As his control over the country collapsed, Batista made use of his plane and left the country, enabling Castro to take power with the overwhelming support of the population. He was, by his own assertion, not a Communist at this point. However, since the only nations willing to recognize the Castro regime were the Communist bloc, Cuba was forced into a new political allegiance.

▶ **Makarov pistol**

Revolutionary Forces, Sierra Maestra, May 1956

Easily concealed handguns like the Makarov were ideal weapons for urban insurgents, who were willing to exchange fire with the police on the streets of the national capital.

Specifications

Country of Origin: USSR	Barrel Length: 91mm (3.5in)
Date: 1951	Muzzle Velocity: 315m/sec (1033ft/sec)
Calibre: 9mm (.35in) Makarov	Feed/Magazine: 8-round detachable box
Operation: Blowback	magazine
Weight: .66kg (1.46lb)	Range: 40m (131ft)
Overall Length: 160mm (6.3in)	

Specifications

Country of Origin: United States

Date: 1936

Calibre: 7.62mm (.3in) US .30-06

Operation: Gas

Weight: 4.37kg (9.5lb)

Overall Length: 1103mm (43.5in)

Barrel Length: 610mm (24in)

Muzzle Velocity: 853m/sec (2800ft/sec)

Feed/Magazine: 8-round internal box magazine

Range: 500m (1640ft) +

▲ **M1 Garand**

Cuban Army, Oriente Province, August 1958

By the late 1950s, the US military had no further need of the World War II-era M1 Garand, and many thousands were sold to allies such as the Cuban Army, and French forces in Indochina.

Guatemala and Nicaragua
1960s–1990s

Central America was the scene for several revolutions and counter-revolutions, some of which became proxy wars between East and West.

MANY OF THE WEAPONS used in both Guatemala and Nicaragua were of Western European or Eastern European origin, in many cases purchased in large numbers by the government and then captured or stolen by insurgents. Other weapons were supplied to various factions by the United States and the Soviet Union.

As elsewhere in the world, the Soviet Union was willing to support a revolution that might bring about a friendly government. Conversely, US opposition to the spread of Communism prompted the supply of arms, often accompanied by CIA advisors to train personnel in their use.

Central American revolutions

In the wake of the successful Cuban revolution, it seemed that suitably determined insurgent forces could be successful in many other countries. One adherent of this idea was Ernesto 'Che' Guevara, one of Castro's lieutenants. Guevara attempted to foster a rural insurgency in Bolivia but was killed by the security forces in 1967

Guevara's failure in Bolivia was largely due to lack of popular support. He had hoped to create the conditions necessary for a successful revolution by undertaking attacks on government and military targets. The general population were not motivated to join the insurgency or even support it to any great degree. What Guevara had failed to appreciate was that a successful revolution requires an opportunity – it cannot simply be imposed.

A suitable opportunity did exist in Guatemala as the result of blatant corruption within the government. Coups and sham elections created a succession of military governments that damaged the economy and undid generally popular social reforms.

A large segment of the population was disaffected and some, such as indigenous Mayan peoples, were actively persecuted. In 1960, therefore the Guatemalan civil war began in earnest. A group of military officers launched a coup against the existing government while guerrilla activity began in the cities. These were separate events, and both were easily put down. The military rebels moved to remote areas of the country and began a long civil war under the banner of MR-13 (*Movimiento Revolucionario 13 Novembre*), a name derived from the date of the abortive coup.

The Guatemalan government, corrupt as it was, received support from the CIA. This fact was largely due to its anti-Left leanings; a corrupt Guatemala was a more desirable neighbour for the United States than a Communist one. US advisors were sent to assist the Guatemalan government in dealing with the insurgency. A separate insurgency movement existed until 1968, when it merged with MR-13. This organization, named FAR (*Fuerzas Armadas Rebeles*,

or Rebel Armed Forces) was composed of various different groups and lacked cohesion. Its forces were unable to obtain a foothold in the countryside, so they moved into the cities in keeping with a principle of revolutionary warfare put forward by the Brazilian Communist Carlos Marighela. It was hoped that by pulling security forces into the urban centres, the pressure on rural insurgent groups would be reduced. The Guatemalan government responded with extreme brutality and permitted vigilante groups to operate more or less at will. Bloody clashes took place in the towns between insurgents armed with whatever weapons they could get and the better-

▲ FN 49

Guatemalan Security Forces, 1960s

The FN 49 was deployed by the security forces of Argentina, Brazil, Colombia and Venezuela. It saw considerable action during street battles with insurgents in Rio de Janeiro in the late 1960s.

Specifications

Country of Origin: Belgium	Overall Length: 1116mm (43.54in)
Date: 1949	Barrel Length: 590mm (23.23in)
Calibre: Various, including 8mm (.314in)	Muzzle Velocity: 710m/sec (2330ft/sec)
Operation: Gas	Feed/Magazine: 10-round fixed box magazine
Weight: 4.31kg (9.5lb)	Range: 500m (1640ft

▲ Madsen M45

Guatemalan Security Forces, Guatemala City, May 1967

The Guatemalan government's counter-terror campaign in the cities relied on crushing any resistance with heavy and often indiscriminate firepower. The Danish-made Madsen borrowed concepts from wartime expedient weapons such as the British Sten.

Specifications

Country of Origin: Denmark	Overall Length: 800mm (31.49in)
Date: 1945	Barrell Length: 315mm (12.40in)
Calibre: 9mm (0.35in)	Muzzel Velocity: 365m/sec (1197.5ft/sec)
Operation: Blowback	Feed/Magazine: 32-round box magazine
Weight: 3.15kg (6.94lb)	Range: 100m (328ft)

organized and more ruthless security forces. Yet despite extreme repression, the insurgency continued and in 1980 gained additional impetus.

By the mid 1990s Guatemala's economy had improved and along with it conditions for the majority of the population. With reduced cause for disaffection, a gradual move towards peace and stability resulted. Thus despite extreme measures the Guatemalan civil war was won, or at least ended, by civil reform rather than military action.

Nicaragua

Conflict in Nicaragua had been ongoing for many years when the FLSN (*Frente Sandinista de Liberacion Nacional*, or Sandinista National Liberation Front) was created in 1961. This force took its name from Augusto Sandino, who led a guerrilla force to fight US forces in Nicaragua. He was betrayed and murdered by Anastasio Somoza Garcia, who later took power in a coup. Opposition to the Somoza regime was intermittent and usually unsuccessful

Specifications

Country of Origin: USSR	Barrel Length: 415mm (16.34in)
Date: 1947	Muzzle Velocity: 600m/sec (1969ft/sec)
Calibre: 7.62mm (.3in) Soviet M1943	Feed/Magazine: 30-round detachable box
Operation: Gas	magazine
Weight: 4.3kg (9.48lb)	Range: 400m (1312ft)
Overall Length: 880mm (34.65in)	

▲ **AK-47 assault rifle**

Sandinista guerrilla forces, Managua, 1978

The Soviet Union delivered up to 100,000 AK-47s to the Sandinistas, both before and after they took power in Nicaragua. As in other theatres, the hardy AK-47 proved a superb weapon in jungle conditions.

▲ **Sa23**

Nicaraguan National Guard, June 1970

The Czech Sa23 used its trigger as a selector. A light pull fired one round; full movement initiated automatic fire.

Specifications

Country of Origin: Czechoslovakia	Overall Length: 686mm (27in)
Date: 1950	Barrell Length: 284mm (11.18in)
Calibre: 9mm (0.35in)	Muzzle Velocity: Not known
Operation: Blowback	Feed/Magazine: 24- or 40-round box magazine
Weight: 3.27kg (7.20lb)	Range: 100–200m (328–656ft)

until the foundation of the FLSN, which is usually taken as the start date for the Nicaraguan revolution. The FLSN carried out campaigns in both rural and urban areas, and worked hard to win over the people of the regions where it operated.

The FLSN organization remained small and achieved little until 1972, when the Somoza government blatantly misappropriated international relief funds after a serious earthquake. This action alienated a large segment of the population, and resulted in a rapid expansion of the FLSN as well as increased opposition through legal political channels. The government response was to increase repression.

A spectacular guerrilla success in 1978 weakened the government to the point where a coup was narrowly avoided. Insurgents were able to capture the

National Palace and several hundred government officials. FLSN support increased to the point where a large-scale campaign could be launched throughout the country.

Supplied with arms from Cuba and the Soviet Union and facing demoralized government troops, the insurgents took control over the major urban areas. Despite heavy urban fighting the security forces could not dislodge the guerrillas and as a result of international pressure as well as internal collapse, the Somoza government was ousted. Here was the 'official' end of the revolution, though internal conflict continued afterwards. As with other Latin American nations, it was not armed force that decided the issue but the support or lack of it by the majority of the population.

▲ Samonabiject Puska vz52

Nicaraguan Security Forces, Managua, June 1979

After being replaced in Czech service by the vz58, large numbers of vz52 rifles were supplied to overseas users. The vz52 saw action in the street battles for the Nicaraguan capital, Managua.

Specifications

Country of Origin: Czechoslovakia	Overall Length: 843mm (33.2in)
Date: 1952	Barrel Length: 400mm (15.8in)
Calibre: 7.62mm (.3in) M52 or 7.62mm (.3in)	Muzzle Velocity: 710m/sec (2330ft/sec)
Soviet M1943	Feed/Magazine: 10-round detachable box
Operation: Gas	magazine
Weight: 3.11kg (6.86lb)	Range: 500m (1640ft) +

Specifications

Country of Origin: United States	Barrel Length: 508mm (20in)
Date: 1963	Muzzle Velocity: 1000m/sec (3280ft/sec)
Calibre: 5.56mm (.219in) M193	Feed/Magazine: 30-round detachable box
Operation: Gas	magazine
Weight: 2.86kg (6.3lb)	Range: 500m (1640ft) +
Overall Length: 990mm (39in)	

▲ M16A1 assault rifle

US Military Advisors, Panama, 1979

US forces trained and equipped 'Contra' counter-revolutionary forces in neighbouring countries after the fall of the Nicaraguan government.

Falklands War: Argentine forces
1982

Ownership of the Falkland Islands has been a subject of dispute between Britain and Argentina for many years. In 1982, the Argentine government decided to invade.

IN 1955, A MILITARY COUP replaced the democratic government of Argentina with a junta that presided over a rapid economic decline and significant urban unrest. In 1972, former president Juan Perón returned from exile to take over the reins of power but could do little to improve matters. While the countryside was relatively peaceful, the streets of major cities became battlegrounds, especially in the mid 1970s.

In 1976, a further coup created another military junta that held on to power through the usual means of intimidation and repression. Led by General Leopoldo Galtieri, the government sought some means to distract the population from internal issues and hit upon a not-uncommon solution: an external conflict.

Argentina claims the Falkland Islands under their Spanish name the Malvinas, and had been

▶ **Captured small arms**
A British soldier stacks Argentine weapons following the capture of Port Stanley by UK forces. The Argentine and British forces used virtually the same small arms, including the FN MAG, FN FAL and M1919 Browning .30-calibre machine gun (being held here).

Specifications

Country of Origin: Argentina	Barrel Length: 533mm (21in)
Date: 1960	Muzzle Velocity: 853m/sec (2800ft/sec)
Calibre: 7.62mm (.3in) NATO	Feed/Magazine: 20-round detachable box
Operation: Gas	magazine
Weight: 4.31kg (9.5lb)	Range: 800m (2620ft) +
Overall Length: 1053mm (41.46in)	

▲ **FM FAL**

10th Mechanized Infantry Brigade / 7th Regiment, Wireless Ridge, 13 June 1982

The Argentinian version of the FAL rifle was locally produced by Fabricaciones Militaires, hence the 'FM' designation. Argentine FALs were capable of fully automatic fire.

negotiating with Britain over their sovereignty for some years. The Falkland islanders themselves had voted overwhelmingly to remain British, however. Reasoning that Britain lacked the means and the will to mount an amphibious campaign in the South Atlantic, Galtieri's government decided to take the islands by force.

Tensions were running high with Chile at the time, so many of Argentina's best troops were deployed to protect against a Chilean attack. They included mountain troops who were trained for cold-

environment wafare. Many of the conscripts who were sent to the islands were not similarly trained, and suffered accordingly.

The initial invasion was spearheaded by Argentine special forces, who had orders to avoid inflicting casualties if possible. It was hoped that minimal force might reduce British resolve to take back the islands. In the event, the small force of Royal Marines stationed on the island put up a spirited resistance until the situation was obviously hopeless, at which point they surrendered.

Once the islands were secured, they were garrisoned primarily with conscript troops, mostly of low quality. It was not expected that the British

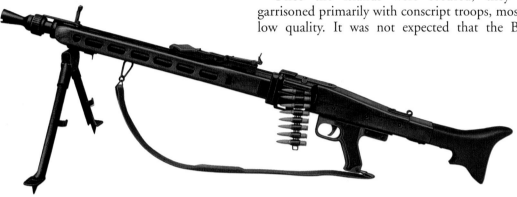

▲ Rheinmetall MG3

3rd Mechanized Infantry Brigade / 12th Regiment, Goose Green,
26 May 1982

The MG3, chambered for the same 7.62mm (.3in) ammunition as the FN FAL rifle, was the standard Argentine Army light support weapon.

Specifications

Country of Origin: West Germany	Barrel Length: 531mm (20.9in)
Date: 1966	Muzzle Velocity: 820m/sec (2690ft/sec)
Calibre: 7.62mm (.3in) NATO	Feed/Magazine: 50- or 100-round belt (50-round
Operation: Short recoil, air-cooled	belt may be contained in drum)
Weight: 11.5kg (25.35lb)	Cyclic Rate: 950–1300rpm depending on bolt
Overall Length: 1220mm (48in)	Range: 2000m (6562ft) +

Specifications

Country of Origin: Argentina	extended; 770mm (30.3in) stock folded
Date: 1960	Barrel Length: 436mm (17.1in)
Calibre: 7.62mm (.3in) NATO	Muzzle Velocity: 853m/sec (2800ft/sec)
Operation: Gas	Feed/Magazine: 20-round detachable box
Weight: 4.36kg (9.61lb)	magazine
Overall Length: 1020mm (40.15in) stock	Range: 500m (1640ft) +

▲ FM FAL (Paratroop version)

9th Infantry Brigade / 25th Infantry Regiment, Goose Green,
26 May 1982

The folding-stock version of the FAL was used by paratroops and some other formations, including the 25th Infantry, a unit similar to the US Army Rangers.

would try to recapture the Falklands, and once it was obvious that this was going to be undertaken it became problematic to reinforce the garrison by sea due to the presence of British submarines.

The Argentine garrison was strongly deployed around the capital, Port Stanley, and along the land approaches to it. Other forces were positioned at key points or held in reserve to oppose a British landing. The strength of the Argentine defence at Port Stanley made a direct assault impractical, so it was expected – correctly – that the British would land elsewhere and move on Stanley overland.

Other forces were deployed to islands in the region, such as South Georgia and Pebble Island, but these were considered peripheral to the conflict, as was the large island of West Falkland. In the final analysis, the fate of the Falkland Islands would rest

upon who controlled the capital and main population centre at Port Stanley.

The Argentine infantry deployed to the islands were mostly just out of basic training and were not adequately trained for conditions on the Falklands. Nor were they up to the task of mobile warfare even if this had been practical. However, since much of the islands' terrain was impassable to vehicles and there were several obviously strong defensive positions, the conscripts were expected to be able to hold their own against even a major attack.

The key weaknesses of the Argentine forces were lack of training and the absence of mutual confidence between the officers and the enlisted men. Argentine forces were somewhat brittle; they were capable of putting up a good fight under favourable conditions, but might disintegrate when faced by setbacks.

▲ FARA 83

Under development

The FARA 83 rifle was under development as a possible replacement for the FM FAL. It is possible that some examples may have been taken to the Falklands for combat evaluation purposes.

Specifications

Country of Origin: Argentina	745mm (29.3in) stock folded
Date: 1981	Barrel Length: 452mm (17.8in)
Calibre: 5.56mm (.219in) NATO	Muzzle Velocity: 980m/sec (3215ft/sec)
Operation: Gas, rotating bolt	Feed/Magazine: 30-round detachable box
Weight: 3.95kg (8.71lb)	magazine
Overall Length: 1000mm (39.4in) stock extended;	Range: 500m (1640ft) +

Specifications

Country of Origin: Argentina
Date: 1974
Calibre: 9mm (.35in) Parabellum
Operation: Blowback, closed bolt
Weight: 3.4kg (7.49lb)
Overall Length: 693mm (27.2in)
Barrel Length: 290mm (11.4in)
Muzzle Velocity: 400m/sec (1312ft/sec)
Feed/Magazine: 25- 32- or 40-round detachable
   box magazine
Range: 100m (328ft)

▲ FMK-3

602nd Commando, Mount Kent, 31 May 1982

The FMK-3 was developed to meet the Argentine Army's need for a close-combat weapon. It is well-balanced enough to be fired one-handed.

Falklands War: British forces
1982

It is widely accepted that 3:1 odds are needed for a successful offensive. The British could not deploy anything like enough troops to achieve this superiority.

THE BRITISH RESPONSE to the invasion of the Falkland Islands was impressively fast, but was constrained by the amount of maritime transport available. Even by converting liners and container ships to naval auxiliaries, the force that could be deployed to the Falkland Islands was severely limited.

Attempts were made to provide adequate logistical support and helicopter mobility, both of which were further reduced by air attacks on the task force as it anchored off the Falklands. Only a handful of Scorpion and Scimitar armoured vehicles, and a very limited amount of artillery, could be deployed. The Falklands campaign was obviously going to be an infantry affair.

With a landing directly at Port Stanley out of the question, San Carlos Water was chosen as the main anchorage. Lying between East and West Falkland, this location provided a fairly sheltered anchorage that could be protected against air attack by naval Harrier aircraft, warships and Rapier missile batteries landed on shore. Despite these precautions, extremely determined Argentine air attacks sank ships and

reduced the resources available to the British ground forces. Perhaps most keenly felt was the loss of several Chinook transport helicopters aboard the container ship *Atlantic Conveyor*.

Air mobility
Peripheral operations by Royal Marines and special forces retook South Georgia and destroyed Argentine ground-attack aircraft based on Pebble Island, but East Falkland was a tougher proposition. Landings at Port San Carlos were more or less unopposed by ground forces, and there was no real chance of a counter-attack due to the Argentine deployments. However, the fleet was very vulnerable close inshore and suffered significant losses to air attack.

It was thus necessary to move quickly, but with few helicopters available, mobility and logistics were serious problems. The only answer was to rely on the toughness and physical fitness of the ground troops, who had to carry what they needed and march to their objectives as infantry had traditionally done. After establishing a secure beachhead the British

▲ **L1A1 Self-Loading Rifle (SLR)**

3 Commando Brigade / 2nd Battalion, The Parachute Regiment, Goose Green, 26 May 1982

The British version of the FN FAL, designated L1A1, was capable of semi-automatic fire only. In the British Army at that time, individual marksmanship was prized more highly than the capability to deliver suppressing fire.

Specifications

Country of Origin: United Kingdom	Barrel Length: 535mm (21.1in)
Date: 1954	Muzzle Velocity: 853m/sec (2800ft/sec)
Calibre: 7.62mm (.3in) NATO	Feed/Magazine: 20-round detachable box
Operation: Gas	magazine
Weight: 4.31kg (9.5lb)	Range: 800m (2625ft) +
Overall Length: 1055mm (41.5in)	

moved first against Darwin and Goose Green. The attacking force was required to march overland carrying huge loads of equipment before attacking a well-defended position. Despite being outnumbered by the defenders the paratroops given the task were able to make a successful frontal assault across a narrow isthmus and capture their objectives.

With the southern flank secured by the taking of Goose Green, British paratroops and marines advanced across the northern part of East Falkland. Their objectives were a series of small coastal settlements, after which the advance on the capital could begin in earnest. The settlements of Douglas and Teal Inlet, as well as the outer defensive positions around Port Stanley, were relatively lightly held. There was no significant counter-offensive, partly due to weather conditions and partly because the Argentine commanders knew that some British infantry were still at sea. These might be used for a direct assault if the defences around Port Stanley were weakened.

Ridge assault

Meanwhile, other British forces began pushing across the southern part of East Falkland. Both the northern and southern arms of the pincer encountered defended positions, which were usually constructed on high ground. These ridges had to be cleared by assault, supported where possible by Harriers from the Royal Navy's carrier force and the artillery, which laid down its heaviest bombardment since the end of World War II.

Between 6 and 13 June, a series of battles were fought to clear defensive positions. These were often close-quarters affairs, characterized by small-scale scrambles for positions in the tumbled rocks of the ridges. Many Argentine units fought stubbornly, though others were less determined.

One factor working in favour of the British was the fearsome reputation of the Gurkha troops who formed part of the ground force. In a close-quarters battle morale is more important than ever, and that of the Argentine conscripts was shaken by the tales they heard about Gurkha units. Some of these were spread, rather unwisely, by Argentine officers who hoped to inspire their men.

The capture of Bluff Cove on 8 June allowed a forward logistics base to be set up, which greatly eased British supply problems. Two landing ships were bombed while unloading, but it was still possible to get troops and supplies ashore.

Final battles

The final battles of the campaign were fought to clear defensive positions from the ridges above Port Stanley. On the night of 13/14 June, Wireless Ridge was taken by The Parachute Regiment while the Scots Guards assaulted Tumbledown mountain. As the Welsh Guards and Gurkhas moved up to attack the final positions at Mount William and Sapper Hill, the Argentine defence collapsed. The Argentine surrender on 14 June made an assault on Port Stanley itself unnecessary.

1st Battalion, Welsh Guards, Rifle Platoon, Rifle Section, 1982

A typical British infantry platoon of the Falklands era was made up of a platoon HQ and three rifle sections. A rifle section would include the following weapons:

2 Sterling SMG, 7 x SLR, 1 x L7A2 GPMG (plus up to 3 M72 LAW)

▲ L7A2 (FN MAG) GPMG

5th Infantry Brigade/2nd Battalion, Scots Guards, Tumbledown, 13 June 1982

The 'Gimpy' (GPMG) was an integral part of British rifle squads, providing effective and accurate automatic fire support even when heavier weapons were not available.

Specifications

Country of Origin: United Kingdom	Barrel Length: 546mm (21.5in)
Date: 1961	Muzzle Velocity: 853m/sec (2800ft/sec)
Calibre: 7.62mm (.3in) NATO	Feed/Magazine: Belt-fed
Operation: Gas, air-cooled	Cyclic Rate: 600–1000rpm
Weight: 10.15kg (22.25lb)	Range: 3000m (9842ft)
Overall Length: 1250mm (49.2in)	

◀ L2A2 HE fragmentation grenade

3 Commando Brigade/42 Commando / Royal Marines, Mount Harriet,
12 June 1982

Grenades are an effective weapon in assault operations if they can be properly placed. A lobbed grenade can drop into a position protected from direct fire.

Specifications

Country of Origin: United Kingdom	Height: 84mm (3.25in)
Date: 1960	Detonation Mechanism: Timed friction fuse
Type: Fragmentation	Filling: Composition B
Weight: .395kg (.87lb)	Lethal Radius: 10m (32.8ft)

Colombia
1960s–PRESENT

Colombia has seen more than five decades of low-intensity warfare between government forces and a variety of insurgent groups.

COLOMBIA SUFFERED PERIODS of significant unrest before the 1960s, interspersed by relatively peaceful times. Some of the causes of the current violence date back to these old disputes, but the present conflict began in the early to mid 1960s.

A number of operations were mounted by the Colombian security forces in the early 1960s, aimed at reducing the activities of insurgent groups operating throughout the country. The insurgents were pushed out of the urban centres and could only maintain bases in very remote rural areas, where they could hide their activities.

Yet by the mid 1970s a new wave of urban unrest had begun. Government countermeasures and initiatives that were intended to find a negotiated settlement calmed the situation by the early 1980s. Up until this point the conflict had been primarily political and ideological in nature, with the motivations of the insurgents varying somewhat.

Narcotic power

The situation became even more complex in the 1980s as drug barons became a potent political force in Colombia. This brought conflict with the guerrillas and with the government, which was under pressure from the USA to act against the narcotics sources.

Both the drug lords and the insurgents used terrorism and assassination to influence political decisions, with the guerrillas increasingly funded by drug money in addition to the more traditional revenue from kidnappings. By the mid 1990s the insurgents were able to carry out direct attacks on bases used by the security forces. This resulted in a withdrawal from some outlying areas.

The redeployment of security forces had some benefits, such as reduced vulnerability to attacks on small bases, but it also meant that the insurgents

could operate freely in many areas. Pro-government vigilante groups began to operate against the insurgents in some areas, using methods every bit as brutal as those of the guerrillas.

The forces deployed by the drugs cartels at times operated as something similar to rifle-armed light infantry, taking control of areas of the countryside to prevent police interference in their operations. In the urban environment, cartel gunmen found small, concealable weapons to be highly useful for security and strikes against their opponents. In addition to handguns, submachine guns were favoured, of which many came from Spanish manufacturers.

The cartels were also involved in international arms smuggling, enabling them to obtain a wide variety of weaponry for their own use, as well as selling arms for profit. Some of these weapons found their way onto the black market in Colombia despite supposedly strict gun control laws.

In recent years, the Colombian armed forces have made some progress at combating the insurgents and drug barons, but the political situation in the country remains volatile. Many of the underlying social and economic problems that caused the unrest remain. In particular, the government's anti-narcotics stance alienates segments of the population who rely on coca cultivation for their income. Since the guerrillas are willing to protect

▲ Star Z70B

M-19 (April 19th Movement) Insurgents, Bogota, 1985

The Star M70B was a developed version of the earlier Z-62, replacing trigger-pressure fire selection with a more conventional safe/semi/full-automatic fire selector switch.

Specifications

Country of Origin: Spain	Barrel Length: 200mm (7.87in)
Date: 1971	Muzzle Velocity: 380m/sec (1247ft/sec)
Calibre: 9mm (.35in) Parabellum	Feed/Magazine: 20-, 30-, or 40-round detachable
Operation: Blowback	box magazine
Weight: 2.87kg (6.33lb)	Range: 50m (164ft) +
Overall Length: 700mm (27.56in)	

the coca farmers from government interference, they receive support and funding that has little to do with ideology or identification with a cause; simple economic necessity drives many people into the arms of the insurgent organizations.

Urban violence

The conflict in Colombia has been characterized by urban violence, kidnapping and assassination, activities that require only small arms and a willingness to use them. Government operations against the coca plantations, and patrols aimed at finding the guerrillas' bases, have been resisted, but for the most part the conflict is fought at a low level. Although the government has achieved some successes in combating drugs gangs in recent years, the conflict is likely to continue in the same manner for some time yet.

▲ Star Z-62

Colombian National Police, Bogota, 1992

Experienced gained from Spanish Army service with the Z-45 resulted in Star creating an improved submachine gun in the late 1950s. This weapon entered service in 1963, as the Z-62. The Z-62 has a different layout, with the pistol grip much closer to the magazine well.

Specifications

Country of Origin: Spain	Barrel Length: 215mm (8.4in)
Date: 1963	Muzzle Velocity: 399m/sec (1312ft/sec)
Calibre: 9mm (.35in)	Feed/Magazine: 25- or 30-round detachable box
Operation: Blowback, open bolt	magazine
Weight: 3kg (6.61lb)	Range: 150–200m (492–656ft)
Overall Length: 615mm (24.2in)	

Specifications

Country of Origin: Israel	Overall Length: 730mm (28.74in)
Date: Not known	Barrell Length: 215mm (8.46in)
Calibre: 5.56mm (.219in); 7.62mm (.3in)	Muzzel Velocity: 710m/sec (2329ft/sec)
Operation: Gas, rotating bolt	Feed/Magazine: 35-round box magazine
Weight: 2.8kg (6.17lb)	Range: 300–500m (984 –1640ft)

▲ Galil ACE 21

Colombian National Army Special Forces Anti-Terrorist Group, Cartagena, 2004

The Galil ACE is the latest version of the Galil assault rifle. It is available with various barrel lengths for use as a support weapon, rifle or carbine.

Chapter 5

Modern Wars

Wars in the modern world are characterized
by their complexity and the predominance of urban combat,
often within an area where non-combatants are trying to go
about the business of daily life. Large-scale engagements
between national armies do happen, but confrontations
between massed armoured formations are less common than
fleeting battles between insurgents and infantry supported
by light armoured vehicles.

Often, troops are involved in 'war-like situations' rather than
straight-up warfare. They are deployed to keep the peace
rather than to fight an enemy, or to deal with an insurgency.
These priorities create ambiguities than can be exploited by
hostiles, and they require a delicate balance of restraint and
aggression if the overall mission is to be a success.

◀ **Checkpoint security**
Armed with an L7A2 general-purpose machine gun, a British Army trooper from the 3rd Battalion, the
Parachute Regiment, keeps watch as part of a vehicle checkpoint during Operation *Iraqi Freedom*, 2004.

Introduction

Warfare has always been about political outcomes rather than military victories. The side that achieves its aims will win, even if defeated in every battle.

THE TERM 'THREE-BLOCK WAR' was coined to describe a situation in which troops might be involved in humanitarian aid, peacekeeping and direct combat operations at the same time, all within a three-block radius. It reflects the complexity of many conflicts and the many missions that must be carried out in order to succeed.

Direct conflict between national armies creates a relatively straightforward situation – the goal is to defeat a clearly identifiable enemy using technology and tactics. Even here, complexities arise when combatant forces seek to limit the suffering of the enemy population. Many national governments have less regard for their own people than their enemies,

and will try to hide their facilities among innocents. Positioning command posts and arms factories beside hospitals and schools may limit the willingness of a hostile force to attack them.

Much of this complexity is inadvertent, however. It is very rare to encounter a theatre of conflict where there are absolutely no civilians, so military forces must take care only to engage properly identified targets. This situation of course allows hostiles to hide among the innocent population in order to gather information or approach their targets, but while making war without regard to the suffering of innocents might be simpler, it is also horrific and politically costly.

▲ **Sniper security**

A US Army sniper team scan for enemy activity during a foot patrol near Forward Operating Base Mizan, Afghanistan, 2009. The sniper is armed with a Barrett M82 'Light' .50-calibre anti-materiel rifle. The soldier with binoculars carries an M4 carbine slung from his shoulder. In the background (left) appears to be an abandoned Soviet-made PKM light machine gun.

▲ **Classic Soviet LMG**
Armed with an RPK light machine gun, an Iraqi army soldier from 5th Iraqi Army Division undergoes training in Kirkush Military Training Base, Iraq, 2011.

Operations are particularly difficult where a peacekeeping force is involved in a complex conflict featuring many factions, including irregular forces who might not wear uniforms or identifying insignia. Today's friendlies might be tomorrow's hostiles, and even without the prospect of treachery it can be hard to tell one group apart from another – especially if deliberate deception is employed.

The problem in many cases is not so much dealing with enemy combatants as identifying them and finding their whereabouts. Combatants may conceal themselves in remote mountain bases or fade back into the general population to avoid detection. In either case, once contact is lost it is very difficult to regain, a fact that permits hostiles to make traditional hit-and-run attacks against targets of their choosing.

Modern wars are, for the most part, won in the hearts and minds of the people and, to some extent, their political leadership. Military success plays a part in the outcome, of course, but the overall mission is political. It is not enough to keep on killing guerrillas; if the population is hostile then more will appear. The people must be won over or at least dissuaded from

supporting the insurgents. This means that troops must work with the locals, talk to them, and win their acceptance – perhaps even friendship. Such cannot be done from behind tank armour or a strike jet's cockpit.

The close contact required by foot and light vehicle patrolling, and by operating checkpoints and guarding aid stations, exposes troops to attack with basic weapons. Similarly, when attacking a remote insurgent base it is usually infantry that have to take the brunt of the fighting; other arms cannot always be brought to bear.

Modern ground troops are supported by a wealth of technological equipment: remote-controlled drones, GPS-guided artillery shells and all-but-impervious main battle tanks (MBTs). Yet they still must engage hostiles, clear enemy positions and secure key areas in the same manner as infantry of all eras. Infantry weapons are still, arguably, the most important of military tools. It is the soldier on the ground who makes the shoot/don't shoot decision, and success or failure in the overall mission will be influenced greatly by the combined weight of those decisions.

Former Yugoslavia
1990s

Traditionally referred to as the 'powder-keg of Europe', the Balkans once again ignited into warfare in the early 1990s.

The presence of many different ethnic, religious and political groupings has always made the Balkans a potentially unstable region. In the early years of the twentieth century, national boundaries were redrawn on many occasions. From this complex situation emerged the Kingdom of Yugoslavia, which was invaded by the Axis powers in World War II. After liberation, Yugoslavia became the Socialist Federal Republic of Yugoslavia (SFRY).

Yugoslavia at this time comprised several states, including the republics of Serbia, Croatia and Bosnia-Herzegovina. Within each of these states lived a mix of Christians and Muslims, and most states had significant populations whose ethnic origins differed from the state as a whole. Bosnia, for example, was home to large populations of Serbs and Croats, who were more inclined towards loyalty to Serbia or Croatia than to their ostensible homeland in Bosnia.

Despite this internal complexity, Yugoslavia was a prosperous nation in the post-war years and enjoyed solid economic growth. Although having a Communist government, Yugoslavia was not aligned with the Soviet Union and received support from the West to ensure that it did not become so. Changes in the East–West political situation caused this support to be reduced, and Yugoslavia's economy suffered accordingly.

With international debt increasing and the economy declining fast, the national government granted the member republics greater control over their affairs, encouraging a general move towards independence. Autonomous regions, such as Kosovo in Serbia, were created, which caused resentment in some quarters. Disagreements between the various member states of Yugoslavia caused endless political wrangling, which came violently to a head at the end of the 1980s.

It is hard to pinpoint a precise moment when the breakup of Yugoslavia began, but the announcement of secession from Croatia by Croatian Serbs saw the beginning of armed conflict. Croatia was at that time moving towards independence, and its constitution

▲ **Vz58**

Bosnian Irregulars, Sarajevo, May 1994

The Czech-made Vz58 resembles an AK-47 and uses the same ammunition, but it is a separately developed gas-operated design.

Specifications

Country of Origin: Czechoslovakia	Barrel Length: 390mm (15.4in)
Date: 1958	Muzzle Velocity: 705m/sec (2313ft/sec)
Calibre: 7.62mm (.3in) Soviet M1943	Feed/Magazine: 30-round detachable box
Operation: Gas, falling breech-block	magazine
Weight: 2.91kg (6.42lb)	Range: 400m (1312ft)
Overall Length: 845mm (33.3in)	

seemed to be treating Serbs as second-class citizens. This was unacceptable to Croatian Serbs, who had the support of many Yugoslavian Army officers.

Serb domination

Much of the army's officer class were ethnic Serbs, who were naturally sympathetic to their cousins in Croatia. The Federal Army had taken steps to disarm Croatian forces during the run-up to independence, which gave the Serbs a major advantage. Both sides lacked significant armament at the beginning of the conflict, but the Croatian Serbs were supplied by sympathetic Federal Army officers. The emerging state of Croatia, on the other hand, had to obtain weapons through international channels, often negotiating embargo conditions. Serb forces generally had access to equipment from the former Yugoslav army, and were well equipped with military weapons. These included Zastava assault rifles, which were derived from the AK series. One notable difference was that the Zastava rifles did not use chrome lining in the barrel, which made them less resistant to corrosion. However, they were correspondingly more accurate and proved both robust and reliable in combat situations.

Other factions were badly affected by the arms embargo and were forced to buy weapons on the black market or from criminal groups within their own society. These weapons tended to be suited to urban criminality rather than military combat, and included a range of handguns and submachine guns which were mainly of Eastern European origin.

The emerging conflict was particularly unpleasant, with accusations of atrocities and massacres levelled

▶ Agram 2000

Croatian Irregulars / Croatian War of Independence, 1995

Despite its highly modern appearance, the Agram 2000 was developed from the Beretta Modello 12, which dates back to the late 1950s.

Specifications

Country of Origin: Croatia	Barrel Length: 200mm (7.8in)
Date: 1990	Muzzle Velocity: Not known
Calibre: 9mm (.35in) Parabellum	Feed/Magazine: 15-, 22- or 32-round detachable
Operation: Blowback	box magazine
Weight: 1.8kg (3.96lb)	Range: 100m (328ft)
Overall Length: 482mm (18.9in)	

▶ CZ85 pistol

Serbian Irregulars, Srebrenica, February 1995

The Czech-made CZ85 pistol is an updated version of the CZ75, differing mainly in having an ambidextrous safety and slide stop.

Specifications

Country of Origin: Czechoslovakia	Barrel Length: 120mm (4.7in)
Date: 1986	Muzzle Velocity: 370m/sec (1214ft/sec)
Calibre: 9mm (.35in) Parabellum	Feed/Magazine: 16-round detachable box
Operation: Blowback	magazine
Weight: 1kg (2.2lb)	Range: 40m (131ft)
Overall Length: 206mm (8.1in)	

against both sides; many Croatian leaders were later convicted of war crimes. Attacks on civilians were employed both as a military gambit to weaken the enemy's resolve and also in an effort to remove unwanted ethnic groups from Croatian territory. Croatia was also attacked from outside, notably by Serbian forces, throughout five years of war.

Border clashes

Soon after fighting broke out in Croatia came the declaration of independence by Slovenia. The subsequent clash with the Yugoslavian federal forces became known as the Ten-Day War. This was a fairly minor conflict, with few casualties. Federal Yugoslavian troops generally took up positions on the borders of the republic of Slovenia, and primarily confined themselves to containment operations. After some skirmishing a ceasefire was agreed and eventually the federal forces pulled out, essentially confirming Slovenian independence.

The fate of Bosnia was a particular bone of contention between the various former Yugoslavian factions. After an initial period of heavy fighting, which was marked by atrocities and the murder of surrendered enemy personnel, UN peacekeeping forces attempted to create safe areas within the conflict zone, beginning a long and difficult deployment where their hands were often tied by rules of engagement that, for example, allowed hostiles to walk away unhindered after throwing a

▶ **CZ99 pistol**

Federal Armoured Forces, Slovenian Border, June 1991

Unrelated to Czech 'CZ' pistols, the Zastava CZ99 was produced to meet the needs of the Yugoslavian military and passed into the hands of various forces.

Specifications

Country of Origin: Yugoslavia	Overall Length: 190mm (7.4in)
Date: 1990	Barrel Length: 108mm (4.25in)
Calibre: 9mm (.35in) Parabellum,	Muzzle Velocity: 300–457m/sec (985–1500ft/sec)
10.16mm (.4in) / 40 S&W	Feed/Magazine: 15- (9mm/.35in) or 10/12-round
Operation: Single- or double-action	(10.16mm/.4in) detachable magazine
Weight: 1.145kg (2.5lb)	Range: 40m (131ft)

Specifications

Country of Origin: Czechoslovakia	Barrel Length: 115mm (4.5in)
Date: 1960	Muzzle Velocity: 320m/sec (1050ft/sec)
Calibre: 7.65mm (.301in)	Feed/Magazine: 10- or 20-round detachable
Operation: Blowback, closed bolt	box magazine
Weight: 1.28kg (2.8lb)	Range: 25m (82ft)
Overall Length: 517mm (20.3in)	

▲ **M84 submachine gun (Vz61 Skorpion)**

Serbian Forces, Sarajevo, April 1995

A license-built version of the Czech Vz61 Skorpion, the M84 was adopted by Yugoslavian forces as a personal defence weapon for vehicle crews.

grenade at UN troops or the people they were deployed to protect.

From 1992 onwards, the conflict spread to Bosnia-Herzegovina. Again, various factions were involved but overall the conflict pitted Serbs against Bosnian and Croat forces. The Serbs were in general well equipped, with support from both Serbia and Serbian sympathisers within the federal armed forces. The latter gradually fragmented, with most heavy equipment and stocks of ammunition ending up in Serb hands.

Early in the conflict, Serbian forces attempted to capture Sarajevo, capital of Bosnia. Although they were able to penetrate the city and took control of some key points, the numerous but poorly equipped defenders were able to prevent the city's fall. The

Specifications

Country of Origin: Yugoslavia	Overall Length: 875mm (34.4in)
Date: 1968	Barrell Length: 415mm (16.33in)
Calibre: 7.62mm (.3in)	Muzzle Velocity: 720m/sec (2362ft/sec)
Operation: Gas (rotating bolt)	Feed/Magazine: 30-round detachable box
Weight: 3.70kg (8.16lb)	magazine
	Range: 410m (1345ft)

▲ **Zastava M70**

Serbian Forces, Sarajevo, March 1993

Fitted with a telescopic sight, the M70 assault rifle was adequate as a sniping weapon in a medium-range urban context, when fired from tall buildings along the streets of Sarajevo.

Specifications

Country of Origin: Yugoslavia	Barrell Length: 542mm (21.33in)
Date: 1972	Muzzel Velocity: 745m/sec (2444ft/sec)
Calibre: 7.62mm (.3in)	Feed/Magazine: 30- or 40-round box magazines
Operation: Gas, rotating bolt	or 75-round drums
Weight: 5.5kg (12.12lb)	Range: 400m (1312ft)
Overall Length: 1025mm (40.35in)	

▲ **Zastava M72**

Slovenian Provisional Forces, Ljubljana, June 1991

A light support version of the M70 rifle, the M72 served with the Yugoslavian armed forces and was thus obtained by most successor forces.

▲ **Balkans battle**
Unidentified irregulars move warily through a street somewhere in the former Yugoslavia, armed with Zastava assault rifles.

ensuing battle for the city remains the longest siege of a capital city in modern times. Sarajevo was more or less entirely cut off by Serbian positions in the surrounding hills.

With no means of reply to shelling by Serb artillery, located in fortified firebases, the people of Sarajevo and the defenders were forced to live under constant fire, which was directed at civilian targets as well as military ones. Snipers in tall buildings deliberately attacked civilians as part of a campaign to wear down the defenders.

Despite their advantages in heavy weapons, Serb forces were still unable to take complete possession of the city, although they dominated some areas. Assaults intended to increase Serbian control resulted in street fighting, with blocks changing hands in bitter close-range firefights. The Bosnians managed to get hold of enough small arms to mount a defence

against these attacks, though they lacked the large-scale military capability required to break out or force a supply corridor through the siege lines.

UN aid

UN aid was brought into Sarajevo via the airport, a hazardous business that required the deployment of peacekeeping troops to protect the aid shipments and the airport itself. The UN involvement gradually expanded into air strikes on Serbian artillery and later logistics assets, with the combined effect of easing the pressure on the Bosnian forces to the point at which they could begin to take offensive action.

This conflict, which became known as the Bosnian War, was ended by a negotiated ceasefire in 1995. Increasing Bosnian success in the field, coupled with threats of additional UN airstrikes, contributed to a willingness to bring the war to a close. The siege of

Sarajevo was lifted by Serb withdrawal rather than a relief operation.

Much of the conflict in the former Yugoslavia was fought by paramilitaries and militias, many of whom regarded civilians as legitimate targets. Although heavy weapons and artillery were available and were used liberally, much of the fighting was expressed by small-arms engagements between personnel armed with much the same equipment on both sides.

The UN embargo on arms shipments to Yugoslavia affected the Serb forces less than other factions, as they had extensive access to the armouries of the Federal Army. Most other factions were forced to obtain whatever weaponry they could by smuggling, black market sales or scrounging from battlefields.

Most of this weaponry was Eastern European in origin, i.e. heavily influenced by Soviet equipment. Assault rifles were ubiquitous, but in urban combat around towns, villages and the suburbs of major cities, submachine guns proved to be an effective close-range weapon.

▶ PM-63

Kosovan Irregulars, Kosovo, March 1992

The PM-63 uses a slide that is integral with the breech-block, rather like an automatic pistol. Accurate automatic fire would not be possible with the PM-63, with so much reciprocating weight moving around.

Specifications

Country of Origin: Poland	Barrel Length: 152mm (6in)
Date: 1964	Muzzle Velocity: 320m/sec (1050ft/sec)
Calibre: 9mm (.35in) Makarov	Feed/Magazine: 15- or 25-round detachable box
Operation: Blowback	magazine
Weight: 1.6kg (3.53lb)	Range: 100–150m (328–492ft)
Overall Length: 583mm (23in)	

Specifications

Country of Origin: FR Yugoslavia	Overall Length: 540mm (21.25in)
Date: Not known	Barrell Length: 254mm (10.0in)
Calibre: 7.62mm (.3in)	Muzzel Velocity: 678 m/sec (2224 ft/sec)
Operation: Gas-operated, rotating bolt	Feed/Magazine: 30-round detachable box
Weight: 3.5kg (7.72lb)	magazine
	Range: 200m (656ft)

▲ Zastava M92

Croatian Armed Forces, post-Conflict

The M92 was developed from the M85, itself a copy of the Soviet AKSU-74. The weapon is chambered for 7.62x39mm, the M85 for 5.56x45mm.

Wars in the Caucasus
1994–PRESENT

The breakup of the Soviet Union exposed old tensions and created new ones, creating a volatile situation on Russia's southern flank.

WITH THE DISSOLUTION of the Soviet Union, most of its former territories entered into treaties with Russia defining their new relationship. Chechnya was a notable exception, and after some internal conflict a government emerged which was committed to full independence from Russia. Moscow made a military response, but this was rapidly withdrawn.

After many years of relying on the venerable AK series, Russian forces began to move towards a new generation of more sophisticated weapons influenced by concepts developed elsewhere. Many of these weapons were chambered for 'Western' calibres and are compatible with a variety of rail-mounted accessories, increasing their attractiveness to international buyers. Although these weapons proved themselves effective, the move away from AK-series rifles was slowed by the sheer numbers of Kalashnikov-based weapons available. Despite its longevity, the AK series remains effective, and serves to arm second-line units or else are sold on the open market, ensuring that they will be available for a long time to come.

Chechnya

Chechnya soon began to suffer economic problems in addition to repeated coup attempts and outright civil war. Economic difficulties were exacerbated by the exodus of thousands of non-ethnic Chechens,

▲ **Ammo belt**

An Azeri soldier adjusts a light machine-gun's ammo belt during the Nagorno-Karabakh border conflict, 1992.

▶ **PSM pistol**

Russian Peacekeeping Forces, South Ossetia, January 2008

The PSM fires a weak, small-calibre round but has the advantage of being very small and light, and thus easy to carry.

Specifications

Country of Origin: USSR	Barrel Length: 85mm (3.35in)
Date: 1973	Muzzle Velocity: 315m/sec (1033ft/sec)
Calibre: 5.45mm (.215in) Soviet Pistol	Feed/Magazine: 8-round detachable box
Operation: Blowback	magazine
Weight: .46kg (1.01lb)	Range: 40m (131ft)
Overall Length: 160mm (6.3in)	

many of whom had been experts and skilled workers in key industries. Russian forces became increasingly involved in Chechen infighting, first as covert support for the government's opponents and later more directly. In December 1994 the decision was taken to enter Chechnya and oust the pro-independence government.

The Russian offensive began with air strikes that demolished the Chechen air force, but this success was offset by political difficulties in a complex ethnic situation. Many officials within Russia, and large numbers of Russian Army officers, opposed the conflict. Some of the units detailed for the invasion were at low readiness and struggled even to move to the border. Although the Russian Army enjoyed air superiority and vastly better equipment, the conscript

forces it fielded were ill-trained and unenthusiastic, which permitted the Chechens to launch hit-and-run raids on demoralized troops. Nevertheless, the advance towards the Chechen capital of Grozny could not be halted and soon Russian forces encircled the city.

Initial attempts to push into the city were repulsed with heavy Russian losses, despite major artillery and air support and the use of armoured forces. Instead the Russians were forced to grind their way through the increasingly ruined city street by street, finally achieving what appeared as victory in March 1995.

The weapons used by both sides in this bitter street fighting were much the same Soviet-era assault rifles and other infantry weapons. The AK series of rifles were designed to be used by poorly trained conscripts

▶ PMM pistol

Kchevki Tank Group, Tskhinvali, August 2008

The PMM (or Makarov) was the standard issue sidearm to Soviet-era forces. The huge numbers manufactured ensured that it remained in use for many years afterwards.

Specifications

Country of Origin: USSR/Russia	Overall Length: 165mm (6.49in)
Date: 1952	Barrell Length: 93.5mm (3.68in)
Calibre: 9mm (.35in)	Muzzle Velocity: 430m/sec (1410ft/sec)
Operation: Double action	Feed/Magazine: 12-round box magazine
Weight: .76kg (1.67lb)	Range: 50m (164ft)

Specifications

Country of Origin: Russia	Barrel Length: 405mm (15.9in)
Date: 1994	Muzzle Velocity: 900m/sec (2953ft/sec)
Calibre: 5.45mm (.215in)	Feed/Magazine: 30- or 45-round AK-74-
Operation: Gas	compatible box magazine; 60-round casket
Weight: 3.85kg (8.49lb)	magazine
Overall Length: 943mm (37.1in)	Range: 400m (1312ft)

▲ AN-94 assault rifle

Russian Army / 19th Motorized Rifle Division, Tskhinvali, August 2008

Designed as the successor to the Soviet era AK-74, the AN-94 is a much more complex weapon capable of firing two-round bursts at an extremely high rate of fire, or fire at full automatic on a lower rate.

and militia, and indeed they were in this conflict. At close quarters in urban terrain, firepower and reliability counted for more than long-range accuracy, and here the AK assault rifle excelled.

Having taken Grozny, Russian forces were able to gain ground in the country, pushing the Chechens back into increasingly remote areas. The war became a guerrilla conflict, crossing the line into terrorism through hostage-taking and attacks on civilian targets. Despite some successful counter-attacks and sympathetic insurgency in Russia and elsewhere, Chechen forces were gradually defeated in the field. However, Grozny was twice retaken by the Chechens,

who took advantage of Russian weakness there as troops were massed for operations elsewhere.

A ceasefire was followed by a formal peace treaty in November 1996, but tensions still existed between Russia and its former territory. A general deterioration in the internal security situation in Chechnya led to open combat between the Chechen government forces and various militias. After numerous incidents involving Russian personnel, a second invasion was launched.

Russian intervention began with an air campaign in late 1999, followed by a ground invasion. The Russian advance was methodical and well supported

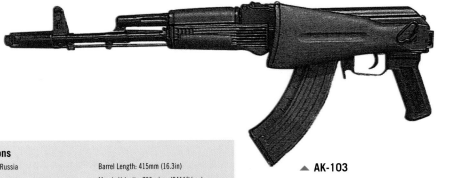

▲ AK-103

Russian Border Forces, South Ossetia, January 2008

The AK-103 is essentially a modernized and re-calibered AK-74M. It is primarily used by law enforcement and border guard units, and has achieved some export success.

Specifications

Country of Origin: Russia

Date: 1994

Calibre: 7.62mm (.3in)

Operation: Gas

Weight: 3.4kg (7.49lb)

Overall Length: 943mm (37.1in)

Barrel Length: 415mm (16.3in)

Muzzle Velocity: 735m/sec (2411ft/sec)

Feed/Magazine: 30-round detachable box
magazine

Range: 300m (984ft) +

▲ AK-107

Russian Army / 20th Motorized Rifle Division, Abkhazia, August 2008

The AK-107 was developed as a cheaper alternative to the AN-94. It is capable of full- or semi automatic fire as well as three-round bursts.

Specifications

Country of Origin: Russia

Date: 1990s

Calibre: 5.45mm (.21in)

Operation: Gas

Weight: 3.8kg (8.38lb)

Overall Length: 943mm (37.1in)

Barrell Length: 415mm (16.3in)

Muzzel Velocity: 900m/sec (2,953 ft/sec)

Feed/Magazine: 30-round detachable box
magazine

Range: 500m (1640ft)

by both artillery and strike aircraft, reaching Grozny by mid October. Other forces drove on major cities in Chechnya, meeting resistance mainly from bands of militia fighters equipped with small arms only. Direct Russian rule over Chechnya was established in May 2000, with a gradual move towards autonomy.

South Ossetia

Elsewhere, the breakup of the Soviet Union created other problems. Conflict in South Ossetia during 1991–92 and Abkhazia in 1992–93 left parts of these regions in separatist hands, and other areas controlled by pro-Russian factions.

During August 2008, Georgia attempted to regain control of South Ossetia, launching an offensive into the region that initially met with success. Georgian forces attacked Tskhinvali, clashing with local forces and also Russian peacekeepers stationed there. The Georgians reached the city centre, but could not hold it in the face of determined resistance

Russia responded to the incursion by sending its own forces into South Ossetia and launching airstrikes against the Georgian advance. Georgian and Russian armoured forces clashed at times, though Russian air power prevented Georgian tanks from having much effect on the conflict. Much of the

▲ AK-200

Under development

The AK-200 is the latest Russian assault rifle, developed from the AK-74. It reflects modern preferences for accessory rails and advanced materials, allowing the attachment of modular equipment, including advanced optical sight combinations, laser illuminators, flashlights, vertical foregrips, bipods and grenade launchers.

Specifications

Country of Origin: Russia
Date: 2010
Calibre: 5.56mm (0.21in)
Operation: Gas, rotating bolt
Weight: 3.8 kg (8.38 lb)
Overall Length: 943mm (37.1in)

Barrell Length: 415mm (16.3in)
Muzzle Velocity: 900m/sec (2953ft/sec)
Feed/Magazine: 30-round detachable box
  magazine
Range: 500m (1640ft)

Specifications

Country of Origin: Russia
Date: Early 1990s
Calibre: 7.62mm (.3in)
Operation: Gas, rotating bolt
Weight: 4.68kg (10.3lb)
Overall Length: 1225mm (48.2in)

Barrell Length: 560mm (22.2in)
Muzzel Velocity: 830m/sec (2,723ft/sec)
Feed/Magazine: 10-round detachable box
  magazine
Range: 800m (2624ft)

▲ SVD-S Dragunov sniper rifle

76th Pskov Air Assault Division, Abkhazia, August 2008

The SVD-S is a modified version of the proven SVD sniper rifle. It is intended for airborne troops and has a folding stock.

ground fighting was urban combat between Georgian infantry and local irregulars. Ossetian forces inflicted casualties on Georgian vehicles in close-range ambushes with RPG-7 anti-tank weapons.

Russian operations were hampered by the need to funnel reinforcements through a narrow route, but gradually the balance of forces came to favour Russia. Despite counter-attacks, the Russians were able to

drive Georgian forces out of Tskhinvali and, ultimately, from South Ossetia. Russian forces then pushed into Georgia, advancing on the city of Gori. After heavy fighting the Georgians retreated and the city was taken.

The conflict came to an end with a ceasefire that was followed by a Russian withdrawal from the occupied territories.

Specifications

Country of Origin: Russia
Date: 1999
Calibre: 7.62mm (.3in)
Operation: Gas
Weight: 8.7kg (19.18lb)
Overall Length: 1155mm (45.47in)

Barrell Length: 640mm (25.19in)
Muzzle Velocity: 825m/sec (2706ft/sec)
Feed/Magazine: 100- and 200-round belt fed
magazine
Range: 1500m (4921ft)

▲ **'Pecheneg' Kalashnikov infantry machine gun**
Russian Army / 19th Motorized Rifle Division, Tskhinvali, August 2008
The Pecheneg is a development of the PKM machine gun, chambered for 7.62x54mm. It does not have a quick-change barrel and is aimed at the squad support weapon niche rather than the general-purpose machine gun role.

Iraqi Army and insurgent weapons
2003–PRESENT

The 1991 Gulf War was limited by its UN remit to removing Iraqi forces from Kuwait. The 2003 invasion was a wholly different prospect, launched with the goal of regime change in Iraq.

AT THE END OF THE 1991 GULF WAR there was a significant 'on to Baghdad' sentiment among the Coalition forces that had driven the Iraqi Army from Kuwait. Many people forecast that there would be another Gulf War in the near future, suggesting that the dictator Saddam Hussein could be toppled while he was weak, or else a far more costly war would be required in the future.

Despite internal uprisings, the Saddam regime managed to survive its catastrophic defeat in 1991, and brutally put down all attempts at resistance. By

2003 the Iraqi forces had rebuilt their strength and were, at least on paper, formidable. However, the equipment fielded by this impressively large army was outdated. Armed with Soviet-era weaponry for the most part, the Iraqi Army was a generation or more behind the international forces it faced in 2003.

Internally, too, the Iraqi military was weak. The regular army was composed largely of ill-trained conscripts, many of whom were opposed to the regime. Few were active supporters. The officer class was more loyal, but the Iraqi Army as a whole was neither skilled nor motivated. Indeed, concerns about its loyalty were among the reasons for the original formation of the Republican Guard.

The Republican Guard was a political force as much as a military one, intended to counterbalance the army's power. Loyal to the Saddam regime, it received the best equipment and had far higher morale than the purely military formations. Small arms and light support weapons used by both formations were the same, being Soviet-era weaponry well suited to use in harsh desert conditions by conscript troops.

Under the codename Operation *Iraqi Freedom*, the United States and the United Kingdom led the invasion of Iraq in March 2003. British forces aimed for Iraq's second city of Basra, while the US military drove on Baghdad itself. Led by armoured forces, the advance on Baghdad was rapid. However, attacks against the logistics 'tail' that followed the 'teeth' formations demonstrated that a significant will to resist existed.

Many Iraqi Army formations disintegrated under air strikes or armoured assault, or surrendered at the first opportunity. Yet there were increasing numbers of irregulars in civilian clothes, some of whom were army personnel in disguise. These insurgents attacked whatever targets they could, then attempted to disappear into the civilian population. Coalition forces were hampered by a desire to avoid civilian casualties, which required great restraint even under

fire. The policy paid off to a great extent; most ordinary Iraqis hated the brutal Saddam regime and simply stayed out of the way of the fighting. Despite exhortations to rise up and defend the homeland, Saddam's people mostly stood aside as the Coalition demolished what army units tried to stand and fight.

Despite determined resistance here and there, the Iraqi Army could not hope to prevent the fall of Basra and Baghdad, and soon afterwards the rest of the country was in Coalition hands. This victory marked the end of the conflict against the Saddam Hussein regime, but a difficult period lay ahead. Coalition forces found themselves drawn into conflict with all manner of opponents.

Some of these enemies were die-hard supporters of Saddam Hussein and his Ba'ath party. Others were anti-Western Jihadists from Iraq and other countries, who had come to join the conflict as a means to strike at their ideological enemies. Militias loyal to various political and religious figures also clashed in the power vacuum created by the collapse of the dictatorship. Not all of these groups were exclusively opposed to the Coalition. Some fought one another, or took on all-comers for control of a key city or region. In the midst of this chaotic and dangerous situation the Coalition forces attempted to restore order, to hand control to local authorities, and to avoid inflaming the situation by over-reaction.

Once the formal ground campaign was over, and success had apparently been achieved, the Coalition

Specifications

Country of Origin: USSR	Barrel Length: 400mm (15.8in)
Date: 1974	Muzzle Velocity: 900m/sec (2952ft/sec)
Calibre: 5.45mm (.215in) M74	Feed/Magazine: 30-round detachable box
Operation: Gas	magazine
Weight: 3.6kg (7.94lb)	Range: 300m (984ft)
Overall Length: 943mm (37.1in)	

▲ **AK-74**

Fedayeen Saddam, Baghdad, April 2003

The AK-74 is primarily distinguishable from its predecessor AKM/AK-47 by the long groove in the stock and the indentation above the magazine well, as well as its smaller-calibre round.

forces went over to a 'peacekeeping' role, though their enemies did not. Advanced weaponry and heavily armoured tanks were only so much use when trying to maintain law and order in a densely populated city, and foot patrols put Coalition soldiers in a position where any insurgent with a weapon had a chance to cause casualties.

Thus the war to depose Saddam Hussein was largely fought by aircraft, missiles and armoured vehicles, but the fight to control Iraq fell upon the infantry. Highly skilled and well equipped Coalition soldiers had the advantage, man for man, in a firefight, but the insurgents were on home ground and could hide among innocents. With no shortage of weaponry available after the disbandment of the Iraqi Army, the insurgency after the fall of Iraq proved more of a threat than the organized resistance of the Iraqi Army.

▲ PKM

Iraqi Army / Republican Guard / Baghdad Division, Kut, April 2003

A contemporary of the US M60, the PKM machinegun is a robust and effective weapon which has achieved good export sales.

Specifications

Country of Origin: USSR	Barrel Length: 658mm (25.9in)
Date: 1969	Muzzle Velocity: 800m/sec (2600ft/sec)
Calibre: 7.62mm (.3in) M1943	Feed/Magazine: Belt-fed (belts contained in
Operation: Gas, air-cooled	boxes)
Weight: 9kg (19.84lb)	Cyclic Rate: 710rpm
Overall Length: 1160mm (45.67in)	Range: 2000m (6560ft) +

▲ RPG-7

Iraqi Insurgents, Fallujah, December 2004

Although the RPG-7 is limited in its effectiveness against main battle tanks, it posed a significant threat to lighter vehicles and to buildings used as Coalition bases.

Specifications

Country of Origin: USSR	Overall Length: 950mm (37.4in)
Date: 1961	Muzzle Velocity: 115m/sec (377ft/sec)
Calibre: 40mm (1.57in)	Feed/Magazine: Single-shot, muzzle-loaded
Operation: Rocket motor	Range: c.920m (3018ft)
Weight: 7kg (15lb)	

Iraq and Afghanistan: Sniper weapons and tactics
2000–PRESENT

Marksmanship is of course a key skill for the sniper, but there is more to sniping than hitting the target.

WHILE MOST INFANTRY TACTICS revolve around volume of fire, suppressing an enemy force as other elements move into a better position, sniping is entirely the opposite. A sniper may only fire one shot in an entire engagement. Yet man for man snipers are among the most influential of combat assets.

A sniper must obviously be a good shot, and must be able to hit targets reliably at extreme ranges. This skill necessitates an ability to predict the target's movements, account for wind and bullet drop, estimate the effects of humidity and temperature, and a host of other factors. Just as important, a sniper must be able to get into a good position and remain there undetected. He also needs to be able to escape from an enemy search party if necessary.

Observation and stealth skills are of paramount importance to the sniper, as well as an understanding of human behaviour. It is often possible to predict where an enemy will stop by observing local conditions, allowing a shot to be set up in advance.

Furthermore, when hunting enemy snipers or gunmen, by looking for good places to shoot from, the sniper may be able to figure out where a hostile might hide himself.

A sniper might only take one shot at a target, so that shot must count. He might ignore an ordinary enemy soldier or gunman in the hope that a higher-value target may present himself. By refraining from shooting the first target that appears he gives himself the chance to make a greater difference to the course of the campaign.

High-value target

Eliminating an officer or effective leader can have serious effects on enemy combat capabilities. Communications personnel and specialists are also high-value targets. Snipers are trained to choose a target that will have a significant effect rather than simply hoping to inflict a casualty, though morale can be seriously impaired by general sniper attacks.

▲ **Dragunov SVD**

Taliban Guerrillas, Helmand Province, April 2008

A number of Dragunov rifles were captured by Afghan fighters during the Russian occupation, and have since been used against Western forces.

Specifications

Country of Origin: USSR	Barrel Length: 610mm (24in)
Date: 1963	Muzzle Velocity: 828m/sec (2720ft/sec)
Calibre: 7.62mm (.3in) Soviet	Feed/Magazine: 10-round detachable box
Operation: Gas	magazine
Weight: 4.31kg (9.5lb)	Range: 1000m (3280ft)
Overall Length: 1225mm (48.2in)	

Snipers are also reconnaissance assets, reporting on what they observe or calling in artillery and air support on valuable targets. Here, too, their keen observation skills allow them to gather information or direct fire better than the typical infantry soldier. An enemy unit that does not know it is being observed may be surprised by an air strike or bombardment, suffering more serious casualties.

Teamwork

Snipers rarely work alone. The usual practice is to create two- or three-man teams, often with an experienced sniper educating a less-experienced one in the process. A sniper can only observe in one direction at a time, so having a companion to provide security is useful. A spotter can also report the results of a shot, which may occur out of the sniper's field of

▲ M14 Enhanced Battle Rifle (EBR)

US Army / 10th Mountain Division, Afghanistan, May 2010

Developed directly from the M14 sniper rifle, progenitor of the M21 sniper rifle, the M14 EBR is issued to US Army designated marksmen and US special forces.

Specifications

Country of Origin: United States

Date: 2001

Calibre: 7.62mm (.3in) NATO

Operation: Gas, rotating bolt

Weight: 5.1kg (11.24lb)

Overall Length: 889mm (35in)

Barrell Length: 457mm (18in)

Muzzle Velocity: 975.4m/sec(3200ft/sec)

Feed/Magazine: 10- or 20-round detachable box
    magazine

Range: 800m (2624ft) +

▲ M39 Marksman rifle

US Marine Corps / 2nd Marine Expeditionary Brigade, An Nasiriyah, Iraq, March 2003

Also derived from the M14, the M39 was produced to meet the needs of US Marine Corps marksmen and explosive ordnance disposal teams working in urban areas.

Specifications

Country of Origin: United States

Date: 2008

Calibre: 7.62mm (.3in) NATO

Operation: Gas, rotating bolt

Weight: 7.5kg (16.5lb)

Overall Length: 1120mm (44.2in)

Barrel Length: 560mm (22in)

Muzzle Velocity: 865m/sec (2837ft/sec)

Feed/Magazine: 20-round detachable box
    magazine

Range: 780m (2559ft)

vision, and can direct the sniper onto new targets as they appear.

Snipers in Iraq and Afghanistan have typically made use of fairly large-calibre rifles (7.62mm/.300 being common), which have excellent ballistic properties over long range but are relatively easy to carry. Very large calibre 'anti-materiel rifles' are primarily intended for use against hard targets such as communications equipment and vehicles, but can also be used for extremely long-range sniping. They are very bulky, however, and difficult to transport for a sniper team operating on foot in the mountains of Afghanistan.

Snipers are sometimes deployed in support of an infantry operation, targeting enemy assets such as machine-gun crews and officers with precision fire to facilitate an infantry advance. They are also used as defensive assets. For example, it is not uncommon for a convoy to drop off a sniper team en route to carry out its mission. The sniper team can then observe a road and prevent hostiles from planting explosives or setting up an ambush. The team is then picked up as the convoy returns, or by other assets.

In urban combat such as that encountered in Iraq, snipers are invaluable. Their precision helps reduce the chances of collateral casualties whilst enabling

▲ **M110 Semi-Automatic Sniper System**

US Army /121st Infantry Regiment, Khowst, Afghanistan, September 2009

The M110 was developed to meet US Army requirements, and is being adopted by the Marine Corps to replace the M39.

Specifications

Country of Origin: United States	Barrel Length: 508mm (20in)
Date: 2008	Muzzle Velocity: 783m/sec (2570ft/sec)
Calibre: 7.62mm (.3in) NATO	Feed/Magazine: 10- or 20-round detachable box
Operation: Gas, rotating bolt	magazine
Weight: 6.94kg (15.3lb)	Range: 800m (2625ft)
Overall Length: 1029mm (40.5in)	

Specifications

Country of Origin: United States	Barrel Length: 736mm (29in)
Date: 2000	Muzzle Velocity: 823m/sec (2700ft/sec)
Calibre: 12.7mm (.5in)	Feed/Magazine: 5-round detachable box
Operation: Manually-operated rotary bolt action	magazine
Weight: 11.8kg (26lb)	Range: 1600m (5249ft)
Overall Length: 1448mm (57in)	

▲ **McMillan TAC-50**

Canadian Army / Princess Patricia's Canadian Light Infantry, Shah-I-Kot Valley, March 2002

Firing extremely powerful ammunition adapted from a heavy machine gun round, the TAC-50 was used to make what was then the world's longest confirmed kill in March 2002. Master Corporal Arron Perry killed an enemy combatant from 2310m (7579ft) and Corporal Rob Furlong killed an enemy combatant at a distance of 2430m (7972ft) in the same month.

friendly forces to eliminate hostiles located in an inaccessible area, such as on a rooftop. By the time infantry got to the enemy location through the streets, the hostiles would be long gone. A sniper's bullet can get there a lot quicker, and will not be ambushed en route.

In more open terrain such as the desert, or when shooting from one area of high ground to another in Afghanistan's mountains, snipers can pick off hostiles which might be difficult targets for personnel armed with small-calibre assault rifles. Guerrillas concealed among the rocks above a road in Afghanistan are a hard target for troops armed with assault rifles, but a sniper or designated marksman may be able to deal with them. A designated marksman is not a sniper as such, but uses a similar weapon with a high degree of skill. He is part of an infantry force, and takes difficult or long-range shots when necessary.

Specifications

Country of Origin: United States	Barrel Length: 736mm (29in)
Date: 1987	Muzzle Velocity: 853m/sec (2800ft/sec)
Calibre: 12.7mm (.5in)	Feed/Magazine: 5-round detachable box
Operation: Bolt action	magazine
Weight: 9.53kg (21lb)	Range: 1000m (3280ft) +
Overall Length: 1346mm (53in)	

▲ **Harris M87R**

US Navy Seals, Afghanistan, March 2011

The M87R is used for some US special forces missions. It is too bulky for rapid assault movements, but has a variety of applications as a support weapon.

Specifications

Country of Origin: United Kingdom	Barrel Length: 692mm (27.2in)
Date: 2006	Muzzle Velocity: Not known
Calibre: 12.7mm (.5in)	Feed/Magazine: 5- or 10-round detachable box
Operation: Gas	magazine
Weight: 12.2kg (27lb)	Range: 1500m (4921ft)
Overall Length: 1369mm (53.9in)	

▲ **Accuracy International AS50**

British Army Special Forces, Afghanistan

The AS50 is the largest-calibre rifle produced by Accuracy International. It can deliver explosive or incendiary rounds over extreme distances. The rifle is highly transportable and lightweight. It can be disassembled in under three minutes and serviced without tools.

Iraq and Afghanistan:
Occupation and counter-insurgency
2001–PRESENT

Despite the vast technological resources available, modern conflicts are often won or lost at the squad level. 'Boots on the ground' have never been more important.

THE OVERTHROW OF SADDAM HUSSEIN'S REGIME in Iraq was not by any means an easy task, but at least there were obvious targets to aim for. The Coalition forces were opposed initially by formal units that could be located and attacked by conventional means; air power, tanks and artillery were highly effective in destroying the Republican Guard and the Iraqi Army.

Even during the Coalition advance towards Baghdad, irregular forces harassed logistics convoys and units attempting to secure ground that had been taken. Although the major formations of the Iraqi military were in disarray, a challenge was still mounted by various insurgency groups.

Some of these irregulars were army personnel cut off from their units and still determined to carry out their orders to defend the nation, but the majority did not belong to the army, at least, not any more.

Army personnel who wanted to continue the fight joined groups of insurgents who lacked heavy weapons, but retained the will to fight. Others came from political or religious groups, some from outside Iraq. Coordination among the insurgents was rare, but their activities were still a distraction and a nuisance for Coalition forces trying to demolish Saddam's regime. These fighters inflicted the occasional real setback, but for the most part were unable to greatly affect the outcome of the campaign at the military level.

Fighting insurgency

After the fall of Baghdad and the end of the war as such, the insurgency did not end. Indeed, it became more complex as groups fought for control of regions and cities. At times some groups entered into ceasefires or cooperation agreements with the

▲ **FN SCAR**

US Navy SEALs, Afghanistan, April 2009

The SCAR was developed to meet the requirements of US special forces personnel. The SCAR-L is chambered for 5.56mm (.219in) ammunition; the SCAR-H uses 7.62mm (.3in) rounds. It is a lightweight and portable support weapon with a sniper capability.

Specifications

Country of Origin: United States	Overall Length: Various, depending on variant
Date: 2009	Barrel Length: 400mm (16in) SCAR-H; 351mm
Calibre: 7.62mm (.3in) SCAR-H,	(13.8in) SCAR-L
5.56mm (.219in) SCAR-L	Muzzle Velocity: 870m/sec (2870ft/sec)
Operation: Gas, rotating bolt	Feed/Magazine: 20-round box magazine
Weight: 3.58kg (7.9lb) SCAR-H;	(SCAR-H) or STANAG box magazine (SCAR-L)
3.29kg (7.3lb) SCAR-L	Range: 600m (1968ft)

Coalition, while others in the same area began a new campaign of violence. The political situation changed constantly, making it hard to keep track of which groups were at any time friendly, neutral, suspect or outright hostile.

Dealing with the insurgency in Iraq was a frustrating business. 'Friendly' locals might turn hostile for no immediately obvious reason, and often local groups would change allegiance. For example, control of the city of Fallujah was handed over to a locally raised and led security force, which soon afterward disbanded and gave its weapons to anti-

Coalition insurgents. US troops were thus forced to fight for the city all over again, an occurrence made even more bitter by the betrayal of trust that brought it about.

Against this backdrop of sudden political shifts, ambushes and attacks with mortars and RPGs against their bases, the Coalition forces struggled to win over the Iraqi people and accomplish their goals. Much of their work was of reconstruction; getting the power back on and clean water flowing to homes in the cities, bringing humanitarian aid and medical assistance to those worst affected by the war.

▲ M16A4 assault rifle

US Marine Corps / 2nd Marine Division, Al Anbar, Iraq, April 2006

The M16A4, used by the US Marine Corps, is capable of taking a range of accessories, including foregrips, scopes and laser sights.

Specifications

Country of Origin: United States	Barrell Length: 508mm (20in)
Date: 1957	Muzzle Velocity: 948m/sec (3110ft/sec)
Calibre: 5.56mm (0.219in) NATO	Feed/Magazine: 30-round detachable
Operation: Gas, rotating bolt	box magazine
Weight: 3.58kg (7.9lb)	Range: 800m (2624ft)
Overall Length: 1003mm (39.5in)	

Specifications

Country of Origin: United States	Overall Length (M203 grenader launcher):
Date: 1969	380mm (15in)
Calibre: 40mm (1.57in)	Barrel Length: 305mm (12in)
Operation: Breech-loaded	Muzzle Velocity: 75m/sec (245ft/sec)
Weight: 1.63kg (3.5lb) loaded	Feed/Magazine: Single shot
	Range: 400m (1312ft)

▲ M16 with M203 grenade launcher

US Army / 4th Infantry Division, Laghman Province, Afghanistan, March 2011

The M203 grenade launcher can deliver a range of ordnance at greater distances than a solider can throw a hand grenade. It is to be replaced in service with the M320 grenade launcher.

▶ **Loophole**

A US soldier aims his M4 carbine through a loop hole in a wall during a firefight with insurgents in Iraq, 2005. Compact and hardy, the M4 has proved an excellent weapon in urban warfare.

Interfering in these tasks was one way the insurgents hoped to discredit the Coalition, so simply pulling out of a dangerous area was not always a solution.

It was here that the key work of the Coalition was done. Fighting the insurgents was a necessary task, as was defending personnel and installations, but any insurgent killed or detained might be replaced by another. By returning the cities of Iraq to something as close to normal as possible, Coalition forces took away many of the factors that fed insurgent recruitment. Operating in the community, and a potentially hostile one at that, required patience and restraint, coupled with watchfulness and a streetwise cunning that allowed Coalition troops to predict insurgent activity. For example, the sudden disappearance of local children from the street would often indicate that an ambush was in preparation.

Different approaches were tried, depending upon the circumstances. Where possible, Coalition forces cooperated with local leaders and tried to allow the local police or friendly militias to keep order. This would make their presence seem less intrusive and helped support the gradual handover of control to Iraqi authorities.

However, when attacked, or when control of an area was lost, Coalition forces had to respond with precise but overwhelming force.

Specifications

Country of Origin: United States	Barrel Length: 368mm (14.5in)
Date: 1997	Muzzle Velocity: 884m/sec (2900ft/sec)
Calibre: 5.56mm (.219in) NATO	Feed/Magazine: 30-round detachable box
Operation: Gas	magazine or other STANAG magazines
Weight: 2.88kg (6.36lb)	Range: 400m (1312ft)
Overall Length: 838mm (33in)	

▲ **Colt M4 carbine**

US Army / 82nd Airborne Division, Fallujah, January 2004

The M4 carbine is fitted with picatinny rails under the barrel and atop the receiver, enabling the use of various accessories. Swapping accessories is a simple matter.

Despite bold attempts to make a quantum leap in small arms technology in recent years, US forces were armed for the most part with a developed version of the venerable M16 family. However, this M16A4 and M4 carbine are significantly improved over their predecessors. Capable of taking a range of accessories using standardised rail systems, the M4 in particular has shown itself to be a versatile and effective combat weapon. Light and easily manoeuvred for urban combat, its telescopic stock can be quickly tailored to a specific user and accessories can be swapped for different missions.

On the other hand, events in Afghanistan and Iraq showed that some weapons were due for upgrade or replacement. Many of the M249 SAWs in use are now over 20 years old and are becoming worn out. These weapons remain effective, but the specific examples in use are showing their age.

Armoured vehicles proved useful in supporting raids, securing static checkpoints and dealing with insurgents in strong defensive positions, but the burden fell mainly upon infantry, who operated on foot or from lightly protected vehicles. At times, almost any movement within some cities was prone to attacks by snipers and RPG-armed gunmen. This made even routine movements such as resupply or

US INFANTRY SQUAD, 2006		
Unit	Equipment	Men
Squad leader	1 x M4 carbine	1
Medic	1 x M4 carbine	1
Fireteam 1	1 x M249 LMG (SAW) 2 x M16 or M4 rifles 1 x M16/M203 grenade launcher	4
Fireteam 2	1 x M249 LMG (SAW) 2 x M16 or M4 rifles 1 x M16/M203 grenade launcher	4

personnel transfers problematic in the extreme. The British found the 'multiple' to be a useful combat force. Essentially a half platoon, the multiple provided enough sets of eyes and sufficient firepower to be effective in close urban terrain without becoming unwieldy or requiring manpower that was often simply not available. At times, quite sizeable forces were committed to an operation, but counter-insurgency work is a manpower-intensive activity and often small units had to cover a wide area for lack of enough men to do the job properly.

Both the British and US forces faced grim battles for cities such as Fallujah and Basra, dealing with uprisings and insurgent attacks whilst remaining

US Infantry Squad, 2006

A US Army infantry squad consists of 9–13 soldiers led by a staff sergeant. Each squad is composed of at least two fire teams. Each fire team consists of four men, led by a corporal. A fire team is made up of two riflemen (one being the team leader), a grenadier and an automatic rifleman, armed with an M249 LMG. Sometimes a squad can be enhanced with advanced marksmen depending on the mission requirements.

Leader (1 x M4 carbine)   **Medic (1 x M4 carbine)**

Fireteam 1 (1 x M249 SAW, 2 x M4 carbine, 1 x M16/M203 grenade launcher)

Fireteam 2 (1 x M249 SAW, 2 x M4 carbine, 1 x M16/M203 grenade launcher)

mindful of the surrounding population. Most combat in this environment was at close quarters and multiple levels, with gunmen on rooftops and upstairs windows as well as at street level. The RPG-7 was used liberally against buildings and personnel as well as vehicles.

While a tank or infantry combat vehicle would likely survive even multiple hits, the Land Rovers and Humvees used by infantry formations were very vulnerable. The best response to an RPG ambush was rapid and accurate return fire, hopefully eliminating the operator or forcing him to take cover before firing, or at least to take a hurried shot rather than aiming carefully. More open roads had their own hazards, ranging from ambushes to roadside bombs. The logistical apparatus required to keep the Coalition forces in fighting condition, plus that required for reconstruction, was an inviting target for the insurgents. Detecting and removing Improvised

Explosive Devices (IEDs) was a vital task for Coalition forces, who used a range of methods and technologies, including specialized bomb disposal equipment, alongside more traditional bomb-defusing skills. Powerful rifles were used by some Explosive Ordnance Disposal (EOD) personnel to destroy IEDs from a safe distance.

IEDs were also a major threat in Afghanistan, though some characteristics of the campaign were quite different. The invasion of Afghanistan came about as a result of the same world events as the Iraq campaign, notably the 11 September 2001 terrorist attacks on the USA, and here, too, there was an initial military campaign aimed at regime change followed by a lengthy insurgency.

Afghanistan

In 2001, at the time of the invasion, Afghanistan was under the control of the fundamentalist Islamic

▲ **Squad assault**

A US Marine squad manoeuvres during the fighting for the town of Fallujah, 2004. While one machinegun team gives covering fire with their M240 LMG, another machine-gun team dashes across open ground to etsablish a new position.

Taliban, which openly sponsored terrorism against the West. After years of Soviet occupation and internal turmoil, Afghanistan was not in a position to offer significant opposition to the initial campaign, which deposed the Taliban and established an interim government, followed by democratic elections.

The new government of Afghanistan was supported by an international coalition, which protected the capital, Kabul, and the immediate area. However, much of the country remained beyond effective government control. Various factions, many

of them tribal in nature, controlled parts of Afghanistan's provinces. Among these factions were guerrillas loyal to the ousted Taliban, or at least its fundamentalist ideals.

The invasion of Afghanistan was followed by an attempt to locate and apprehend the leaders of the al-Qaeda terrorist organization, notably Osama bin Laden. While this was eventually accomplished, it was a slow process. So, too, was the loosening of the insurgents' grip on the provinces. As in Iraq, the support of the population for the new government

Specifications

Country of Origin: United States	Barrel Length: 560mm (22.04in)
Date: 1994	Muzzle Velocity: 860m/sec (2821ft/sec)
Calibre: 7.62mm (.3in) NATO	Feed/Magazine: Belt-fed
Operation: Gas, air-cooled	Cyclic Rate: 550rpm
Weight: 8.61kg (18.98lb)	Range: 1100m (3609ft) +
Overall Length: 1067mm (42in)	

▲ **M60E3 GPMG**

US Navy SEALs, Afghanistan, March 2011

The E3 version of the M60 was adopted by the US Marine Corps. It is still used by some special operations units, but has generally been replaced by the M240.

Specifications

Country of Origin: Belgium/United States	Barrel Length: 630mm (24.8in)
Date: 1977	Muzzle Velocity: 853m/sec (2800ft/sec)
Calibre: 7.62mm (.3in) NATO	Feed/Magazine: Belt-fed
Operation: Gas, open bolt	Cyclic Rate: 650–1000rpm
Weight: 11.79kg (26lb)	Range: 800m (2625ft)
Overall Length: 1263mm (49.7in)	

▲ **M240 general-purpose machine gun**

US Marine Corps / 2nd Marine Division, Al Anbar, Iraq, April 2006

The M240 was originally adopted by the US military as a vehicular weapon, but eventually supplanted the M60 in the general-purpose machinegun role.

largely depended upon proving that the government could defeat the guerrillas and protect its people.

Infiltration and guerrilla tactics

While the Taliban were generally pushed out of the major cities, they were able to infiltrate back in to carry out attacks. They were also able to take control of many provincial towns and villages, supporting their activities with funds and supplies extorted from those who would not give them willingly. Breaking the hold of the Taliban on any given town was not an immense problem, but keeping them out was a different matter.

The Afghan people have been fighting guerrilla wars against various invaders for most of their history, sometimes with the very same weapons their ancestors used. Taliban fighters were encountered armed with weapons taken from the Russian or earlier invasions, such as Lee-Enfield rifles and even weapons from before the twentieth century. They have in some cases used the same ambush points above the few passes though Afghanistan's mountains that their predecessors did.

Dealing with such skilled guerrilla fighters was a matter of breaking their power in any given region and helping the local population gain the strength and confidence to prevent the Taliban from coming back. More importantly, the locals had to be convinced that it was in their interests to do so. This

meant a 'boots on the ground' presence, patrols, and the creation of local security and police forces. The security/police units were at times infiltrated by Taliban fighters who thus gained training and knowledge of their enemies' methods before gong 'over the wall' to return to their comrades. Some went so far as to attack their supposed allies before fleeing.

Despite such frustrations, the task of nation-building lies at the heart of defeating any insurgency. The enemy's ability to fight must also be weakened, which meant taking the war to the insurgents. Thus alongside operations to win over and strengthen the local population, the Coalition launched attacks on Taliban strongholds in remote areas. Many of these strongholds lay in steep mountain valleys, which reduced the opportunities for using artillery and armour, except with the new generation of precision munitions available.

GPS- and laser-guided shells and bombs permitted strikes in areas previously immune to such attacks, and huge penetrator bombs threatened apparently impregnable cave and tunnel strongholds. However, success required that the Taliban be confronted in the countryside and the mountains, and defeated on the ground.

Over the years there has been a steady move towards smaller-calibre weapons. 7.62x51mm battle rifles gave way to 5.56x45mm assault rifles. For the most part, experience has shown this to be the right

▲ **M249 Squad Automatic Weapon (SAW)**

US Army / 82nd Airborne Division, Fallujah, January 2004

The M249 is a squad-level support weapon, and is often used in assault tactics.
It can take rifle magazines in addition to the more usual linked belt.

Specifications

Country of Origin: United States	Barrel Length: 521mm (21in)
Date: 1982	Muzzle Velocity: 915m/sec (3000ft/sec)
Calibre: 5.56mm (.219in) NATO	Feed/Magazine: 30-round STANAG magazine or
Operation: Gas, open bolt	200-round belt
Weight: 7.5kg (17lb)	Cyclic Rate: 750–1000rpm
Overall Length: 1041mm (41in)	Range: 910m (2985ft)

▶ **Overwatch mission**

Armed with an Accuracy International L96 sniper rifle, a British Royal Marine sniper team return enemy fire in Lakari Bazaar, Afghanistan, July 2009. The rifle stock and barrel has been covered with tape to stop light reflections giving away their position.

choice. A smaller-calibre weapon can be just as lethal at most likely combat ranges as a heavier calibre, and is accurate to a distance far beyond that at which the average soldier can hit anything.

Most modern combat takes place at fairly short ranges, where firepower is more important than accuracy. Thus most assault rifles are effective out to 300–400m (984–1312ft), which is more than enough in most cases. But when ambushed by Taliban riflemen hidden among rocks several hundred metres away and above the road, troops equipped with weapons such as the M4 or M16 may find that their weapons lack the accurate range. Marksmanship training at such ranges may also be lacking.

Thus the 'designated marksman rifle' proved itself invaluable in Afghanistan. A larger calibre weapon

with a greater accurate range, in the hands of a solider trained almost to sniper standards, permits precision return fire against an ambush while other soldiers use automatic suppressive fire. Larger-calibre weapons are also useful when firing across a valley at hostiles on the far side.

However, the majority of troops deployed to Afghanistan were still equipped with 5.56mm (.219in) assault rifles, and these performed satisfactorily in most engagements. The firepower

▲ **Diemaco C8**

Canadian Army / Princess Patricia's Canadian Light Infantry, Paktia Province, Afghanistan, March 2002

The C8 is a Canadian-made version of the M4 carbine. The Canadian equivalent to the M16 is designated C7.

Specifications

Country of Origin: Canada	Barrel Length: 508mm (20in)
Date: 1994	Muzzle Velocity: 900m/sec (3030ft/sec)
Calibre: 5.56mm (.219in) NATO	Feed/Magazine: Various 30-round STANAG
Operation: Gas, rotating bolt	magazines
Weight: 3.3kg (7.3lb) unloaded	Range: 400m (1312ft)
Overall Length: 1006mm (39.6in)	

Specifications

Country of Origin: United Kingdom

Date: 1985

Calibre: 5.56mm (.219in) NATO

Operation: Gas

Weight: 3.71kg (8.1lb)

Overall Length: 709mm (27.9in)

Barrel Length: 442mm (17.4in)

Muzzle Velocity: 940m/sec (3084ft/sec)

Feed/Magazine: 30-round detachable

box magazine

Range: 300m (984ft)

▲ L22 carbine

British Army / 7th Armoured Brigade, Afghanistan, July 2011

The L22 is an shortened version of the L85 assault rifle. It is used by some British vehicle crews and other personnel needing a very compact weapon.

Specifications

Country of Origin: United Kingdom

Date: 1997

Calibre: 7.62mm (.3in) / .300 Winchester

Magnum, 8.58mm (.338in) / .338 Lapua

Magnum

Operation: Bolt action

Weight: 6.8kg (15lb)

Overall Length: 1300mm (51in)

Barrel Length: 686mm (27in)

Muzzle Velocity: c.850m/sec (2788ft/sec)

Feed/Magazine: 5-round detachable box

magazine

Range: 1100m (3609ft) .300 Winchester; 1500m

(4921ft) .338

▲ L115A3 / AWM

*British Army / Household Cavalry, Helmand Province, Afghanistan,
November 2009*

The world record for the longest sniper kill – actually two kills in rapid succession – was established by British corporal Craig Harrison at 2475m (8119ft) using the L115A3 rifle.

▲ L129A1 sharpshooter rifle

*British Army / 16 Air Assault Brigade, Helmand Province, Afghanistan,
March 2011*

The L129A1 was procured to meet an urgent need for longer-range capability within an infantry force. A semi-automatic weapon, it offers greater firepower than a bolt-action sniper rifle such as the L96.

Specifications

Country of Origin: United Kingdom

Date: 2010

Calibre: 7.62mm (.3in) NATO

Operation: Gas, semi-automatic

Weight: 4.5kg (9.92lb)

Overall Length: 990mm (38.9in)

Barrel Length: 406mm (16in)

Muzzle Velocity: Not known

Feed/Magazine: 20-round detachable box

magazine

Range: 800m (2625ft)

offered by a small squad of infantrymen equipped with assault rifles, squad support weapons and perhaps a general-purpose machine gun is impressive. When outnumbered and defending a checkpoint or forward base, this degree of firepower can be the decider between defeat and victory – or at least holding on long enough for help to arrive.

The use of under-barrel grenade launchers, which give an infantry squad a measure of indirect area fire capability, have also added greatly to infantry capabilities. A skilled grenadier can drop a 40mm (1.57in) grenade among a group of hostiles, even if they are behind cover. He can then switch back to using his rifle, ensuring that his grenade-launching capability does not rob the squad of a rifle. For a small unit, even just one rifle is a significant asset.

▲ Heckler & Koch HK416

German Army / German Mechanized Infantry Brigade 41, Kunduz Province, Afghanistan, May 2009

Based on the US M4 Carbine, the HK416 uses a gas piston system derived from the G36 rifle. It has four picatinny rails for a range of accessories. The weapon is also used by the US military and Norwegian armed forces.

Specifications

Country of Origin: Germany
Date: 2005
Calibre: 5.56mm (0.21in)
Operation: Gas, rotating bolt
Weight: 2.950kg (6.50lb)
Overall Length: 690mm (27.2in)

Barrell Length: 228mm (9.0in)
Muzzle Velocity: Varies by barrel length and type
of round used
Feed/Magazine: 20-, 30-round STANAG magazine
or 100-round Beta C-Mag box magazine
Range: 365m (1200ft)

Specifications

Country of Origin: Germany
Date: 2005
Calibre: 5.56mm (.219in) NATO
Operation: Gas, rotating bolt
Weight: 8.15kg (17.97lb)

Overall Length: 1030mm (40.6in)
Barrel Length: 482mm (19in)
Muzzle Velocity: 920m/sec (3018ft/sec)
Feed/Magazine: Disintegrating link belt
Cycle Rate: 850rpm
Range: c.1000m (3280ft)

▲ Heckler & Koch MG4

German Army / German Airborne Brigade 26, Kunduz Province, Afghanistan, July 2009

The MG4 was developed in the 1990s as a squad support weapon. It has a folding stock, which greatly shortens the weapon when moving in and out of vehicles or helicopters. It can be fired with the stock folded.

▲ **Khaybar KH 2002**

Islamic Jihadists, Iraq, post 2004

Developed from the M16 by way of a Chinese assault rifle, the Iranian Khaybar
may have found its way into the hands of Islamic fighters resisting the Coalition
occupation, despite efforts to prevent arms smuggling in the region.

Specifications

Country of Origin: Iran	Barrel Length: Not known
Date: 2004	Muzzle Velocity: 900–950m/sec
Calibre: 5.56mm (.219in)	(2952–3116ft/sec)
Operation: Gas, rotating bolt	Feed/Magazine: Various STANAG magazines
Weight: 3.7kg (8.15lb)	Range: 450m (1476ft)
Overall Length: 730mm (28.7in)	

Tensions in East Asia
1980–PRESENT

**Tensions in the Far East are a consequence of both age-old rivalries as well as unresolved
issues from the Cold War.**

MANY OF THE CONFLICTS that exist today in Asia
are historic in origin, and often it is difficult to
find a root cause of a current war. This in turn makes
it hard to find lasting solutions, as there are rivalries
and enmities in the region going back decades or even
centuries.

World War II and the Chinese Civil War (which
began before 1939 and ended in 1949) had very
significant effects upon the region. Not only was
Western colonial influence greatly reduced in East
Asia but the rise of a Communist state in China
added a new ideological conflict to an already
bubbling pot. The clash of Communism versus
democracy was, as we have seen, a key factor in the
Vietnam War and the Korean Conflict. The latter
resulted largely from the arbitrary partition of Korea
at the end of World War II. The north of the country

was occupied by Soviet troops and became a
Communist state, while the south was pro-Western,
with large numbers of American and other Allied
troops present.

After attempts to reunify the country by
negotiation and open warfare failed, an armed
standoff began which continues to this day. Matters
are complicated by disputes over ownership of islands
off the Korean coast. Any nation is of course entitled
to position forces in its sovereign territory, but the
presence of forces on islands close to the border has
been cited as a threat and a provocation at times.

Open conflict between North and South Korea has
not occurred since the 1950s, but both Koreas today
maintain strong military forces; incidents are not
uncommon. North Korea obtained much of its
military technology from China and the Soviet

Union, and uses a military system common in 'Communist bloc' countries. Weaponry tends to be fairly low-tech and is recognizably derived from Russian equipment or Chinese copies of it.

South Korean military equipment tends to be heavily influenced by Western designs, and is usually compatible with items like M16 magazines and standard optical sights. Gear tends to be more high-tech than Northern equivalents, and is interoperable with the equipment issued to US forces that would almost certainly assist South Korea in repelling a renewed invasion from the North.

Taiwan also faces the possibility of invasion. At the end of the Chinese Civil War the defeated Nationalists retreated to what is now Taiwan, establishing the Republic of China. The mainland became dominated by the People's Republic of China. Both, as their names suggest, assert that they are the legitimate government of all China. Taiwanese (i.e. Republic of China) equipment is Western

▲ **Norinco Type 86S**

People's Liberation Army (PRC), mid-1980s

Despite its appearance, the Type 86S has many of its internal workings in common with the AK assault rifle series. It was not adopted for general service.

Specifications

Country of Origin: China	Overall Length: 667mm (26.25in)
Date: 1980	Barrel Length: 438mm (17.2in)
Calibre: 7.62mm (.3in)	Muzzle Velocity: 710m/sec (2429ft/sec)
Operation: Gas	Feed/Magazine: 30-round box magazine
Weight: 3.59kg (7.91lb)	Range: 300m (984ft)

Specifications

Country of Origin: China	Barrel Length: 445mm (17.5in)
Date: 1977	Muzzle Velocity: 720m/sec (2362ft/sec)
Calibre: 7.62mm (.3in)	Feed/Magazine: 30-round detachable box or
Operation: Gas, rotating bolt	75-round drum magazine
Weight: 3.4kg (7.5lb)	Cyclic Rate: c.650rpm
Overall Length: 955mm (37.6in)	Range: 500m (1640ft)

▲ **Type 81**

People's Liberation Army (PRC), early 1990s

Clearly derived from the AK series, the Type 81 was produced in assault rifle and light machinegun configurations. It can feed from a 75-round drum or a standard rifle magazine.

influenced and sometimes derived from US designs, while the arms and equipment of the People's Republic of China (PRC) is heavily influenced by Soviet/Russian designs. Much of the PRC's early military equipment was directly copied from Soviet arms, although relations between these two Communist nations cooled in the latter half of the twentieth century.

The PRC is a major force in world affairs, and is closing the technological gap between its equipment and that of more advanced nations. Modern Chinese weapons may still show Soviet-era influences, but they are becoming more refined as China gains experience in developing new military systems.

The Chinese military still emphasizes huge available manpower over technological excellence. Equipping such a large force necessitates designs produced with an eye to their cost and ease of maintenance, so many Chinese weapon systems have traditionally been simple and robust.

Specifications

Country of Origin: China	Barrel Length: 463mm (18.2in)
Date: 1997	Muzzle Velocity: 930m/sec (3050ft/sec)
Calibre: 5.8mm (.228in) DBP87	Feed/Magazine: 30-round box or 75-round drum
Operation: Gas, rotating bolt	magazine
Weight: 3.25kg (7.2lb)	Range: 400m (1312ft)
Overall Length: 745mm (29.3in) rifle	

▲ **QBZ-95**

People's Liberation Army (PRC), 1995

Chinese designers produced an entirely new family of weapons built around a specially developed cartridge. Rifle, carbine and light machine gun versions exist.

Specifications

Country of Origin: China	Overall Length: 960mm (37.79in) stock extended;
Date: 2003	710mm (27.95in) stock folded
Calibre: 5.8mm (.228in) DBP87,	Barrel Length: Not known
5.56mm (.219in) NATO	Muzzle Velocity: 930m/sec (3050ft/sec)
Operation: Gas-operated, rotating bolt	Feed/Magazine: 30-round detachable box
Weight: 3.5kg (7.71lb)	magazine
	Range: 400m (1312ft)

▲ **QBZ-03**

People's Liberation Army (PRC), 2005

Disappointment with the QBZ-95 caused Chinese designers to return to a more conventional weapon derived from the Type 81. The standard-issue rifle can launch rifle grenades without requiring an adapter.

It is inconceivable that Taiwan could launch an invasion of mainland China; its forces would simply be swallowed up by the vast numbers facing them. Were tensions to boil over, an invasion of Taiwan by the PRC would pit the relatively high-tech forces of Taiwan against overwhelming numbers. The main defence of Taiwan is its island location and the force-multiplying effect of defending a shoreline. It is possible that Chinese troops could be prevented from getting ashore in sufficient numbers to overpower the defenders, at least long enough for overseas assistance to arrive.

Taiwan has links with the West and would probably receive rapid assistance. However, it is never good strategy to reinforce defeat, so the Taiwanese forces' priority would be to demonstrate that they possessed both the means and the will to defend their island unilaterally. The possession of well-equipped armed forces makes a statement to the world that this capability exists.

▲ Type 65

Republic of China Division (Taiwan) Armed Forces, 1985

Heavily influenced by the US M16 family, the Type 65 was introduced in the 1970s and evolved through updated variants into the T65K2.

Specifications

Country of Origin: Taiwan	Overall Length: 990mm (38.9in)
Date: 1976	Barrel Length: 508mm (20in)
Calibre: 5.56mm (.219in) NATO	Muzzle Velocity: 990m/sec (2530ft/sec)
Operation: Gas	Feed/Magazine: Various STANAG magazines
Weight: 3.31kg (7.29lb)	Range: 500m (1640ft) +

▶ Daewoo K1

South Korean Armed Forces, 1990

The K1 assault rifle was developed to meet a South Korean need to replace ageing M3 submachine guns and other US weapons then in service. Because of this lineage, it is sometimes designated as a submachine gun, although it fires rifle ammunition.

Specifications

Country of Origin: South Korea	Overall Length: 838mm (32.99in)
Date: 1981	Barrel Length: 263mm (10.35in)
Calibre: 5.56mm (.219in) NATO	Muzzle Velocity: 820m/sec (2690ft/sec)
Operation: Gas, rotating bolt	Feed/Magazine: Various STANAG magazines
Weight: 2.87kg (6.32lb)	Range: 250m (820ft)

▲ **INSAS squad automatic rifle**

Indian Army / 2nd Rajputana Rifles, Kargil District, Kashmir, 1999

Based on a developed version of the AK-47 action, the INSAS (Indian National Small Arms System) rifle is gas-operated and capable of semi- or fully-automatic fire in addition to three-round bursts. The support version of the INSAS assault rifle differs mainly in its heavier barrel, which has different rifling to improve long-range performance. The INSAS saw combat during the 1999 Kargil War with Pakistan, where the rifle had some reliability problems in the very cold climate.

Specifications

Country of Origin: India	Overall Length: 960mm (37.8in)
Date: 1998	Barrel Length:464mm (18.3in)
Calibre: 5.56mm (.219in) NATO	Muzzle Velocity: 900m/sec (2953ft/sec)
Operation: Gas	Feed/Magazine: 20- or 30-round detachable box
Weight: 4.25kg (9.4lb)	magazine
	Range: 800m (2625ft) +

South-East Asia

1980–PRESENT

South-East Asia has a long history of tension and conflict involving both states and stateless organizations striving for nationhood or independence.

THE WITHDRAWAL OF COLONIAL POWERS after World War II and the rise of Communism only added to existing tensions in South-East Asia. The region includes some of the world's most powerful economies and some of the poorest regions on the planet, so it is perhaps inevitable that conflicts frequently arise.

Some of these conflicts are based on economic factors. For example, large numbers of ships pass through the Straits of Malacca between Indonesia and Peninsular Malaysia. In this narrow waterway operate bands of pirates who use helicopters and small boats to attack vulnerable vessels. Despite the best efforts of the world's navies and local law enforcement agencies, these pirates are able to withdraw to villages along the nearby coasts and islands and hide when they are not active.

There is nothing political about the actions of these pirates, except where they exert influence over local government officers. However, in other areas of South-East Asia there are political conflicts. One such

saw the emergence of the world's newest sovereign state, the Democratic Republic of Timor-Leste, better known as East Timor.

This state had its origins in a declaration of independence made when the Portuguese withdrew from their colonies in the region. Independence was forestalled by an invasion from Indonesia, resulting in bloody fighting. A guerrilla war went on through the 1980s and 1990s, until international pressure caused the withdrawal of Indonesian forces and permitted East Timor to finally assert its independence.

Other conflicts in South-East Asia are internal, such as that in Myanmar (Burma). An extremely poor country despite good natural resources, Myanmar suffers from a highly corrupt government. A military coup placed a junta in power in 1962, and although elections were implemented, the exclusion of other political parties made this nothing more than a public relations gesture.

Opposition to the government was dealt with using heavy-handed methods, and racist policies were implemented against groups not recognized by the government as true citizens of Burma. These actions led to a major uprising and coup in 1988, at which time the nation adopted its new name. Internal conflict continued, however, with details hard to come by outside the country. Accusations have been made of forced labour projects and ongoing campaigns to oppress or eradicate groups disliked by the government.

Internal conflicts of this sort are normally fought by infantry and light vehicles, with air support and artillery playing a fairly minor supporting role. There is a fine line between attempting to reassert the

government's control over its sovereign territory and terrorizing the populace into submission, and with few details of operations or clashes available to outside agencies it is hard to establish the true nature of Myanmar's internal troubles.

Despite the support of China for the North Vietnamese in their conflicts with France and the United States, Vietnam and China clashed at the end of the 1970s. The war arose as a result of Vietnamese incursions into Cambodia and the occupation of the Spratly Islands, which China had claimed as its own territory. The Sino-Vietnamese war took the form of a raid in massive force rather than a campaign of

▲ SR-88

Singapore Armed Forces, 1987

Developed from the SAR-80, the SAR-88 achieved good sales to armed forces throughout the region. It can take an M203 under-barrel grenade launcher.

Specifications

Country of Origin: Singapore	Barrel Length: 460mm (18.1in)
Date: 1984	Muzzle Velocity: Not known
Calibre: 5.56mm (.219in) NATO	Feed/Magazine: 30-round detachable box
Operation: Gas, rotating bolt	magazine
Weight: 3.68kg (8.11lb)	Range: 800m (2625ft)
Overall Length: 960mm (37.7in)	

Specifications

Country of Origin: Singapore	Barrel Length: 460mm (18.1in)
Date: 1990	Muzzle Velocity: Not known
Calibre: 5.56mm (.219in) NATO	Feed/Magazine: 30-round detachable box
Operation: Gas, rotating bolt	magazine
Weight: 3.68kg (8.11lb)	Range: 800m (2625ft)
Overall Length: 960mm (37.7in)	

▲ SR-88A

Singapore Armed Forces, 1990

An updated SR-88 using lighter materials, the SR-88A is also available in a short 'carbine' configuration for use by airmobile troops and vehicle crews. Its magazine catch will accept a regular M16 magazine and a C-mag, which is also used in M16 rifles.

conquest. Chinese forces captured some objectives and destroyed infrastructure before retiring. The conflict then simmered on in the form of border skirmishes until 1989, when Vietnam granted the political concessions China wanted. Notably, this included a withdrawal from Cambodia.

Some parts of South-East Asia have seen relatively little conflict in recent years. Singapore, for example, is a highly prosperous island nation with a healthy arms industry. Singaporean weapons are equivalent to many Western systems and can often interchange

accessories and magazines with them. Many of these weapons are exported, creating an alternative to the traditional Western/Russian/Chinese choice facing many importers.

Until fairly recently, a nation seeking weapons had to make a choice between Western and Communist suppliers. Today, however, the range of high-quality weapons on offer has been greatly increased. This is not solely due to the expansion of South-East Asian arms manufacturing, but it has been a significant factor.

▲ SAR 21

Singapore Armed Forces / 2004

The SAR-21 was the world's first assault rifle to incorporate a laser sighting aid as standard fit, inside the carrying handle. Carbine and light support versions are also manufactured.

Specifications

Country of Origin: Singapore	Barrel Length: 508mm (20in)
Date: 1999	Muzzle Velocity: 970m/sec (3182ft/sec)
Calibre: 5.56mm (.219in) NATO	Feed/Magazine: 30-round box magazine;
Operation: Gas, rotating bolt	plastic or STANAG magazines
Weight: 3.82kg (8.42lb)	Range: 460m (1509ft)
Overall Length: 805mm (31.7in)	

Specifications

Country of Origin: Indonesia	Overall Length: 990mm (38.97in)
Date: 2005	Barrell Length: 740mm (29.13in)
Calibre: 5.56mm (0.219in) NATO	Muzzle Velocity: 710m/sec (2329ft/sec)
Operation: Gas, rotating bolt	Feed/Magazine: Various STANAG magazines
Weight: 3.4kg (7.49lb)	Range: 500m (1640ft)

▲ Pindad SS2

Indonesian Armed Forces, 2007

The Pindad SS2 is derived from the FN FNC rifle. It is actually a weapon family, with carbine, rifle and 'para-sniper' versions all based on a common receiver. It can also be fitted with an SPG-1A underbarrel grenade launcher, as illustrated.

Chapter 6

Peacekeeping, Counter-terrorism & Law Enforcement

There have been few 'gentlemen's wars' in history,
where the military situation remained uncomplicated by
humanitarian or social factors. Increasingly, modern military
operations must switch between warfighting and lower-
intensity conflict in which troops are expected to maintain
law and order, enforce a ceasefire or deal with insurgents
amid the mass of ordinary people who need to
get on with their lives. Conversely, law enforcement
agencies may have to deal with heavily armed
opposition from stateless groups such as terrorist
organizations or drugs cartels. Whilst military backup may
be available on call, often it is law enforcement personnel
who are on the frontline.

◀ **Riot control**
Venezuelan National guardsmen fire shotguns at protesters to keep apart militant supporters of President
Hugo Chávez and opposition marchers who were protesting against the government's military takeover of
the city police force, Caracas, November 2002.

Introduction

The line between dealing with criminal activity and military opposition is a fine one. Some criminal organizations are armed with military equipment, while many governments consider paramilitary insurgent groups to be civilian criminals rather than enemy combatants.

WHERE MILITARY FORCES are deployed in an 'aid to civil power' context they have some law enforcement rights, but are usually there to back up the police rather than to replace them. If martial law has been declared then the situation is different, but under normal circumstances the military is present to assist and support the normal law enforcement process. Captured members of paramilitary organizations are tried in the courts and prosecuted for the same offences as anyone else might be – murder, weapons possession and so forth. Unless special legislation is in place then the regular legal system must be followed. Military personnel deployed in aid to the civil power are also bound by rules of

engagement. Where an enemy combatant would be a legitimate target in a war zone, troops assisting police are normally expected to arrest a suspect rather than simply open fire. They may, of course, use their weapons if fired upon, or to protect innocents, but potential hostiles are usually considered criminal suspects rather than enemy combatants until they give clear indication of their intentions.

Peacekeeping forces are in a similar position. They must often operate among a hostile or potentially hostile population, attempting to enforce a ceasefire or international mandate that local political groups do not want. Peacekeepers are, by their presence, targets for hostile groups, but are forced to remain

▲ **Indonesian peacekeepers**

Indonesian Army soldiers board an aircraft at Mombasa, Kenya, to take a flight to Elizabethville, Congo, as part of United Nations peacekeeping operations, 1960. They are armed with M3 submachine guns with flash hider attachments.

▲ **Taking cover**

A wounded British soldier mans a L4 Bren light machine gun on the Ulster/Republic of Ireland border during a patrol, 1977.

within the rules of engagement. These may prevent them from taking pre-emptive action to protect themselves, or force them to remain inactive while snipers fire over their positions at the innocents they are supposed to be protecting.

Combating terrorism

There are philosophical questions about the status of insurgents and guerrillas, i.e., whether they are criminals or enemy combatants, and the situation is often little clearer with terrorists. Any armed group that uses fear to obtain its political, religious or social ends can legitimately be labelled a terrorist organization. Terrorists are criminals under law, but can also be subject to military action. For example, in the situation where a terrorist training camp or weapons cache is identified, it might be raided by law enforcement personnel, or military means might be used to eliminate it.

The latter is more likely if the facility is overseas and beyond the reach of domestic law enforcement agencies. For the most part, domestic counter-terrorism work is the function of specially trained paramilitary law enforcement agencies. These units are equipped with military hardware and very highly trained, but are part of the civilian law enforcement

process. They are not optimized to fight foreign troops but to deal with relatively small terrorist groups or heavily armed criminals. Thus the fight against terrorism involves both military and law enforcement assets.

Urban concerns

Counter-terrorism units and law enforcement agencies generally operate in the urban environment, where innocent people may be close by. Precision is extremely important in this context, and for this reason semi-automatic weapons are often favoured over fully-automatic ones. Combat, if it occurs, is generally at short range and often inside buildings. Even sniping is rarely conducted at ranges greater than 100–200 metres (300–600 feet). One key consideration is over-penetration; law enforcement officers cannot afford to have a shot pass through the target and injure someone else, or a missed shot go through a wall and hit an innocent bystander.

Against these concerns must be balanced the need for a quick 'stop' of the target. Officers are often outnumbered and may have to shoot in order to prevent a hostile from endangering civilians. Lethality is less of a consideration than the ability to immediately disable a criminal or terrorist.

Northern Ireland: British forces
1968–98

The 'Troubles' in Northern Ireland involved several paramilitary organizations as well as the Royal Ulster Constabulary and the British Army.

THE POLITICAL SITUATION in Northern Ireland has always been complex, with Catholic/Protestant religious divides usually but not always paralleling political beliefs. The question of whether Northern Ireland should remain part of the United Kingdom or join Eire provided motivation for some groups involved in the conflict, but others had a different agenda only loosely connected with the political fate of the region.

Opinions differ as to when the Troubles began. There has always been some level of political agitation and sectarian violence in Northern Ireland due to the region's history. However, in the mid 1960s a move towards increased violence began. In August 1969, British troops were deployed to Northern Ireland to assist the civil authorities in maintaining order. This move was prompted by

▲ **Counter-sniper action**

Armed with an SLR fitted with a sniper scope, a British soldier watches out for enemy activity somewhere in Belfast, 1978.

severe rioting which had caused several deaths. The army, however, was unable to prevent an escalation of violence, and the next few years were very difficult for the people of Belfast in particular.

Several paramilitary organizations emerged before or during the Troubles. Loyalist groups such as the Ulster Volunteer Force (UVF) targeted the Catholic community while the Irish Republican Army (IRA) attacked Protestants and the British Army. Both, of course, claimed only to be protecting their own people from aggression. The IRA fragmented in 1969 into the Official IRA, which was primarily concerned with political activity, and the Provisional IRA, which was committed to direct action. Like other paramilitaries in Northern Ireland, the IRA was declared an illegal organization by the government, but was not recognized as a hostile military force. Therefore, the British Army was officially aiding the civil power against criminal groups composed of British citizens. Its powers were limited to supporting the police rather than fighting a war against the IRA.

Peacekeeping role

For three decades British Army units rotated through Northern Ireland, deploying to Belfast and the surrounding area. Troops manned checkpoints and patrolled the streets, supported police operations and worked as peacekeepers rather than combat troops. Some major operations were mounted. In 1972, large areas of Belfast and Derry were barricaded by local people to prevent road access, and had become 'no-go areas' for the authorities. At the end of July, the army mounted Operation *Motorman*, sending thousands of troops into the no-go areas, along with armoured engineering vehicles to dismantle the barricades. Such overwhelming force was used that the IRA did not try to resist the operation.

Some British Army bases were in a state of virtual siege at times. Resupply by helicopter was the only way that some areas could be manned, due to the number of roadside bombs, ambushes or sniper

Specifications

Country of Origin: United Kingdom

Date: 1956

Calibre: 9mm (.35in) Parabellum

Operation: Blowback

Weight: 2.7kg (5.9lb) empty

Overall Length: 686mm (27in) stock extended;
 481mm (18.9in) stock folded

Barrel Length: 196mm (7.7in)

Muzzle Velocity: 395m/sec (1295ft/sec)

Feed/Magazine: 34-round detachable box
 magazine

Range: 200m (656ft)

▲ **Sterling L2A3**

British Army / Royal Engineers, Derry, July 1972

The A3 variant of the Sterling submachine gun was adopted by the British Army in 1956. It was the last Sterling model to go into general service.

▲ **Heckler & Koch HK53**

British Army / 14 Intelligence Company, Northern Ireland October, 1979

The HK 53 was favoured by SAS intelligence operatives for its increased firepower compared to a conventional 9mm submachine gun.

Specifications

Country of Origin: Germany

Date: 1975

Calibre: 5.56mm (.219in) NATO

Operation: Blowback

Weight: 2.54kg (5.6lb)

Overall Length: 680mm (26.8in)

Barrel Length: 225mm (8.85in)

Muzzle Velocity: 400m/sec (1312ft/sec)

Feed/Magazine: 25- or 30-round detachable box
 magazine

Range: 400m (1312ft)

attacks on ground convoys. Parts of Country Antrim were known as 'Bandit Country' by British troops due to the level of support for the IRA there. Operations in this area were very hazardous.

SLR in action

The L1A1 self-loading rifle (SLR) was not ideally suited to operations in a urban environment. Long and heavy, it was designed for engagements at a considerable distance rather than quick movement through urban terrain. However, it did offer good stopping power on a hit. In the rural environment, or when operating from a 'hide' created in a building, the accuracy of the L1A1 made it highly effective. With it, any soldier could disable a vehicle in use by paramilitary gunmen and could engage and suppress a distant sniper who might be immune to return fire from smaller-calibre weapons. This was particularly useful when on patrol in rural areas controlled by the paramilitaries.

Special forces role

British special forces personnel were deployed to Northern Ireland at various times, operating against the paramilitaries in a covert manner. For the most part their duties were intelligence-gathering and surveillance, though they undertook a range of other missions. Special forces personnel made a number of arrests of IRA suspects, approaching the target in a covert manner and striking swiftly, or hunting enemy personnel in the countryside. They were also instrumental in defending Loughgall police station in 1987. Having obtained information that the IRA intended to attack the station, a detachment of the Special Air Service (SAS) troopers laid an ambush. A

group of IRA personnel, using a stolen digger to carry a large bomb, were ambushed whilst approaching the police station. Eight IRA members were killed.

Usually, clashes between the paramilitaries and the army were relatively small-scale affairs. British units learned to make highly effective use of cover whilst on patrol, and evolved excellent urban counter-sniper techniques. The goal was always to arrest anyone attacking the police, army or civilians, but troops were permitted to open fire when necessary. The army took a steady stream of casualties over the years, but was able to keep the situation in Northern Ireland under control while a political solution was sought.

Specifications

Country of Origin: United Kingdom	Barrel Length: 535mm (21.1in)
Date: 1958	Muzzle Velocity: 853m/sec (2800ft/sec)
Calibre: 7.62mm (.3in) NATO	Feed/Magazine: 20-round detachable box
Operation: Gas, self-loading	magazine
Weight: 4.31kg (9.5lb)	Range: 800m (2625ft) +
Overall Length: 1090mm (43in)	

▲ **L1A1 self-loading rifle**

British Army / 2nd Battalion, The Parachute Regiment, Belfast, September 1979

Its powerful round could be a two-edged sword; on the one hand it permitted troops to tackle a sniper hiding behind a typical brick wall, but equally it posed a significant hazard to anyone within a large radius on a ricochet or missed shot.

Specifications

Country of Origin: United Kingdom	Barrel Length: 700mm (27in)
Date: 1970	Muzzle Velocity: 744m/sec (2441ft/sec)
Calibre: 7.62mm (.3in) NATO	Feed/Magazine: 10-round detachable box
Operation: Bolt action	magazine
Weight: 4.42kg (9.7lb)	Range: 500m (1640ft)
Overall Length: 1180mm (46.4in)	

▲ **Enfield Enforcer**

Royal Ulster Constabulary, Belfast, October 1986

The Enforcer was developed for law-enforcement use from the L42A1 sniper rifle, itself derived from the Lee-Enfield Mk 3.

Irish Republican Army (IRA)

1968–PRESENT

The term 'IRA' is most commonly associated with the Provisional IRA, but there have in fact been several organizations using the same name.

THE IRISH REPUBLICAN ARMY (IRA) was formed in the early twentieth century, passing through several incarnations before splitting in 1969 into the Official IRA (OIRA) and the Provisional IRA (PIRA). The latter conducted an armed struggle against the Royal Ulster Constabulary (RUC), British Army and Loyalist paramilitaries and is commonly known as 'The IRA'. Political agreements ended the armed struggle, though some splinter groups of the PIRA still continue to advocate violence and claim the IRA name as their own.

From 1969 until the conflict was declared to be over in 2005, the PIRA carried out a mostly urban guerrilla campaign, intermixed with acts of terrorism. The campaign was largely conducted in Northern Ireland, but attacks were made on the British mainland. Bombs were a favoured weapon, and were used with some sophistication. For example, at times a second bomb would be planted near a suitable point for a command post. When the British Army arrived to deal with the first bomb, their deployment might make the command team susceptible to attack with the second device.

Direct action was also taken against police and army patrols and bases, including mortar and sniper attacks. The weapons used in these attacks were initially of World War II vintage, though some more modern equipment was available. Libya supplied significant quantities of arms at the end of the 1970s and early 1980s, including numbers of RPG-7 launchers and AK-47 assault rifles.

The IRA also obtained weapons from various other sources, including Browning pistols, Heckler & Koch rifles, AR-18 Armalite and M16 automatic rifles from North America. Some were stolen from the military and police, some bought on the black market and secretly shipped into the country, often through the Republic of Ireland. Many of these were basic infantry weapons, but more advanced equipment was also available. Rumours that the IRA had obtained one or more US-made Barrett M82 anti-materiel rifles caused grave concern among the security forces.

Small arms were used to attack the security services of course, but were also used to control and/or intimidate the local population.

▲ Armalite AR-18

Provisional IRA / Belfast Brigade, Belfast, August 1980

Essentially an upgraded AR-15, the AR-18 was not adopted for military service but was obtained in quantity by the IRA, with whom it became closely associated.

Specifications

Country of Origin: United States
Date: 1966
Calibre: 5.56mm (.219in) M109
Operation: Gas
Weight: 3.04kg (6.7lb)
Overall Length: 965mm (38in)

Barrel Length: 463mm (18.25in)
Muzzle Velocity: 990m/sec (2530ft/sec)
Feed/Magazine: 20-round detachable box
   magazine
Range: 500m (1640ft) +

▶ **Browning High Power**

Provisional IRA / Belfast Brigade, Belfast, January 1970

The Browning High-Power was produced in vast numbers for the British Army and became readily available on the black market after World War II.

Specifications

Country of Origin: Belgium/United States	Barrel Length: 118mm (4.65in)
Date: 1935	Muzzle Velocity: 335m/sec (1100ft/sec)
Calibre: 9mm (.35in) Parabellum	Feed/Magazine: 13-round detachable box
Operation: Short recoil	magazine
Weight: .99kg (2.19lb)	Range: 30m (98ft)
Overall Length: 197mm (7.75in)	

▲ **RPG-7D**

Provisional IRA / Belfast Brigade, Belfast, June 1997

RPG-7s supplied by Libya were used to attack Army and Royal Ulster Constabulary armoured vehicles. Not all such attacks were successful.

Specifications

Country of Origin: USSR	Overall Length: 950mm (37.4in)
Date: 1961	Muzzle Velocity: 115m/sec (377ft/sec)
Calibre: 40mm (1.57in)	Feed/Magazine: Single-shot, muzzle-loaded
Operation: Rocket motor	Range: c.920m (3018ft)
Weight: 7kg (15lb)	

International peacekeeping
1980–PRESENT

Peacekeeping forces have been deployed by the United Nations more than 60 times since World War II. There have also been numerous non-UN peacekeeping operations.

PEACEKEEPING IS A RATHER DIFFERENT prospect to warfighting, though troops may find themselves in a deadly combat situation at any time. In many ways, peacekeeping can be more stressful for the personnel involved than open warfare. Peacekeeping operations are invariably of lengthy duration, and personnel are expected to deal with a range of challenges and threats on a constant basis. Peacekeepers are also forced to remain within strict rules of engagement which may prevent them from taking combat actions that their instincts tell them are right.

Peacekeepers are often forced to confront the aftermath of conflict and the human suffering that results from it. They may at times find themselves trying to support a peace process that none of the warring factions seems to want, and may be responsible for the lives of aid workers or innocent non-combatants as well as their own safety. This is a difficult enough prospect at the best of times, but in an environment where it is hard to tell hostiles from innocents it can be a virtually impossible task.

Showing restraint

Peacekeeping forces are supposedly not expected to have to fight. Their role is to support the move towards a lasting peace by verifying compliance with treaties and other agreements, by observing the fairness of elections, and by providing an 'armed presence' to deter interference with aid work or reconstruction. However, even if the political leadership and the majority of members of the opposing groups genuinely want peace, there will usually be some who want to keep fighting and who see the peacekeepers as legitimate targets.

Peacekeeping, correctly defined, takes place after all parties have decided that they want or are willing to accept an end to the conflict. Peacekeepers are thus deployed with mutual consent of combatants. Operations where peace must be imposed upon one or more of the combatants might more properly be defined as 'peace enforcement'. Yet these activities generally fall under the popular conception of peacekeeping.

Most peacekeeping operations are undertaken after a UN resolution, and frequently under the direct control of the UN itself. The personnel involved are contributed by national forces, however; the UN has no armed forces of its own. It has been suggested that a UN army could and perhaps should be raised, but so far this idea has not been implemented.

Operating under UN control, and alongside forces contributed by other nations, can be a serious challenge. Equipment may not be interoperable; ammunition calibres vary and troops may not even speak the same language. Trust and good joint working practices must also be built during the deployment and until they are, efficiency suffers. Efficiency is also a problem due to the way the UN operates. A consensus is needed in order to make many decisions, and this can take time. Peacekeeping operations can thus be cumbersome and slow to react to local conditions.

Somalia

Some peacekeeping operations have been notable successes, although often only after a lengthy period. Others, such as peacekeeping efforts in Somalia, have influenced the situation but not resolved it. The Somali Civil War, which began in 1991, has seen various attempts to intervene under UN and non-UN command, but conflict continues. Intervention in Somalia resulted in the origin of the term 'Mogadishu Line', named for the capital of Somalia. The Mogadishu Line is the point where peacekeeping ends and troops are instead involved in open conflict.

◀ MAB PA-15

Finnish Contingent / EUFOR Althea, Bosnia, December 2004

The French-developed MAB-PA-15 was not adopted by the French armed forces, but was taken up by the Finnish Army and some police forces.

Specifications

Country of Origin: France	Barrel Length: 114mm (4.5in)
Date: 1975	Muzzle Velocity: 330m/sec (1100ft/sec)
Calibre: 9mm (.35in) Parabellum	Feed/Magazine: 15-round detachable box
Operation: Delayed blowback	magazine
Weight: 1.07kg (2.36lb)	Range: 40m (131ft)
Overall Length: 203mm (8in)	

UN peacekeepers were deployed to Somalia in 1992 mainly to support humanitarian relief operations, but became involved in combat against various local factions. Intense fighting in Mogadishu and casualties elsewhere caused the UN to withdraw its peacekeeping forces. There was, in truth, no peace to keep in Somalia at that time. The conflict, with all its associated suffering and damage to the stability of the region, went on unimpeded.

Later interventions in Somalia included strikes by US forces against some factions, but this was connected with efforts against the al-Qaeda terrorist organization and was not a peacekeeping measure. An African Union force deployed to Somalia in 2008 in support of a new coalition government's attempts to create peace and stability. This measure met with fierce opposition from some factions in the civil war, who saw the peacekeepers as intruders in their homeland.

Many peacekeeping troops come from developing nations rather than the world's major powers. The reason is not least due to the fact that the UN pays a subsidy for troops deployed as peacekeepers, which helps less-developed nations support their military establishment and allows their forces to gain operational experience.

Specifications

Country of Origin: West Germany
Date: 1959
Calibre: 7.62mm (.3in) NATO
Operation: Delayed blowback
Weight: 4.4kg (9.7lb)
Overall Length: 1025mm (40.35in)

Barrel Length: 450mm (17.71in)
Muzzle Velocity: 800m/sec (2625ft/sec)
Feed/Magazine: 20-round detachable box
    magazine
Range: 500m (1640ft) +

▲ Heckler & Koch G3
RUF Insurgents, Sierra Leone, July 2000
The HK G3 has been widely exported, in several variants. The G3SG/1 'sharpshooter' version is essentially the same weapon with a scope and a modified stock.

▲ Heckler & Koch G41
German Special Forces, Counter-terrorism Operations, post-1987
The G41 was to have replaced the G3 in German Army service, but proved too expensive. A few examples found their way into the hands of special forces units. Others appeared on the open market.

Specifications

Country of Origin: West Germany
Date: 1987
Calibre: 5.56mm (.219in) NATO
Operation: Roller-delayed blowback
Weight: 4.1kg (9.04lb)
Overall Length: 997mm (39.3in)

Barrel Length: 450mm (17.7in)
Muzzle Velocity: 920m/sec (3018ft/sec) SS109
    cartridge; 950m/sec (3117ft/sec) M193
    cartridge
Feed/Magazine: Various STANAG magazines
Range: 100–400m (328–1312ft)

The equipment requirements for peacekeeping are different to warfighting, to some extent. Peacekeepers generally only need personal small arms and light support weapons as they are unlikely to be engaged by major enemy forces. Such equipment is inexpensive, and in many cases outdated weapons will suffice. A peacekeeping force needs patience, training and diligence more than state-of-the-art military technology, and these human factors can be supplied by any nation.

Most of the time peacekeepers are policemen, security guards, observers and advisors. Their weapons are a deterrent rather than their main asset. However, when local factions turn on the peacekeepers, the possession of effective weapons and the training to use them becomes essential to survival.

▲ FAMAS F1

French Army / 8th Marine Infantry Parachute Regiment, 'The Red Line', Chad, January 1984

The FAMAS F1 was adopted in 1978 by the French Army. It suffered from a number of defects and was followed by the improved G1 version.

Specifications

Country of Origin: France	Overall Length: 757mm (29.8in)
Date: 1978	Barrel Length: 488mm (19.2in)
Calibre: 5.56mm (.219in) NATO	Muzzle Velocity: 960m/sec (3100ft/sec)
Operation: Gas	Feed/Magazine: 25-round box magazine
Weight: 3.61kg (7.96lb)	Range: 300m (984ft)

Specifications

Country of Origin: Austria	Barrel Length: 508mm (20in)
Date: 1980	Muzzle Velocity: 970m/sec (3182ft/sec)
Calibre: 9mm (.35in) Parabellum,	Feed/Magazine: 25-, 32-round (9mm/.35in) or
5.56mm (.219in) NATO	30-, 42-round (5.56mm/.219in) detachable
Operation: Gas, rotating bolt	box magazine
Weight: 3.6kg (7.9lb)	Range: 2700m (8858ft)
Overall Length: 790mm (31.1in)	

▲ Steyr-Mannlicher AUG

Austrian Contingent / EUFOR Althea, Bosnia, January 2010

The AUG uses a two-stage trigger to select semi-automatic or full-automatic fire. Some models have a blocking projection that prevents the trigger from being moved far enough for full-automatic operation when in position.

Heckler & Koch support weapons
1960s–PRESENT

Heckler & Koch created a family of closely related support weapons capable of meeting the needs of law enforcement, counter-terrorist units or military formations.

GENERAL-PURPOSE MACHINE GUNS (GPMGs) generally use a fairly heavy rifle calibre round; typically 7.62mm (0.3in). They are usually belt-fed, firing from an open bolt. This means that the bolt starts the firing cycle in the rear position, running forward to chamber a round before firing takes place. The open-bolt system reduces accuracy somewhat, but GPMGs are not precision weapons. They are intended to put a lot of rounds into a general area. Operating from an open bolt improves cooling, which is an asset during sustained fire

GPMGs are heavy and ammunition belts are cumbersome. Lighter automatic weapons, fed from a box or drum and firing an intermediate assault rifle cartridge, are more mobile and thus easily integrated into a rifle squad. Using a light support weapon derived from an assault rifle has the additional advantages that ammunition can be shared and troops can be quickly trained to operate and maintain a similar weapon to the standard service rifle.

In the early 1960s, Heckler & Koch began producing a light support weapon derived from the G3 rifle. Designated the HK21, this weapon was somewhere between the light support and GPMG categories. The gun was belt-fed, firing 7.62x51mm ammunition, but

this was fed from underneath, like a rifle, rather than from the side in more typical machine-gun style. The HK21 also fired from a closed bolt, meaning that the bolt began the firing cycle locked in the forward position. This improved accuracy but reduced sustained-fire capability due to greater heating.

The HK21's unusual feed system enabled it to be fitted with a magazine adapter, converting it from belt to magazine feed. It therefore allowed the use of rifle magazines, turning the weapon into a heavy rifle. Large-capacity drum magazines were also produced, giving an infantry squad effective fire support

▶ **H&K stalwart**
US Navy SEALs have employed the highly effective Heckler & Koch MP5 submachine gun on operations. The weapon is also used by FBI Hostage Rescue Teams, the British SAS, and dozens of other countries around the world.

capability without impairing the mobility of the soldiers using the weapon.

From this weapon, a range of variants appeared. A numerical system was used to describe them, giving rise to model numbers. The first digit indicated the weapon's type or intended use, which was largely dictated by feed mechanism. The HK21's '2' indicated belt feed and an intended role as a GPMG. A '1' indicated a magazine-fed light machine gun. The second digit was used to indicate calibre, with a '1' indicating 7.62x51mm NATO and a '3' indicating 5.56x45mm NATO.

A few examples were produced in 7.62x39mm Soviet calibre, which was designated by a '2'. Thus an H&K22 would be a belt-fed GPMG chambered for 7.62mm Soviet. However, this chambering was not produced in significant numbers.

The designation system is confused by the fact that conversion from belt to magazine feed is a simple matter of using an adapter, and similarly most weapons in the family can be converted from one calibre to another by changing the barrel. All recent models have a quick-change barrel, to facilitate sustained fire, so in theory a member of this weapon

▲ Heckler & Koch HK11

Hellenic Army (Land Forces of Greece), 1980

The 7.62mm (.3in) HK11 is basically an assault rifle with a bipod. It is instantly familiar to anyone trained on the G3 assault rifle.

Specifications

Country of Origin: West Germany
Date: 1970
Calibre: 7.62mm (.3in) NATO
Operation: Delayed blowback, selective fire
Weight: 8.15kg (17.97lb)
Overall Length: 1030mm (40.55in)

Barrel Length: 450mm (17.72in)
Muzzle Velocity: 800m/sec (2625ft/sec)
Feed/Magazine: 20-round detachable box or 80-round drum magazine
Range: 1000m (3280ft) +

▲ Heckler & Koch HK13

Unknown

The HK13 is accurate enough to be used for precision fire, using semi-automatic or three-round burst mode. This is attractive to law-enforcement or counter-terrorism units.

Specifications

Country of Origin: West Germany
Date: 1972
Calibre: 5.56mm (.219in) NATO
Operation: Roller-locked delayed blowback, air-cooled
Weight: 8kg (17.64lb)

Overall Length: 1030mm (40.55in)
Barrel Length: 450mm (17.72in)
Muzzle Velocity: 925m/sec (3035ft/sec)
Feed/Magazine: 20- or 30-round detachable box magazine or belt-fed
Range: 1000m (3280ft) +

family can be converted to any other designation in a matter of moments.

In practice, they are all the same weapon, built around the same delayed-blowback action, and the designation is simply a way of determining the configuration of the weapon. Some models also have an 'E' designation, which indicates an export model with a longer receiver. The accuracy and lightness of these weapons, and the three-round burst capability

of later examples, make them popular with law enforcement and special operations units, as well as the regular armed forces of many nations. The optional vertical foregrip facilitates 'assault' firing and, combined with a large-capacity drum magazine, gives the individual soldier high firepower without weighing all that much more than a standard rifle.

▲ HK21

Royal Malaysia Police (RMP), Pasukan Gerakan Khas (Counter-terrorism Police Squad), 2000

The light machine gun member of the family, the HK21 can carry the belt in a metal container, which fixes to the feed mechanism. It can also take loose belts.

Specifications

Country of Origin: West Germany	Overall Length: 1021mm (40.2in)
Date: 1970	Barrel Length: 450mm (17.72in)
Calibre: 7.62mm (.3in) NATO	Muzzle Velocity: 800m/sec (2625ft/sec)
Operation: Delayed blowback	Feed/Magazine: Belt-fed
Weight: 7.92kg (17.46lb)	Range: 2000m (6560ft)

▲ HK23

Turkish Gendarmerie, 2005

Chambered for 7.62mm (.3in) ammunition, the HK23 is at the 'light' end of the machine-gun spectrum, in terms both of weight and sustained-fire capability. The trade-off between mobility and firepower is always a difficult one.

Specifications

Country of Origin: West Germany	Barrel Length: 450mm (17.71in)
Date: 1981	Muzzle Velocity: 925m/sec (3035ft/sec)
Calibre: 5.56mm (.219in) NATO	Feed/Magazine: 20- or 30-round box magazine,
Operation: Delayed blowback	100-round drum magazine or 50- or
Weight: 8.7kg (19.18lb) on bipod	100-round belt
Overall Length: 1030mm (40.5in)	Range: 1000m (3280ft) +

Peacekeeping forces specialist weapons

1990–PRESENT

Precision rifles give peacekeeping and security forces the ability to deal with snipers and other threats without endangering non-combatants.

THE PRESENCE OF PEACEKEEPING FORCES often forces insurgent groups to adopt a different style of warfare. Rather than launching direct attacks, they might resort to long-range sniping or harassing fire. The planting of IEDs is also a common tactic. Both avoid the need to come into direct contact with peacekeepers, which might trigger a response in force that the insurgents cannot deal with.

Bombs and sniper bullets are also deniable, in that it is hard to prove who launched the attack. This suits the agenda of some groups, who wish to continue their war while still benefiting from overseas aid provided by the same nations that sent the peacekeepers. Proof that a group has broken a ceasefire or attacked either peacekeeping forces or the people they are protecting might result in aid being withdrawn or exclusion from negotiations aimed at ending the conflict.

Thus it is not uncommon for combatant groups to act friendly or at least avoid obvious hostile actions when close to overseas observers or peacekeepers, and instead try to strike from a distance when the opportunity presents itself. Peacekeepers are often bound by strict rules of engagement that permit only a very precise response against personnel undertaking immediately hostile actions.

Sniper rifles are among the few weapon systems that are precise enough to deal with these threats. Most sniping weapons use a fairly heavy cartridge such as 7.62x51mm or .308. By definition, any hostile who is close enough to shoot is within range of a sniper's return fire. His muzzle flash may give away his location, or thermal sensors might be used to find him, at which point an almost certainly more

▲ **PGM Hecate II**

French Commandement des Opérations Spéciales (COS), Afghanistan, 2001

In addition to sniping work, the Hecate II is used by Explosive Ordnance Disposal (EOD) personnel to deal with unexploded bombs and shells, using high-explosive ammunition.

Specifications

Country of Origin: France	Barrel Length: 700mm (27.6in)
Date: 1993	Muzzle Velocity: 825m/sec (2707ft/sec)
Calibre: 12.7mm (.5in) .50 BMG	Feed/Magazine: 7-round detachable box
Operation: Bolt action	magazine
Weight: 13.8kg (30.42lb)	Range: 2000m (6560ft) +
Overall Length: 1380mm (54.3in)	

skilled marksman will undertake to eliminate him. A single shot poses minimal hazard to non-combatants, although some hostiles will shoot from populous areas in the hope that the security forces will be reluctant to return fire.

Sniper weapons also give security forces the reach to eliminate bomb-planters who may be fairly distant, or enemy personnel on a rooftop separated by several streets. Even very strict rules of engagement will not be violated by a single shot aimed at a gunman who is firing his weapon or a hostile in the act of planting an IED. His heavily-armed but not actively hostile companions may not be legitimate targets under certain rules of engagement, which

would make engagement with less precise weapons or automatic fire problematic, but a sniper would still be able to take his shot with legal confidence.

Very heavy rifles such as 12.7mm (.5in) and even 14.5mm (.57in) weapons now available, have tremendously long effective ranges and are sometimes used to tackle difficult targets at extreme distance. Their massive projectiles give an excellent chance of a one-shot kill, which is necessary at such ranges. A second chance is unlikely once the target realizes he is under fire and moves or takes cover. However, these weapons are not really intended for personnel targets.

Extremely heavy rifles are termed 'anti-materiel rifles' and are descended from the anti-tank rifles of

▲ Heckler & Koch MSG90

US Hostage Rescue Team (HRT) / FBI, Quantico, Virginia, 2000

The MSG90 was produced as a cheaper alternative to the PSG-1 sniping rifle, which is favoured by many police forces. Although lighter, it is robust and extremely accurate.

Specifications

Country of Origin: Germany	Barrel Length: 600mm (23.6in)
Date: 1997	Muzzle Velocity: 815m/sec (2675ft/sec)
Calibre: 7.62mm (.3in) NATO	Feed/Magazine: 5- or 20-round detachable box
Operation: Roller-delayed blowback	magazine
Weight: 6.4kg (14.1lb)	Range: 600m (1968ft)
Overall Length: 1165mm (45.8in)	

Specifications

Country of Origin: West Germany	Overall Length: 905mm (35.63in)
Date: 1982	Barrel Length: 650mm (25.59in)
Calibre: 7.62mm (.3in) /.300 Winchester	Muzzle Velocity: c.800m/sec (2624ft/sec)
Magnum	Feed/Magazine: 6-round detachable box
Operation: Gas	magazine
Weight: 8.31kg (18.32lb)	Range: 1000m (3280ft) +

▲ Walther WA2000

German Bundespolizei (BPOL), 1986

One of the finest and, not coincidentally, expensive sniping weapons ever created, the WA2000 is better suited to law-enforcement use and security work than the rigours of general military use.

the early to mid-twentieth century. These weapons can use explosive or armour-piercing ammunition and are intended primarily for attacking equipment. A well-placed .50-calibre rifle round will disable a vehicle by smashing the engine block, enabling the occupants to be arrested or prevented from driving a truck bomb into their target.

Communications equipment is another key target for sniping attack. Disrupting communications can degrade an enemy force's capabilities far more than eliminating one member of the formation, though long-range sniping has also been used to take out a known insurgent or terrorist leader, which can have a similarly debilitating effect on enemy operations.

Heavy rifles are also used to deal with explosive devices, which may be too dangerous to approach. A heavy-calibre round can break up an explosive device and render it harmless, or may cause it to explode prematurely while personnel are kept at a safe distance. In order to make use of these weapons' long ranges, advanced sighting aids are employed. Even something as basic as a telescopic sight is a precision optical instrument, toughened to survive not only the rigours of field operations but also the recoil of the weapon it is mounted on, without going out of alignment. Low-light and thermal sights allow observation and shooting even in darkness, enabling the sniper to protect an area round the clock.

▲ Gepard M6
Indian Army special forces, 2000

The M6 fires an extremely powerful 14.5mm (.57in) round, whose accuracy is questionable beyond about 1000m (3280ft). It is highly effective as an anti-materiel weapon, but is not useful for very long-range sniping.

Specifications

Country of Origin: Hungary	Overall Length: 1125mm (44.29in)
Date: 1995	Barrel Length: 730mm (28.7in)
Calibre: 14.5mm (.57in)	Muzzle Velocity: 780m/sec (2559ft/sec)
Operation: Semi-automatic	Feed/Magazine: 5-round magazine
Weight: 11.4kg (25.1lb)	Range: 600–1000m (1968–3280ft)

Specifications

Country of Origin: Austria	Overall Length: 1370mm (54in)
Date: 2004	Barrel Length: 833mm (33in)
Calibre: 12.7mm (.5in) / .50 BMG	Muzzle Velocity: Not known
Operation: Bolt action	Feed/Magazine: Single shot
Weight: 12.4kg (28.5lb)	Range: 1500m (4921ft)

▲ Steyr HS .50
Iranian military, 2007

The HS .50 is a bolt-action, single-shot weapon available in .50 calibre and also in .460. The HS .50 M1 is an upgraded version fed from a five-round magazine.

Special operations handguns
1970–PRESENT

Handguns are normally carried as a backup weapon, but in some cases they can give special operations personnel an additional capability.

TRADITIONALLY, REGULAR INFANTRY personnel did not carry sidearms in addition to their individual weapons. Handguns might be issued for security duties, but for the most part they were carried by personnel whose main function was not direct combat with the enemy, and who thus did not need or could not carry a rifle. Handguns have traditionally been associated with officers, rear-echelon personnel, vehicle crews, specialists and possibly medics.

There has been a move in some quarters towards providing infantrymen with a backup weapon, but this is by no means prevalent. Even without considering the cost, troops are already carrying enough weight and the majority will never need a handgun. It is fairly rare for rifles or other longarms to jam or malfunction, and on most of those occasions a soldier can take cover and clear his weapon, or obtain a replacement from a casualty.

For special operations personnel, the situation is a little different. Handguns might at times be the only weapons they can carry, for example when concealed firearms are necessary. At other times, a handgun provides an emergency backup or close-range weapon that can be deployed quickly.

Close quarters

Handguns are easy to use at close quarters or in a confined space, but that is about the limit of their advantages. They lack stopping power, possibly requiring several shots to halt a charging hostile, and do not carry much ammunition. They are also inaccurate beyond a short distance, even if the user is a skilled marksman. However, for a small team involved in an intense fight, the ability to swap to another weapon when ammunition runs out or a longarm malfunctions can be vital.

A soldier who is able to draw his handgun is still in the fight even if his capabilities are limited. A soldier whose only weapon has been dropped or is otherwise out of commission deprives the team of a significant proportion of its firepower. Thus handguns are

▲ **S&W Model 39 'Hush Puppy'**
US Navy SEALs, 1980
Developed from the general-issue Model 39, the 'Hush Puppy' was used primarily to eliminate guard dogs. It featured a slide lock to reduce the mechanical noise of a shot.

Specifications

Country of Origin: United States
Date: 1967
Calibre: 9mm (.35in) Parabellum
Operation: Recoil, locked-breech
Weight: .96kg (2.1lb)
Overall Length: 323mm (12.75in)

Barrel Length: 101mm (3.9in)
Muzzle Velocity: 274m/sec (900ft/sec)
Feed/Magazine: 8-round detachable box
  magazine
Range: 30m (98ft)

routinely carried as backup weapons by special operations personnel. Most are fairly standard weapons, though usually of high quality. Some are more specialist pieces.

Handguns with either a fixed or detachable suppressor are a useful tool for eliminating sentries or guard dogs without alerting other hostiles, and have been a staple of special operations armament for decades. A suppressor does not completely eliminate the sound of a weapon, but it makes it likely that a gunshot will not be noticed or recognized over other background noise.

A range of high-end pistols have been produced for special operations use. In many cases, these firearms have emerged via input at the design stage by experienced users, whose expertise was valuable to a project not specifically aimed at creating a special forces weapon. Other projects have produced weapons that have no possible civilian use, and whose capabilities are unlikely to be required even by regular military personnel.

Examples of the pure special forces weapon are specialist underwater pistols. Both the USA and Russia produced successful underwater weapons for

▶ Heckler & Koch P11

German Navy / Kampfschwimmer ('Combat Swimmers'), Operation Enduring Freedom, 2002

Developed from an earlier underwater weapon, the P11 uses a five-shot barrel cluster. The less bulky Russian equivalent weapon has four barrels but is broadly similar.

Specifications

Country of Origin: West Germany	Barrel Length: N/A
Date: 1976	Muzzle Velocity: N/A
Calibre: 7.6mm (.3in)	Feed/Magazine: 5 rounds in disposable barrel
Operation: Electric-actuated	cluster
Weight: 1.2kg (2.7lb) loaded	Range: 30m (98ft) in air; 10–15m
Overall Length: 200mm (7.87in)	(33–49ft) underwater

▲ Heckler & Koch VP70

Portuguese National Republican Guard, 1990

The VP70 was the world's first polymer-framed handgun. It could deliver three-round bursts at 2200rpm, and could be fitted with a stock to create a carbine-like weapon.

Specifications

Country of Origin: West Germany	Overall Length: 204mm (8in)
Date: 1970	Barrel Length: 116mm (4.6in)
Calibre: 9mm (.35in) Parabellum	Muzzle Velocity: 350m/sec (1148ft/sec)
Operation: Blowback	Feed/Magazine: 18-round box magazine
Weight: .82kg (1.8lb)	Range: 40m (131ft)

use by special forces divers. These are not conventional handguns; they shoot a metal dart rather than a standard bullet, Firing is electrically initiated rather than using the mechanical initiation of a primer.

These weapons use a 'pepperbox' configuration – a cluster of pre-loaded barrels which, when empty, is swapped for another rather than being reloaded in the field. Underwater weapons of this sort are limited in their applications. They do work in air, but accurate range is very short and they are inefficient compared to a standard firearm. Thus they are issued only for specialist applications.

Special operations units tend to use the best weapons they can obtain – which is often a matter of personal preference. They are often permitted to choose their own weapons, either from an approved list or at will. Cost factors that would preclude a given weapon from being issued in the thousands to combat troops will not prevent an elite operator from carrying one.

The precise balance of size, magazine capacity, accuracy, calibre and other factors favoured by any one individual can vary somewhat, but certain weapons have emerged as favourites either due to a single essential feature or, more commonly, simply because they are very good handguns. Perhaps the most vital factor for any special operations weapon is reliability – with so few personnel in a team, weapons must function when they are needed. An otherwise excellent but temperamental weapon is simply not an option.

▶ Heckler & Koch SOCOM Mk23

Royal Malaysia Police (RMP), 2000

Developed to meet the needs of special forces personnel, the SOCOM Mk 23 is supremely rugged and reliable. Its subsonic .45-calibre round offers good stopping power and is suitable for use with a silencer.

Specifications

Country of Origin: Germany/United States	Barrell Length: 150mm (5.9in)
Date: 1996	Muzzel Velocity: 260m/sec (850ft/sec)
Calibre: 11.43mm (.45in)	Feed/Magazine: 12-round detachable box
Operation: Short recoil	magazine
Weight: 1.1kg (2.42lb)	Range: 25m (82.02ft)
Overall Length: 245mm (9.64in)	

◀ FN Five-Seven

French Groupe d'Intervention de la Gendarmerie Nationale (GIGN), 2005

Sharing a specially developed 5.7mm (.22in) round with the P90 carbine, the Five-Seven offers similar ballistic performance to a 9mm (.35in) but is more accurate due to the flatter trajectory of its high-velocity round.

Specifications

Country of Origin: Belgium	Barrell Length: 122mm (4.8in)
Date: 1998	Muzzel Velocity: 625m/sec (2050ft/sec)
Calibre: 5.7mm (.22in)	Feed/Magazine: 20-round detachable box
Operation: Delayed blowback	magazine
Weight: .744kg (1.64lb)	Range: 50m (164ft)
Overall Length: 208mm (8.18in)	

Law enforcement shotguns
1980–PRESENT

Shotguns have limited utility in a military combat situation, but are highly useful in security and law enforcement operations.

SHOTGUNS ARE SMOOTHBORE WEAPONS designed to deliver a group of projectiles rather than a single bullet. The size of the shot used can vary considerably; heavy buckshot offers good knockdown power whilst lighter birdshot increases the chance of a hit. For combat applications, heavy shot is generally used, though lighter shot may be substituted when needed, perhaps on occasions where causing superficial wounds and pain are preferable to disabling or killing hostiles.

Shot is not aerodynamic and loses velocity quickly due to friction from the air. Heavier shot remains dangerous out to a greater distance, but even so the lethal range of a shotgun is strictly limited. This is one reason why shotguns are not normally carried by combat personnel.

The spread of shot is controlled by the 'choke' of the weapon, which is either a fixed or variable narrowing of the bore. For combat applications a fairly tight choke is desirable, ensuring a close shot pattern. More dispersed shot patterns reduce the chances of 'stopping' the target (i.e. stopping him doing whatever it is he intends), which is often more important than lethality. Highly dispersed shot may also pose a hazard to bystanders.

Shot does not penetrate well. This limitation makes shotguns ineffective weapons for shooting through light cover, but at the same time it reduces the hazard to innocents who may be on the other side of a thin urban wall. This lack of penetration actually contributes to stopping power – a high-velocity bullet may tear right through a non-critical part of a human

▲ **Riot squad**
Armed with riot shields and shotguns, Venezuelan police clash with protesters in Caracas, November 2002.

being, taking much of its energy with it. A shotgun dumps all of its energy into the target. Light body armour might prevent the shot from entering the body, but the impact will still cause injury.

Shotguns are popular longarms for law enforcement and security personnel for these and other reasons. They are effective but do not cause much property damage or risk hitting a secondary target after overpenetration. Just as importantly, they are intimidating in a way that a handgun simply is not; criminals who might try their luck against a police officer armed with a semi-automatic pistol will often give up without a fight in the face of a shotgun.

In a military context, shotguns are sometimes used as counter-ambush weapons. They enable scouts or point men to return fire rapidly into a general area, hopefully forcing ambushers to take cover. In this application, the weapon's lack of precision is an asset; the aim is to get as much lead moving towards suspected ambush positions as possible rather than hitting an individual target.

Shotguns can also be used to breach locked doors or deliver specialist ammunition. Some specialist rounds are gimmicky or of marginal use, such as mixed heavy and light shot loads. Others are extremely effective. These include solid ball or 'slug' rounds, which consist of a single extremely heavy projectile. Range is still limited, but a slug round has immense stopping power and will penetrate much of the cover found in the urban environment.

Other specialist ammunition includes gas delivery shells, which can penetrate a door before discharging

▲ Atchisson assault shotgun

Unknown

The first full-automatic shotgun to be produced, the Atchisson assault shotgun was constructed largely from parts of other weapons. The trigger group came from a Browning M1918 and the forearm and stock from an M16.

Specifications

Country of Origin: United States	Barrel Length: 457mm (17.99in)
Date: 1972	Muzzle Velocity: 350m/sec (1100 ft/sec)
Gauge/Calibre: 12-gauge	Feed/Magazine: 7-round detachable box or 20-
Operation: Forced gas blowback, selective fire	round drum magazine
Weight: 7.3kg (16.09lb)	Range: 100m (328ft)
Overall Length: 991mm (39.01in)	

▲ Franchi SPAS-12

Indonesian Komando Pasukan Katak (Kopaska), East Timor, 1990

The SPAS-12 can be set for pump-action or semi-automatic use, enabling the use of specialist ammunition between shots with standard shells. Indonesian security forces used the shotgun in fighting rebels in East Timor.

Specifications

Country of Origin: Italy	Barrel Length: 460mm (18.11in)
Date: 1979	Muzzle Velocity: Variable
Gauge/Calibre: 12-gauge	Feed/Magazine: 7-round integral tubular
Operation: Pump action/gas	magazine
Weight: 4.2kg (9.26lb)	Range: 100m (328ft)
Overall Length: 930mm (36.6in)	

tear gas into a room, and 'beanbag' ammunition, consisting of shot contained in a soft bag. Designed to stun and knock down a target whilst being far less lethal than penetrating shot, beanbag ammunition can be used to make an arrest under conditions where lethal force would otherwise be necessary.

By far the most common use of shotguns in law enforcement is for combat with standard ammunition, or to deter potential hostiles by the shotgun's visual threat. Most shotguns used by police departments and security personnel are simple, robust pump-action weapons. These have the advantage of an extremely rugged action and the ability to eject a misfired cartridge and chamber the

next by manually working the action. Some pump-action shotguns have a magazine cut-off, which allows a specialist shell to be loaded directly into the breech and fired, followed by normal shot if necessary.

The main drawbacks with pump-action shotguns are that they are slow to load and fire. Shells must be manually loaded into the internal magazine one at a time, and firing rate is slowed by the need to work the action between shots, a process that also takes the weapon off target. Thus many law enforcement agencies use semi-automatic shotguns for hostage-rescue and other high-threat units. A semi-automatic shotgun may still be slow to load, but once ready it

▲ Franchi SPAS-15
Serbian Land Forces / Special Brigade, 2008
Magazine feed makes the SPAS-15 much quicker to load than most combat shotguns. It can be switched to pump-action mode to make use of low-pressure less-lethal rounds.

Specifications

Country of Origin: Italy	Barrel Length: 450mm (17.71in)
Date: 1985	Muzzle Velocity: Variable, depending on type of
Gauge/Calibre: 12-gauge	ammunition
Operation: Pump action / gas	Feed/Magazine: 10-round detachable box
Weight: 3.9kg (8.5lb) or 4.1kg (9lb)	magazine
Overall Length: 980mm (38.58in)	Range: 100m (328ft)

▲ Benelli M4 Super 90
Royal Malaysian Customs (RMC), Straits of Melaka, 2005
The semi-automatic M4 is favoured by US Marine Corps security teams, and by numerous special police units such as SWAT and counter-terrorist teams throughout the world.

Specifications

Country of Origin: Italy	Barrel Length: 470mm (18.50in)
Date: 1998	Muzzle Velocity: Variable
Gauge/Calibre: 12-gauge	Feed/Magazine: 6-round under-barrel integral
Operation: Gas, semi-automatic	tubular magazine
Weight: 3.8kg (8.37lb)	Range: 100m (328ft)
Overall Length: 1010mm (39.76in)	

can deliver several rapid shots, which is usually enough to disable any opponent.

Where even more firepower is desirable, a number of full-automatic shotgun designs exist. These are military weapons for the most part, designed for base security or urban combat applications. Usually fed from a drum or box magazine, automatic shotguns are bulky and heavy but offer massive firepower at short range, albeit with ferocious recoil that can make these weapons difficult to handle for some personnel.

Like rifles and submachine guns, combat shotguns can often take a range of accessories and modifications to increase their utility. Advanced sights are common, along with laser pointers and tactical flashlights. Some weapons offer the choice of a fixed or folding stock, and in cases the latter can be configured as an elbow hook rather than a stock, facilitating one-handed shooting. However, firing any shotgun one-handed is inadvisable for all but the most substantial people.

Specifications

Country of Origin: South Korea	Barrel Length: 460mm (18.11in)
Date: 1992	Muzzle Velocity: 400m/sec (1300ft/sec)
Gauge/Calibre: 12-gauge	Feed/Magazine: 10-round box or 20-round drum
Operation: Gas	detachable magazine
Weight: 5.5kg (12.12lb)	Range: 200m (656ft)
Overall Length: 960mm (37.79in)	

▲ **USAS-12**

Korean National Police Agency (KNPA), 2000

Heavily influenced by the Atchisson assault shotgun, the USAS-12 achieved respectable sales to various military and security users in East Asia.

▲ **AA-12**

Unknown

The AA-12 can deliver normal shot or a range of specialist ammunition including high-explosive and fragmentation rounds designed to detonate in the air, showering the target with small projectiles.

Specifications

Country of Origin: United States	Barrel Length: 330mm (13in)
Date: 2005	Muzzle Velocity: 350m/sec (1100ft/sec)
Gauge/Calibre: 12-gauge	Feed/Magazine: 8-round detachable box or
Operation: Forced gas blowback, selective fire	20- or 32-round drum magazine
Weight: 5.7kg (12.6lb)	Range: 200m (656ft) FRAG-12 ammunition
Overall Length: 966mm (38in)	

Law enforcement and counter-terrorism

1980–PRESENT

A range of light automatic weapons are available to personnel who require a high-firepower weapon but cannot carry a full-sized rifle.

WITHIN THE MILITARY there are many personnel who may be expected to go into harm's way, but whose main duties do not include direct combat with the enemy. Yet vehicle crews, artillerymen, logistics personnel, specialists such as communications operators, combat pioneers and many officers still have need of an effective weapon.

Many of these personnel cannot make proper use of a rifle while encumbered by their equipment, or when within a vehicle. Others cannot carry the weight of a rifle and ammunition along with their specialist equipment. One solution to this problem is to issue a pistol, but handguns are at best marginally effective. A more potent weapon is desirable.

Submachine guns and carbines have at times been issued to these personnel, and are also used by security troops who are likely to operate in the confined spaces of a base or naval vessel. Engagement ranges for these troops tend to be short, making volume of fire more important than accurate range. Pistol-calibre ammunition is also lighter than an equivalent number of rifle rounds, reducing the load on a soldier.

In a law enforcement and security context, submachine guns or carbines are excellent weapons. Most law-enforcement personnel, even those operating in a paramilitary environment such as hostage rescue or counter-terrorism, tend to engage at short ranges where submachine guns are effective.

Bodyguards

Bodyguards also find light, high-firepower weapons useful. If the threat is fairly distant, the most effective response is likely to be to move the principal

▲ **Colt 9mm SMG**

US Drug Enforcement Administration (DEA), 1995

Colt's 9mm submachine gun/carbine is rather bulky for a weapon of its calibre, but its weight does reduce felt recoil to almost nothing.

Specifications

Country of Origin: United States

Date: late 1980s

Calibre: 9mm (.35in) Parabellum

Operation: Blowback, closed bolt

Weight: 2.6kg (5.75lb)

Overall Length: 730mm (28.9in)

Barrel Length: 267mm (10.5in)

Muzzle Velocity: 396m/sec (1300ft/sec)

Feed/Magazine: 32-round detachable box magazine

Range: 300m (984ft)

Specifications

Country of Origin: West Germany

Date: 1966

Calibre: 9mm (.35in)

Operation: Delayed blowback

Weight: 3.08kg (6.8lb)

Overall Length: 700mm (27.6in)

Barrel Length: 225mm (8.9in)

Muzzle Velocity: 285m/sec (935ft/sec)

Feed/Magazine: 15-, 30- or 32- round detachable
box magazine

Range: 200m (656ft)

▲ **Heckler & Koch MP5**

German Bundespolizei (Federal Police), 1995

The H&K MP5 achieved huge market success, with a vast range of specialist variants produced. Accurate and compact, this personal defence weapon has proved very popular with special forces and law enforcement agencies around the world.

▲ **FN P90**

Belgian Special Forces Group (SFG), Gulf War, 1991

The FN P90 personal defence weapon uses the same cartridge as the Five-Seven Pistol. The gun has a novel loading system whereby rounds are carried in a clear plastic cartridge situated at a right-angle to the barrel. Ejection is via the hollow grip.

Specifications

Country of Origin: Belgium

Date: 1990

Calibre: 5.7mm (.22in) FN

Operation: Blowback

Weight: 2.8kg (6.17lb)

Overall Length: 400mm (15.75in)

Barrel Length: 263mm (7.75in)

Muzzle Velocity: 850m/sec (2800ft/sec)

Feed/Magazine: 50-round detachable box
magazine

Range: 200m (656ft) +

quickly to cover or out of the threat zone. Shooting the attackers is only a priority if the threat is at close range. The ability to respond with overwhelming firepower is of paramount importance under such circumstances.

Thus for many years the submachine gun fulfilled an intermediate role between handguns and rifles. Submachine guns generally (but not always) use a pistol-calibre round but, possessing as they do a longer barrel than a handgun, have a greater effective range and higher accuracy. Various types of submachine guns have emerged over the years,

ranging from large, almost rifle-like weapons down to overgrown pistols.

Personal defence weapons

In recent years the term 'personal defence weapon', or PDW, has emerged. This name to some extent refers to a role rather than a specific type of weapon. Most PDWs are identifiable as submachine guns; they are light, pistol-calibre automatic weapons. However, a number of different approaches have been taken to the PDW concept. Some are extremely small, representing an attempt to cram submachine gun firepower into something little larger than a pistol. Others are definitely longarms, but again offer unusually high firepower for their size. This, more than anything else defines a PDW. It is a weapon intended for self-defence rather than full-scale combat, providing a heavy punch in a small package. Some PDWs use specially developed advanced ammunition, while others are chambered for existing calibres.

PDWs are in many ways ideal weapons for law enforcement personnel, as their small size makes them easy to manoeuvre inside buildings or vehicles. A short, light weapon can be brought on target quickly when moving through a cluttered area, and a high rate of fire enables hostiles to be quickly disabled before they can pose a threat to innocents or law enforcement personnel.

One approach to the PDW concept is demonstrated by the Colt 9mm (.35in) submachine gun. This is a version of the M4 carbine converted to 9mm calibre and is rather large for a submachine gun, being more of a 9mm carbine. However, it is smaller and lighter than a rifle, yet can be used by anyone familiar with the M16 or M4 rifle with minimal conversion training. This weapon would be severely limited on the battlefield, but is well suited for security or emergency self-defence use. It is favoured by some law enforcement agencies, whose agents may have to face opposition armed with automatic weapons.

Weapons such as the FN P90 carbine are similarly sized but very different in approach. Using a 5.7mm (.22in) round in common with the Five-Seven pistol, the P90 was designed to pack as much firepower as possible into a small weapon. Its ammunition was designed to give superior performance against body armour to existing 9mm rounds, and is carried in a 50-round cassette. Although it was developed specifically as a PDW, most users of the P90 treat it as an offensive rather than defensive arm, issuing it as main armament rather than an emergency weapon for personnel less likely to engage in combat.

At the other end of the scale are weapons such as the Russian-made PP2000. This is a very small

▲ **Colt SMG**

Firing 9mm Parabellum rounds, the Colt submachine gun closely resembles the M16 assault rifle in shape and appearance. It has proved popular with special forces and law enforcement agencies.

weapon, not much larger than a typical pistol. It is chambered for standard 9mm ammunition, but also capable of using an armour-piercing round. Its intended users were those who might need more firepower than a handgun, but could not necessarily carry assault rifles or full-sized submachine guns.

Somewhere between these two extremes lie most typical PDWs. Some are versions of existing submachine guns, usually made as small as possible, while others are custom designed for the role. While certainly effective, these weapons face the same challenges that traditional submachine guns have

▲ **Heckler & Koch MP7**

Austrian EKO Cobra (Einsatzkommando Cobra), 2003

Like some other purpose-designed PDWs, the MP7 was built around custom ammunition, giving enhanced penetrative capabilities over standard submachine gun calibres.

Specifications

Country of Origin: Germany	Barrel Length: 180mm (7.1in)
Date: 2001	Muzzle Velocity: c.725m/sec (2379ft/sec)
Calibre: 4.6mm (.18in)	Feed/Magazine: 20-, 30-, 40-round detachable
Operation: Gas, short-stroke piston, rotating bolt	box magazine
Weight: 1.9kg (4.19lb) without magazine	Range: 200m (656ft)
Overall Length: 638mm (25.1in)	

Specifications

Country of Origin: Germany	Overall Length: 690mm (27.2in)
Date: 1999	Barrel Length: 200mm (7.9in)
Calibre: 11.4mm (.45in) / 45 ACP, 10.16mm	Muzzle Velocity: Not known
(.4in) .40 S&W, 9mm (.35in) Parabellum	Feed/Magazine: 25- or 30-round detachable box
Operation: Blowback, closed bolt	magazine
Weight: 2.3kg (5lb)	Range: 100m (328ft)

▲ **Heckler & Koch UMP (Universal Machine Pistol)**

US Customs and Border Protection, 2005

Aimed mainly at the law enforcement marketplace, the Universal Machine Pistol (UMP) was made available in a range of powerful calibres, including .45 ACP and .40, with a 9mm version following soon afterward.

since the invention of the assault rifle. With small, lightweight rifles available, the light automatic weapon niche has been squeezed, and many PDW designs do not offer sufficiently great advantages over a carbine version of an existing assault rifle.

Yet although the gap between handguns and assault rifles has shrunk, it does still exist. The larger submachine guns and carbine-type PDWs may face competition from weapons like the M4 carbine, but the smaller ones do seem to have a promising future.

A weapon that can be carried in a hip or shoulder holster but which can deliver automatic fire and perhaps even defeat body armour offers capabilities that no other weapon can deliver.

Thus while the larger PDWs have joined the assault rifle/submachine gun marketplace and may or may not prosper, it is likely that the smaller ones will find continued favour with law enforcement and special operations personnel, bodyguards, and possibly other non-infantry military personnel.

▶ Steyr TMP

Gruppo di Intervento Speciale, Italy, 2003

The Steyr Tactical Machine Pistol is primarily a defensive weapon. The foregrip helps reduce muzzle climb when delivering automatic fire. Both Austrian police and anti-terrorist units have adopted the TMP.

Specifications

Country of Origin: Austria	Barrel Length: 130mm (5.1in)
Date: 2000	Muzzle Velocity: 380m/sec (1247ft/sec)
Calibre: 9mm (.35in) Parabellum	Feed/Magazine: 15- or 30-round detachable box
Operation: Short recoil, rotating barrel	magazine
Weight: 1.3kg (2.9lb)	Range: 100m (328ft)
Overall Length: 282mm (11.1in)	

▲ CZW 438 M9

Unknown

The CZW 438 was originally chambered for 4.38x30mm ammunition. The M9 variant uses vastly more common 9x19mm rounds, but shares almost all components with the original weapon.

Specifications

Country of Origin: Czech Republic	Barrel Length: 220mm (8.66in)
Date: 2002	Muzzle Velocity: Not known
Calibre: 9mm (.35in) Parabellum	Feed/Magazine: 15- or 30-round detachable box
Operation: Lever-delayed blowback	magazine
Weight: 2.7kg (5.95lb)	Range: 200m (656ft)
Overall Length: 690mm (27.1in)	

Appendix: Service Rifles Today

Below is a list of the main service rifles in use with national forces today.

AK-47/AKM series:
Afghanistan, Algeria,
Cambodia, Egypt, Hungary

AK-74 series:
Russia, Ukraine

AK-103:
Venezuela

Beretta AR70/90:
Italy

C7A1:
Canada

FAMAS G2:
France

FN FAL:
Brazil

FN FNC:
Belgium

FX-05:
Mexico

H&K G3:
Pakistan, Portugal

H&K G36:
Germany, Spain

IMI Tavor TAR-21:
Israel, Thailand

INSAS:
India

L85A2 (SA80):
UK, Jamaica

M4 carbine:
United States Army, Georgia

M16:
Afghanistan, Argentina,
US Marine Corps

SAR 21:
Singapore

S&T Daewoo K11:
Republic of Korea

Steyr AUG:
Argentina, Australia, Austria,
New Zealand

QBZ-95:
China

Type 56:
Vietnam

Index

Page numbers in *italics* refer to illustrations and tables.